The People between
the Rivers

ASIA/PACIFIC/PERSPECTIVES

Series Editor: Mark Selden

The Korean War: An International History
  by Wada Haruki
The United States and China: A History from the Eighteenth Century to the Present
  by Dong Wang
The Inside Story of China's High-Tech Industry: Making Silicon Valley in Beijing
  by Yu Zhou

The People between the Rivers

The Rise and Fall of a Bronze Drum Culture, 200–750 CE

Catherine Churchman

ROWMAN & LITTLEFIELD
Lanham • Boulder • New York • London

Published by Rowman & Littlefield
A wholly owned subsidiary of The Rowman & Littlefield Publishing Group, Inc.
4501 Forbes Boulevard, Suite 200, Lanham, Maryland 20706
www.rowman.com

Unit A, Whitacre Mews, 26-34 Stannary Street, London SE11 4AB, United Kingdom

British Library Cataloguing in Publication Information Available

Library of Congress Cataloging-in-Publication Data
Names: Churchman, Catherine, 1975– author.
Title: The people between the rivers : the rise and fall of a bronze drum culture, 200–750
    CE / Catherine Churchman.
Description: Lanham : Rowman & Littlefield, [2016] | Series: Asia/Pacific/perspectives |
    Includes bibliographical references and index.
Identifiers: LCCN 2016017187 (print) | LCCN 2016019695 (ebook) |
    ISBN 9781442258600 (cloth : alkaline paper) | ISBN 9781442258617 (electronic)
Subjects: LCSH: Pearl River Region (China)—Antiquities. | Red River Region (China
    and Vietnam)—Antiquities. | Indigenous peoples—China—Pearl River Region—
    History—To 1500. | Indigenous peoples—Red River Region (China and Vietnam)—
    History—To 1500. | Bronze drum—China—Pearl River Region—History—To 1500.
    | Bronze drum—China—Red River Region (China and Vietnam)—History—To 1500.
    | Social archaeology—China—Pearl River Region. | Social archaeology—Red River
    Region (China and Vietnam) | Pearl River Region (China)—Social life and customs. |
    Red River Region (China and Vietnam)—Social life and customs.
Classification: LCC DS793.P437 C47 2016 (print) | LCC DS793.P437 (ebook) | DDC
    951.201—dc23
LC record available at https://lccn.loc.gov/2016017187

♾™ The paper used in this publication meets the minimum requirements of American
National Standard for Information Sciences—Permanence of Paper for Printed Library
Materials, ANSI/NISO Z39.48-1992.

Printed in the United States of America

To Li Tana: teacher, mentor, and friend

Contents

Maps and Table

MAPS

TABLE

Acknowledgments

Most of the research for this book was undertaken in the Division of Pacific and Asian History in the now-defunct Research School of Pacific and Asian Studies (RSPAS) at the Australian National University. I was very fortunate to be able to work closely with Li Tana, a skilled and imaginative historian with a deep knowledge of sources in Chinese, Vietnamese, and English. I would not have managed to write anything like this without her guidance, friendship, and generosity with time, and it is therefore to her that I wish to dedicate this book. I am also extremely grateful to David Marr, who kindly offered many useful insights and constructive comments through his careful reading and discussion of all my chapter drafts, and also to the late Nicholas Tapp, who read many of my chapters and suggested a wealth of useful literature and concepts of which I would otherwise have been blissfully unaware. I extend warm thanks to Nola Cooke, whose critical reading of my very first ideas aided me greatly in breaking away from some very well-worn themes in the historiographies of China and Vietnam, as well as in the improvement of my writing style. Thanks must also go to Benjamin Penny, who made insightful criticism of my ideas and offered much help with tricky translations and the location of materials, and to Judith Cameron, for her sagacious advice that kept me from straying too far into wild speculation regarding archaeological matters. Geoff Wade and Charles Holcombe also offered many useful comments and corrections to the manuscript, for which I am most grateful. During the long period of research and writing, I also enjoyed and benefited greatly from intellectual conversations, advice, support, and encouragement from friends and colleagues at RSPAS and elsewhere. Thanks are particularly due to my office mate and friend Dane Alston, but also to Jenny Alexander, Geremie Barmé, Noel Barnard, Duncan Campbell, Rafe de Crespigny, Anthony Garnaut, Jamie Greenbaum, Igor de Rachewiltz, Phillip Taylor, and Nathan Woolley. I was also fortunate during my research and writing for the book to be able to meet and discuss my work with scholars in the United States, among whom James Anderson, Bradley Davis John Phan, and John Whitmore offered particularly helpful advice. I am grateful to have had the financial support of the Chiang Ching-kuo Foundation for providing funding to undertake research in Taipei for two months in 2006, and the Australia Netherlands Research Collaboration, which funded six weeks of travel to Leiden for research in 2009. There I was able to meet Leonard Blussé, Peter Boomgard, Pál Nyiri, Oscar Salemink, and Heather Sutherland, all of whom gave me helpful advice and criticism on my developing concept. During my fieldwork in China, I was lucky enough to meet Li Qingxin of the Guangdong Academy of Social Sciences, Xu Jian of Sun Yat-sen University, David Faure at the Chinese University of Hong Kong, Fan Honggui and Huang Xingqiu of the Guangxi University for Nationalities, and Deng Xiaohua of Xiamen University, all of whom aided me greatly with ideas and materials as I struggled to explain my subject to them in my halting Chinese. I would also like to thank Karina Pelling, Kay Dancey, and Jennifer Sheehan of the RSPAS cartography unit for their advice and help in creating the beautiful maps in the book, Darrell Dorrington for helping with the collection and discovery of source materials at the Menzies Library, and the administrative staff of the former Pacific and Asian History division, Oanh Collins, Maxine MacArthur, Dorothy MacKintosh, Indranee Sandranam, and Marion Weeks, for their constant help and support. For long periods of free accommodation during my research I must thank Heather Sutherland, Sim Lee, and Ku Naisheng, but most of all Eleanora O'Connor Risch, without whose generosity the book would have ended up much shorter. Finally, thank you to my friends and colleagues Eugenie Edquist and Edwina Palmer, who kindly helped me with proofreading the manuscript at various stages of its production.

A Note on Transcription and Referencing Systems

As one approaches the edges of the Chinese-speaking world, one must begin to make choices about how to transcribe Chinese names, as those beyond China's borders who have historically used Chinese characters have their own traditions of transcription. Pinyin has become ubiquitous for the transcription of Chinese characters in any work dealing with China in any period, an unfortunate trend that obscures significant changes in the phonology of Chinese through the ages and encourages a false idea of the unity and continuity of the speech of Chinese, past and present. Because Western readers are used to Chinese transliterated into Pinyin, I was obliged to abandon my original ideal transcribing according to the Sino-Vietnamese or Hán-Việt system for ease of recognition, even though the character readings of this system are phonologically richer than those of Pinyin and also reflect a language somewhat closer to what was spoken during the time period covered by this study. I have retained Hán-Việt transcription for a few personal names and occasional toponyms that are more commonly known in English through their Vietnamese transcription. In the glossary, Hán-Việt alternatives are also provided for some names where I thought they might be useful. In the few cases where there are two different Chinese names that end up with identical transcription in Pinyin without tone marks, I have added these to some characters in order to distinguish them so that the corresponding Chinese characters can be easily found in the glossary. An exception to all of these rules is the name of the city of Guangzhou, which I invariably refer to by its English name, Canton, in part to simplify the problem of the various names used to refer to it throughout the first millennium CE, but mainly in order to avoid confusion with the province of Guangzhou, ruled from that city over most of the period discussed.

The referencing system used for premodern editions of primary sources is according to the traditional system of fascicle number followed by colon and page number, with a suffixed letter a or b indicating on which side the citation is to be found. Citations of modern editions of primary sources use the abbreviation ch. to indicate fascicle number, followed by the page number. Citations from all other works use standard bibliographic referencing.

Chinese Dynasties

Han 206 BCE–220 CE
Wu 222–280
Western Jin 265–316
Eastern Jin 317–420

Southern Dynasties
Liu-Song 420–479
Qi 479–502
Liang 502–557
Chen 557–589
Sui 581–618
Tang 618–907
Song 960–1279

Introduction

This book tells the story of a vanished culture that flourished in the mountain ranges in the south of the East Asian Mainland between the fourth and seventh centuries CE. This culture left behind a sizable collection of bronze kettledrums in the archaeological record, but nothing in the way of a written tradition until the descendants of the drum makers began to use Chinese writing themselves, by which time they had been assimilated to Chinese culture to such an extent that they no longer recognized the people who made the drums as part of their own biological ancestry and wrote about them instead as the relics of an ancient people.

To write a history of a culture that has left behind no written records, one can start by reading what others wrote about them, but eventually a point is reached at which a purely textual approach is no longer effective and one must begin to search for sources elsewhere. My own interest in the history of the indigenous, pre-Sinitic cultures of southern China began after learning some Hokkien and Hakka as an undergraduate in Taiwan in the late 1990s. Early on I became aware that many common words in these two languages had no fixed written form in Chinese characters, and that these words were often simply left as blank squares in a Chinese text with the Romanization to supply the meaning. I soon learned, to my great fascination, that the origins of many such words could be traced back to the languages of the indigenous, pre-Sinitic cultures of southern China who lived there before migrants from the north began arriving in the first millennium CE.

The significance of the gaps in the Chinese character set that sparked my initial interest is not to be underestimated, as these words that cannot be written in characters are signposts to historical materials bypassed by the Chinese literary tradition. The peripheries of the Chinese empires correspond more or less to the peripheries of detailed Chinese knowledge, and as one approaches

1

the outer limits of the empires, the textual record grows patchy and descriptions of those who dwell there ever more fragmentary and fantastic. Those who wrote in Chinese in the first millennium CE were not particularly interested in describing the lifeways of peoples they encountered on their southern borderlands, nor did they busy themselves with the enterprise of ethnological and linguistic categorization of peoples that characterizes modern scholarship and government. Chinese descriptions of the cultural life of these peoples were as a consequence often limited either to the exaggerations of travelers' tales or to offhand mentions of habits they found particularly distasteful.

Despite their own inability to speak to us through text on their own terms, the indigenous peoples of southern China must have possessed entire cultural worlds of their own of which they were the center, speaking their own languages, living within their own political systems, and following their own social rules. They are also certain to have had their own ideas about ways of dealing with their huge neighbors—the succession of empires we are accustomed to group under the collective name of "China." To obtain a detailed and nuanced picture of how these societies of pre-Sinitic peoples might have functioned, how they saw themselves, and how they dealt with the Chinese, reliance on the Chinese written texts alone is insufficient. A Sinocentric view is inherent in all the textual sources and must be counterbalanced by reference to other materials, reading against the grain of the texts, looking not for where the Chinese were, but for where they were not, and augmenting this reading with the fruits of research into historical linguistics, archaeology, and anthropology of the modern period. This is the methodological approach upon which the study is based.

In the chapters that follow, I hope to offer fresh perspectives on the long history of indigenous engagement with the Chinese empires by challenging some widely held assumptions about the history of ethnic relations and political structures related to China's southward expansion, in particular the following four: (1) that close contact with the Chinese empires necessarily leads to acculturation to Chinese social and political norms, (2) that economic development of southern China was wholly due to the influx of Chinese migrants to the area, (3) that the names given ethnic groups in Chinese texts refer to identifiable coherent ethnic or linguistic groups over time, and (4) that the people of the Red River Plain formed a distinct group that resisted assimilation to Chinese imperial rule, which was the underlying reason for the later emergence of the states that are considered ancestral to present-day Vietnam.[1]

This study presents counterarguments to these four points. First, it demonstrates that between the Red and Pearl Rivers, for at least four centuries, interactions with the Chinese state actually strengthened the political autonomy of indigenous societies and that these societies were capable of assimilating Chinese migrants from the north to their own social and political norms. Second, it argues that indigenous chiefdoms often held the economic advantage in trade interactions with the Chinese and were able to use this to ensure that they were safe from Chinese military incursions into their territory. Third, it offers an alternative explanation of the various names for the non-Sinitic peoples on the southern Chinese periphery, demonstrating that the usage of names in Chinese texts is more closely connected to the geographical location and political structures of the referents than it is to differences in ethnicity or language group perceived by the Chinese. Fourth, it also offers a new perspective on the historical tendencies toward political autonomy in the Red River Plain by demonstrating how the rise of indigenous chiefdoms in the lands between the plain and the other provinces of the Chinese empires was an important contributing factor to the eventual growth of a future Vietnamese polity, as the chiefdoms effectively isolated the Red River Plain from the rest of the Chinese Empire, creating fertile ground for the growth of local rule.

I offer the work in the hope that it will stimulate new ways of thinking about the larger historical processes involved in the southward expansion of China.

NOTE

1. An abridged version of the general argument has previously appeared in the books the *Tongking Gulf through History*, edited by Nola Cooke, Li Tana, and James A. Anderson, and *China's Encounters on the South and Southwest*, edited by James K. Anderson and John K. Whitmore.

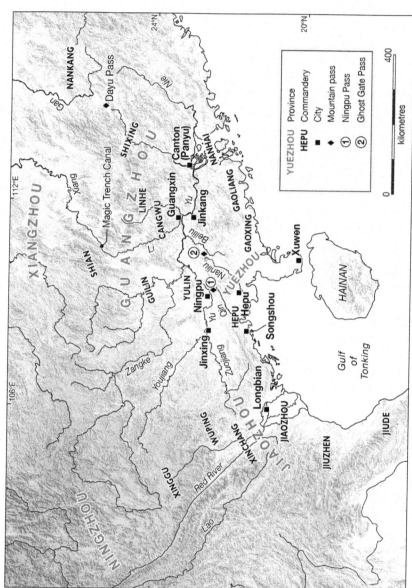

Map 1. The Two Rivers Region, ca. 500 CE

Chapter 1

Digging Up Drums

Every few years, in the lands to the west of Canton and south of the Pearl River, a farmer digging a ditch or plowing a field will strike upon the hard green metal of a buried bronze kettledrum. The history of excavating bronze drums in this region began over a thousand years ago, with the earliest record from the early 870s relating to the unearthing of a drum during the repair of the city walls of Gongzhou ordered by Zhang Fangzhi, the newly arrived provincial inspector.[1] Around the same time, another drum was discovered in Gaozhou by a cowherd who had stumbled upon it by digging in a hole in pursuit of a croaking toad, which was purportedly the spirit of the drum itself.[2] Writing in the 1170s, the Song authors Zhou Qufei and Fan Chengda both mentioned finds of the drums in the area, the former noting that they were sometimes discovered during plowing[3] and the latter that they were frequently dug out of the ground and had formerly been used by the ancient Man people of the south.[4] A later and more detailed description of the circumstances of the discovery of drums in eastern Guangxi comes from Xie Qigun's *Guangxi Tongzhi* (Provincial Gazetteer of Guangxi), composed in 1800:

> In the eighth year of the reign of Emperor Yongzheng [1730], in Beiliu County in Guangxi, a peasant found a bronze drum in perfect condition without any corrosion, in kingfisher green and cinnabar red, variegated in the old colours. It wasn't something that should be kept as a private treasure, and was thus respectfully presented to His Majesty. In the autumn of the same year, on a sandbar in the river known as the "Bronze Drum Sandbar" it had been observed that there was a hidden protuberance just below the surface of the water being lapped at by the waves, a fisherman assembled people to use their combined strength to pull it up, and with a clang up came yet another bronze drum.[5]

Such discoveries are still being made at the rate of one every two to three years, most recently at Yangjiang[6] and Enping[7] in Guangdong, and in Rong County,[8] Beihai,[9] and Wuming[10] in Guangxi.

Bronze drums have been made and used by many different peoples and are found as far to the north and west as Yunnan and Guizhou Provinces in China and as far south as the eastern islands of Indonesia, though the earliest bronze drum casting tradition was probably in the area known as Dian (present-day central Yunnan), close to the headwaters of both the Red and Pearl Rivers. There are several different types of drum and many different typologies by which they are categorized. This study employs Franz Heger's typology of 1902 because all subsequent classification schemes advanced by both Chinese and Vietnamese scholars ultimately have this as their underlying structure.[11] An additional reason for retaining Heger's typology is to avoid the practice in present-day Chinese and Vietnamese scholarship of attaching contemporary toponyms to the drums and in a sense claiming them as the heritage of their respective countries; for this reason in particular, I have avoided using the Vietnamese name *Đông Sơn* in relation to the drums. Although this name has often been used as a catch-all term for bronze kettledrums of southern China and Southeast Asia, the term should properly refer only to artifacts directly related to the Đông Sơn archaeological culture centered on the Đông Sơn excavation site in Thanh Hóa Province in northern Vietnam.[12] This culture produced the most well known type of bronze kettledrum, belonging to type I in Heger's classification, and finds of drums of this type are distributed on both sides of the Sino-Vietnamese border in Yunnan and northern Vietnam, as well as (more rarely) in Guangxi. Heger I drums are notable for the intricacy of their decorations, which usually consist of ringed scenes of warships and warriors in feather headdresses in concentric circles around a radiating sun in the center of the tympanum, upon which sit relief models of stylized frogs. The drums that are central to this study belong to a later group classified by Heger as type II. These have mainly been found to the south of the Pearl River, but examples of the type have also been excavated from the hill country to the west of the Red River Plain. Heger II drums are decorated in a much plainer style than type I, which consists mainly of geometric patterns rather than figures, but still share certain decorative features on the tympanum with the Heger I drums, such as the frogs and radiating sun motif. What the Heger II drums lack in their decorative beauty they make up for in physical size; type II drums measure sometimes as much as 150 cm across the tympanum,[13] making them over twice the size of the largest Heger I drums, which have radii of only 70–79 cm.[14] Heger II drums are also impressive for their sheer numbers; more Heger II–type drums have been unearthed in Guangdong and Guangxi than those of any other type of bronze kettledrum of the first millennium CE in any other place on earth.[15] Two hundred and fifteen examples of Heger II–style kettledrums were known in China by 1990,[16] in contrast to the 144 drums of any type known in Vietnam by 1988.[17] Despite their numbers and impressive size, the Heger II drums of south China have drawn relatively little attention from scholars outside China, while the Heger I drums of the Đông Sơn culture are much better studied. This neglect of Heger II drums in Western-language scholarship is due to both the difficulty of accessing materials written in Chinese and the fact that (unlike the Heger I drums in Vietnam) they are simply less obvious to outsiders, having never been promoted as a national treasure or national symbol to the outside world.

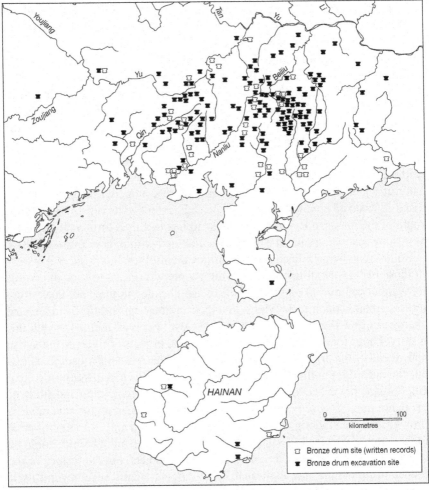

Map 2. The Distribution of Heger II Bronze Drums Excavated in South China by 1982 (after Jiang, *Yueshi tonggu*, p. 142)

The tradition of Heger II drum casting west of Canton began in the second or perhaps third century CE and lasted until around the end of the eighth century. Its demise after this time is marked in the written record by a decrease in mentions of the active use of drums and an inversely proportional increase in records of old drums being dug out of the ground and treated as curios or rarities.[18] The main period of drum production roughly corresponds to what Western historians of China usually call the Early Medieval period, or what Chinese historians refer to as either the Six Dynasties or Wei, Jin, Northern, and Southern Dynasties period from 220 to 589 CE.[19] This was a long period of political disunity in the Chinese-speaking world that followed the fragmentation of the Han Empire into three warring kingdoms in 220 CE, of which Wu, ruled from Jinling (now Nanjing), controlled the southern provinces. The Empire of Jin formed from their territories lasted from 285 to 316, ruling both the north and the south, and a second Empire of Jin based in the south of China from 317 to 420, with its capital at Jiankang (also the city now known as Nanjing), the north of China having been overrun by a succession of steppe peoples who eventually founded their own empires there on the Chinese model. In the south, the period from 317 onward was characterized by four relatively short-lived and successively smaller empires of the Liu-Song, Qi, Liang, and Chen, ruled from Jiankang and known collectively as the Southern Dynasties. Not only were these empires engaged in constant warfare with rival empires in the north of China, they were also highly politically unstable. It was not until the Sui Empire conquered the Chen in 589 that a centralized empire from the north again extended its rule over the lands south of the Yangtze River, but this was to last less than forty years before a new, long-lasting empire, the Tang, was founded within its territories in 618.

Rather than being a history of the drums themselves, this work is a history of those behind the drum culture, of the people who cast and used the drums throughout the period of production, of the changes in their political structures, in their economic activities, and their military capabilities, and also the changes in how they were viewed by those who wrote of them. Through this history, I hope to illuminate the mechanisms and processes involved in the rise and spread of the drum culture, as well as those that eventually caused its disappearance. My aim in writing such a history is to fill a gap in knowledge that Geoff Wade described succinctly as "a need for the recognition and study of the major non-Chinese polities that existed in the Lingnan region (the modern provinces of Guangdong and Guangxi and the northern half of Vietnam) prior to the Tang."[20] The lack of a detailed study on an understudied topic should be reason enough in itself for a monograph on the subject, but the history of the bronze drum culture has additional, wide-ranging significance beyond itself to the consideration of many important and long-discussed questions, such as how the Chinese empires expanded into new territories and how non-Sinitic peoples on the imperial periphery interacted with these empires, and whether or not they were eventually absorbed into the Chinese state through their acculturation to Chinese linguistic, cultural, and political norms—a process usually referred to as Sinification or Sinicization. An additional significance of this study is that it offers a new perspective on the histories of the areas surrounding the heartland of the drum culture, particularly on the nature of the relationships between the peoples of the Red River Plain and the Chinese empires in the first millennium CE.

Like many peoples known to posterity only through their mentions in Chinese sources, it is not possible to know what the makers of the drums actually called themselves. Among the various names given to them by chroniclers writing in Chinese, those that were applied more specifically and consistently throughout the period under consideration were the three terms *Li*, *Lao*, and *Wuhu*, though whether the people thus referred to actually applied such names to themselves or even perceived themselves as single or discrete groups of people remains a mystery. They have left no linguistic record of themselves save their place names and a few dozen words of substrate vocabulary in the various Chinese languages spoken in the areas they once inhabited, and all of these strongly suggest that they spoke languages belonging to the Kadai linguistic family, or more specifically the Tai branch of that family.[21] A precise answer to the question of what their names actually signified remains elusive, especially when one factors in written records of groups of people known as Li or Lao in areas where there is no evidence for the historical use of Tai or Kadai languages, or in areas where there is archaeological record of bronze drums or a related material culture. Such records make it highly unlikely that the names are representative of linguistic groupings or coherent material cultures, and Chinese naming practices for those they perceived as different were inconsistent to the point that a whole chapter of this book is devoted to trying to untangle the mess. Although they will appear with great regularity in this work, the names Li and Lao or Li-Lao do not refer to an ethnic group; they are nothing more than an easy shorthand for "the people who produced bronze drums in the Early Medieval period in what are now the two southern provinces of Guangdong and Guangxi,"[22] with the occasional geographical qualification "between the Two Rivers" or "between the Rivers" as a reminder that other people who did not produce drums or who lived in other areas were also referred to as Li and Lao in the Chinese textual tradition.

The term *Two Rivers* refers to the location of the heartland of the Li and Lao drum culture, about halfway between the mouths of the Pearl and Red Rivers. The geographical center of the culture was the Yunkai and Yunwu mountain ranges, which lie along the watershed between rivers that drain northward into the Yu River and enter the sea through the Pearl River at Canton,[23] and those that drain southward into the Gulf of Tongking and the Red River. From the third to the late fifth centuries, this watershed also represented a rough division between lands theoretically subject to the two southern provinces of Guangzhou and Jiaozhou, controlled from cities near the mouths of the two great rivers. I have added "theoretically" because it is highly unlikely that these were provinces that controlled territories within neatly delineated boundaries; indeed, the most fitting description for what they did control would be "spheres of influence" rather than territories. Commanderies and counties subordinate to Guangzhou were clustered along the waterways that drain into the Pearl River Delta and the South Sea west of the Leizhou Peninsula, whereas those subordinate to Jiaozhou were clustered in the Red River Plain and along the rivers that drained into the Gulf of Tongking. The territories inhabited by the Li and Lao lay about halfway between the two spheres and beyond the control of both.

The idea of the Li and Lao as people who dwelled between these two rivers also carries a secondary conceptual meaning in addition to the reference to geographical location; in historical consciousness, the Li and Lao are squeezed somewhere in between two better-studied fields of Chinese and Vietnamese national history and are regularly omitted from both. In the context of Chinese national history, the Li and Lao are an unimportant, eternally peripheral minority people whose bronze drums are a mere window dressing to the larger splendors of the Chinese national culture. In a Vietnamese context, they are considered unimportant because, despite their proximity to the heartland of Vietnamese proto-states in the Red River Plain, their territory lay outside the boundaries of what would become the Vietnamese state in later centuries. As a result, they have been denied a voice in both of these mainstream narratives, and when they have been studied at all it is usually in a Chinese context, relegated to the obscure field of minority history or *minzushi,* which generally denies them a voice of their own outside the retrospective historical narratives of the modern nation-state.[24]

THE TWO RIVERS REGION AND ITS WIDER REGIONAL CONTEXT

Addressing issues of center and periphery in Southeast Asian historiography, O. W. Wolters noted that "every center is a center in its own right as far as its inhabitants are concerned."[25] I have kept this statement in mind throughout the process of writing this book. As it is a history of peoples who have only been recorded lurking at the edges of the better-known Chinese and Vietnamese stories, it is important that they are placed firmly in the center of the narrative. It is for this reason that I have named the larger region surrounding the lands the Li and Lao drum makers inhabited the "Two Rivers" Region, to remove them conceptually from their minor role in the story of the great southern expansion of China[26] and to accentuate the difference between the shared historical development of the two urban centers of Guangzhou and Jiaozhou at the river mouths and that of the Li and Lao who lived between these centers.

The idea that human activities in China south of the Yangtze River originally had more in common with mainland Southeast Asia than with the Central Plains in the north began to appear in the 1940s and 1950s in the works of Chinese writers such as Xu Songshi and Luo Xianglin and the Japanese writer Matsumoto Nobuhiro.[27] Wang Gungwu considered the area as part of a unit he called "Ancient Southeastern Asia," arguing that Southeast Asia exclusive of southern China came into being only after political and cultural developments of the tenth century CE.[28] From the 1970s onward, these ideas were echoed in the works of Western archaeologists such as Don Bayard,[29] William Meacham,[30] and Wilhelm J. Solheim,[31] who began to consider southern China in prehistoric and early historic times as a northward extension of Southeast Asia rather than a southward extension of China. Charles Higham devoted a whole chapter to the Two Rivers Region as a coherent entity in itself within the larger context of the Southeast Asian Bronze Age.[32] This trend in Western archaeological scholarship of Southeast Asia to include the Pearl River drainage area as the northern extremity of Southeast Asia in prehistoric and early historic times is only just beginning to be carried over into the discipline of history.[33]

Although the French historian Denys Lombard agreed with the archaeologists in proposing that South China and Southeast Asia could not be considered in isolation from each other,[34] and Yoshikai Masato has argued for the recognition of the Two Rivers Region as a distinct historical region in its own right,[35] the trend among postwar historians who have studied the Two Rivers Region has been overwhelmingly to view it from a Sinocentric perspective as the exotic southernmost extremity of the Chinese Empire. This is largely due to the influence of thought patterns filtered through the available textual sources, which are all in Chinese. A few studies of the region exist made from this Chinese viewpoint,[36] and the most famous of these in English is undoubtedly Edward Hetzel Schafer's *The Vermilion Bird*.[37] No monograph since has described the region in such detail or such splendor as does Schafer's. Much of his scholarship on the flora and fauna of the region remains unsurpassed, and because he utilizes many sources dating from the Southern Dynasties rather than the Tang, I direct readers who are interested in the environmental history of the Two Rivers Region toward the two chapters on plants and animals in *The Vermilion Bird* rather than unnecessarily repeating his findings here.[38]

More recently, Charles Holcombe wrote two articles on the region from the Han to the Tang, again mainly relying on Chinese textual sources. His scholarship is particularly important, as he was the first to emphasize the similarities between the societies on the Pearl River and Red River Plains in contrast to those of the country that lay between them, rather than treating the former as distinctly Chinese and the latter as distinctly Vietnamese.[39] I argue a similar point that the most important distinction to be made is between the two river plains taken as a whole and the uplands between them, and extend the distinction to show how it was a reflection of the meeting of two larger cultural areas we would now distinguish as East and Southeast Asia. The provincial capitals on densely populated urbanized plains and the smaller outposts along the rivers and the coast were the southernmost permeations of the Chinese administrative and military culture, and these areas of the Two Rivers Region can rightly be considered the southernmost extension of an East Asian or Chinese cultural world. At the same time, however, the hill country away from the riversides and plains was the subtropical homeland of peoples who spoke languages belonging to the great mainland Southeast Asian language families (Austroasiatic and Kadai), whose folkways were closer to those now associated with upland Southeast Asian material and political cultures, including betel chewing, tattooing, dental modification by lacquering or filing, and living in stilt houses, in addition to the casting and use of bronze drums. It is for this reason that the Two Rivers Region, and its upland regions in particular, can be considered the northernmost extension of a Southeast Asian cultural world. For an inhabitant of the region during the Early Medieval period, this would have manifested itself in a clear upland-lowland distinction, far more significant than a supposedly observable Chinese and Vietnamese difference between the two urban centers of Guangzhou and Jiaozhou.

PREVIOUS STUDIES OF THE LI AND LAO PEOPLES

Scholarship specifically related to the peoples named Li and Lao in Chinese texts has mainly been carried out in Chinese and it is therefore necessary to approach it cautiously, armed with knowledge of the underlying assumptions and concerns of the writers. There are two particularly pervasive problems in Chinese-language scholarship on the indigenous peoples of the Two Rivers Region. One is the assumption that Chinese names for people equaled named realities and the other is the denial of indigenous agency. These problems stem in part from the minority politics of the People's Republic of China (PRC) and partly from uncritical readings of the original texts.

With regard to the meaning of names, both Chinese and non-Chinese writers often assume that the authors of ancient Chinese texts had sufficient knowledge about peoples other than themselves to distinguish between different ethnic groups, and that as a consequence names of peoples in Chinese texts must have referred to concrete and definable realities.[40] The results of this assumption at its most simplistic level are that the distribution of names in ancient texts is treated as proof of the geographical spread of ethnic groups, meaning that the appearance of an ethnonym in a new location is taken as evidence of *völkerwanderung*, and the disappearance of older names and appearance of new ones in the same geographical area is taken as an indication of a change in the area's ethnic groupings. This results in simplistic pedigrees such as the "Lao developed from the Luoyue" and the "Zhuang are descendants of the Li and Lao, who are descendants of the Hundred Yue." This is especially typical of Chinese scholarship that touches on the Li and Lao or bronze drums as part of larger comprehensive histories stretching over longer periods of time, such as the history of Guangdong province,[41] or of minority groups such as the Tai-speaking Zhuang whose invention was a product of ethnic classifications in the 1950s.[42] Writing the Li and Lao into the history of the Zhuang using modern ethnic classifications to interpret the texts of the past under the assumption that patterns of culture have remained stable over centuries is a practice referred to as "upstreaming,"[43] a bias on ethnic continuity over extremely long periods, and is a depressing characteristic of the vast majority of post-1949 Chinese scholarship on the history of many non-Sinitic peoples in China. A better class of Chinese scholarship does exist, however, and can generally be found in the writings of those who have dealt with a narrower time scale and subject matter, studies limited to, for example the Li and Lao specifically within the Early Medieval period. These writings tend to contain more nuanced readings of the texts and admit some disparity between named names and lived realities.

Ruey I Fu carried out some of the very best Chinese-language scholarship on the Li and Lao in the 1950s. His comprehensive *Laoren kao* (Investigations into the Lao) was notable in particular for its being the earliest collection of widely scattered original primary sources dealing with social customs and material culture.[44] Ruey collected as many descriptions as possible from old Chinese texts of the Li and Lao and Wuhu in the mode of a scientific survey, concluding that they were three distinct peoples based on what was observed from their different customs and cultures. In a similar manner to Ruey, Wolfram Eberhard believed that there were identifiable discrete cultures in the south of China that could be determined by records of their cultural characteristics over space and time, and he distinguished a definite Lao culture (although he always transcribed the name as "Liao").[45] Inez de Beauclair also distinguished such a culture by this name, tracing very carefully those who bore the names Gelao and Lao from the past down to the present.[46] All of these works were based on the belief that the name *Lao* always referred to the same groups of people over time.

Schafer began to question the idea that Lao was fixed as the name of a discrete ethnic group, noting instead that the name began with this meaning but was "gradually extended to all southern savages as a term of contempt,"[47] and that the identification of the name with certain cultural characteristics in the manner of Ruey was doubtful given the wide chronological range of the sources.[48] As far as the term *Li* was concerned, Schafer still believed this to be a more definite term indicating peoples related to the modern Li (Hloi) of Hainan.[49] In the 1980s, Xu Hengbin collected similar materials as Ruey relating specifically to the use of Heger II bronze drums, taking a view similar to Schafer's that the Li were a specific ethnic group, but identifying Li as the name for the creators of the bronze drums, a conclusion he based on a comparison of where this name was used with the distribution of drum finds. On the other hand, Xu considered Lao to be a generalized pejorative term for a native southerner similar to Man and Yi that was sometimes used in place of the term *Li*, which he considered the "correct" term for the ethnic group who created the bronze drums.[50] Taiwanese historian Liao Youhua's recent discussion of the Li and Lao is more concerned with ethnic identity problems as she debates whether certain individuals were "really" Li or Lao or were actually "Han Chinese" who had ended up being thus called.[51] The most careful discussion of the etymology of Li and Lao to date has been made by Edwin G. Pulleyblank, who made no attempt to pin the terms down as indicators of specific ethnic groups, concluding only that in the Guangdong region the terms *Li* and *Lao* were used to refer to the local non-Chinese inhabitants and conjecturing that "Lao was used in a broad sense to refer to the Tai-related populations of South China and that there was some basis for this in native usage."[52] Aside from Pulleyblank, the aforementioned writers were often concerned with the question of whether ethnonyms were being correctly applied or not, rather than questioning the essential significance of the names themselves as indicators of ethnic identity. In the end, attempting to discover who the Li and Lao "really" were as ethnic groups is an impossible task because it is based on texts that frequently contradict one another by referring to the same people with different names and using the same names for a widely dispersed variety of peoples. An easier question to answer, which also provides an explanation for the contradictions in the sources, is why such names were applied to people in the first place. One of the key arguments throughout this study is that application of the terms *Li* and *Lao* was not based on linguistic categories or obvious similarities in material culture, but instead was based loosely on a combination of factors including people's geographical location, their relationship to the Chinese empires, and observations of how their social structures and systems of government differed from those of the people who wrote about them in Chinese. Li and Lao societal structures, social behavior, and governmental systems were never static or fixed, nor were those that the writers of Chinese texts considered the norm for themselves, so the significance and application of the names not only differed from writer to writer, but also altered significantly over time. The method of choosing local administrators under the Southern Dynasties differed significantly from the practices of the Han Empire. The Southern Dynasties' tendency toward fragmentation of provinces into ever smaller units and their tolerance of localized gubernatorial dynasties ran parallel to a tendency toward local dynasties of Li-Lao chieftains controlling ever larger territories. The result of this convergence was that by the end of the sixth century it had become difficult for chroniclers to decide what terms to use for people. When writers no longer perceived any difference between themselves and groups of people in the Two Rivers Region, they abandoned the use of the terms *Li* and *Lao* and began to refer to them instead as the people or subjects of a locality, such as the "people of Jiaozhou" or "people of Guangzhou." These "nameless" people in the texts are the ordinary subjects of the Chinese empires, the antithesis of the Li and Lao "other," but there was no fixed boundary between the nameless and the named, rather an ever-shifting line between what those who wrote considered to be cultured and barbaric behaviors.

AGENCY AND SINIFICATION

Contemporary usage refers to the "nameless" people as Chinese or Han, but these terms were not used during the Early Medieval period to refer to groups of people,[53] and they should always be used with this qualification in mind. Contemporary historians writing about European peoples are usually careful to make distinctions between Romans and Italians, Gauls and French, Anglo-Saxons and English people,[54] but a lack of close knowledge of Asian history coupled with the Asian nation-states' promotion of their own long and glorious histories to their own citizens has guaranteed that anachronistic use of the terms *Chinese* or *Han* to people who lived thousands of years ago is often passed over without criticism. *China* is a deceptive collective term for what has been a disparate collection of empires, kingdoms, and republics that have controlled territories of widely varying size in the East Asian Mainland, and whose rulers have maintained a tradition of turning to the literature and philosophy of the society that flourished between the Yangtze and Yellow Rivers in the first millennium BCE for their models of political, linguistic, and social behavior. The power and prestige of the idea of "China" masks an infinite variety of "Chinese" people, languages, material, and religious cultures that were constantly changing over time. Unfortunately, because there are no better terms, I have retained the use of *Chinese* in certain situations to avoid long and prolix explanations, limiting it to the description of administrative structures of the various dynasties and those who worked for them, alongside *Sinitic* in reference to the speakers of languages closely related to modern Chinese.

As mentioned previously, influence of the abundance of Chinese-language sources on the Two Rivers Region has meant that historical scholarship of the region has traditionally approached it from a Sinocentric perspective as a small corner of the larger Chinese world. In Chinese-language scholarship, Chinese empires are depicted as either beneficent civilizers or developers (this is particularly prevalent in Chinese works) or as invaders and colonizers (more common in non-Chinese works). This resembles what Victor Lieberman recognized as the school of "externalist historiography" in regard to historical studies of Southeast Asia, a part of the colonial project that entailed ascribing all cultural innovations and advances in Southeast Asian to outsiders, denying indigenous Southeast Asians any agency or creativity of their own. In the works of the externalist school, Southeast Asians were depicted as the passive recipients of the gifts of greater civilizations than their own, such as the Chinese, the Indian, the Islamic, and ultimately the European. This style of scholarship later gave way to an "autonomous" approach, a study of Southeast Asian societies on their own terms, with emphasis on native Southeast Asians as active adopters and adaptors of the various cultural and political models with which they had become acquainted.[55] Although Southeast Asian peoples (including those of the Red River Plain) were long ago rescued from the externalist approach, the study of their relatives in the lands of the Two Rivers Region that have ended up in China still languishes under the influence of a narrative that Nicholas Tapp has described as "the long, slow march southwards of the dominant, conquering Chinese civilization . . . and its inexorable devouring of indigenous traditions."[56] This is the story of the expansion into the south that was the basic theme of the comprehensive works on the subject such as those of Harold J. Wiens[57] and Charles Patrick Fitzgerald,[58] and it leaves little room for indigenous agency.

The history of non-Chinese peoples in contemporary China is still highly politicized and censored, and views of the southward expansion of China current in Chinese scholarship are still largely caught up in the argument of what Stevan Harrell has called the "civilising project," which he described as a premodern narrative of Chinese administrators bringing civilization to benighted and backward savages repainted in Marxist colors as a process whereby the Han Chinese were highest up the ladder of the stages of human development and were merely pulling the minority peoples from "barbarism" or "slave society" up to their own higher social and production level.[59] Most Chinese-language works from the PRC on the Li and Lao portray them initially as economically and socially backward and emphasize the great improvements in their economic life and the advancement of their culture through feudalization (*fengjianhua*) from contact with the Chinese empires, the "opening up" or "development" (*kaifa*) of their lands, and their eventual mixture (*ronghe*) into the mainstream of Chinese society. These were the commonly expressed views until the 1990s and have remained so in historical works for popular consumption in which the Li and Lao are mentioned.[60] In the past, Chinese scholars also tended to deemphasize the role of military force in dealings with the Li and Lao, emphasizing instead a soft approach whereby local rulers were given imperial administrative titles and eventually peacefully mixed into Chinese society through exposure to Chinese culture.[61] This has been questioned in more recent Chinese scholarship intended for academic audiences, in which there has been a shift toward recognizing that violence, warfare, and economic exploitation were involved in the incorporation of the Li and Lao into the Chinese state. An early example is Wu Yongzhang's study of Southern Dynasties policy toward the Li and Lao, which noted that the Li and Lao grew politically and militarily stronger during the Southern Dynasties period, but also that they came under increasing attack and exploitation by the Southern Dynasties.[62] Peng Fengwen's studies of the Southern Dynasties policy toward the Li and Lao went so far as to criticize earlier scholarship for its downplaying of the military aspect of the conquest of the Lingnan region.[63] Despite this shift, the "civilizing project" demands that the Li and Lao are still treated as economically backward passive recipients of Chinese policy, constantly referred to with the anachronism "minority nationality" (*shaoshu minzu*), and are treated as the objects of attack and exploitation, but ultimately as the beneficiaries of civilization and Sinification. No attempts are made to describe the active response of the Li and Lao to contact with the Chinese empires, and therefore the Chinese discussions of Li and Lao history can be regarded as still essentially "externalist" in their approach.

Where politics and actions of the Li and Lao are described in detail, it is usually in terms of their loyalty or hostility toward the Chinese state, ignoring the possibility that they may have had other more localized concerns for their political allegiances or that their professed loyalties might have been more advantageous to themselves in the short term than to the empires they were supposedly serving. The Lady Xian (*Xian furen*), whose family is discussed in detail in chapter 7, the most well-known of the native Li leaders to be portrayed in this manner, is a case in point. She was married to Feng Bao, the governor of Gaoliang on the southern coast of Guangdong during the Chen dynasty (557–586), supposedly as part of a strategic alliance aimed at gaining the cooperation of the Li people with the local Chen administration. Because of her loyalty to the Chen and Sui empires after her husband's death, her influence over the other Li leaders to keep the peace for these empires, and her introduction of Chinese laws and regulations to the people she ruled, she has been frequently lionized in Chinese scholarship for her role in "safeguarding the country's unity."[64] The possibility that she engaged in a strategic alliance with her powerful neighbors with a view to increasing the influence of her own clan over other chieftains and the conquest of new territories is left out of the picture, and yet the result of the Lady Xian's successive alliances with the three empires brought her clan a huge increase in territory and gave her descendants such a strong grip on power in the lands to the southwest of Canton that it took the Tang over a century to wrest administrative power in this region from their grip. As for the question of Lady Xian encouraging the spread of Chinese civilization among her own people, it is true that her grandson Feng Ang was considered "Chinese" to the extent that he served as a trusted official at the Sui court, but in his home environment between the Two Rivers his primary role seems to be that of feared warlord, and his relative Feng Ziyou was still living as a drum-owning chieftain, despite his Chinese ancestry on his grandfather's side.

Two significant exceptions exist to the general Sinocentric externalism in historical scholarship on the Lao people, and can be found in the work of Wolfram Eberhard, who aimed to show how many indigenous southern cultural traditions had become embedded in Chinese mainstream culture, and that of Liao Youhua, who looked into the acculturation of clans from outside to the norms of the Li and Lao, describing them as "southern-barbarised Han" (*Manhua Hanren*).[65] Unfortunately, neither of these works managed to escape from the idea that there were concrete and definable ethnic groups such as "Han" and "Man" to begin with.

The eventual acculturation of the Li and Lao to Chinese norms of behavior and the end of their bronze drum culture between the rivers as long-term historical processes lend support to the larger conclusions of modern PRC nationalist discourse. As such it should not be surprising that the disappearance of the Li and Lao and their assimilation into greater China has received more scholarly attention in Chinese academic circles than their appearance and rise. However, the birth of the bronze drum culture and the growth of strong non-Chinese political structures between the Two Rivers several centuries *after* the conquest of the surrounding river plains and coast calls into question the assumption that close contact with one's Chinese neighbors inevitably led to the abandonment of one's own customs and political structures. Although this did eventually come to pass over the first millennium CE, in the shorter term, from the third to the sixth centuries, trade and contact between the Li and Lao between the rivers and the people of the Chinese-controlled river plains and coast had the opposite effect, triggering a process of territorial expansion of native Li-Lao political structures, ensuring their independence from direct Chinese rule and encouraging the spread of the drum culture. The focus in this work, therefore, is on the agency of the indigenous chieftains in their interactions with the encroaching Chinese.

APPLYING SOUTHEAST ASIAN METHODOLOGIES
TO THE STUDY OF THE LI AND LAO

Previously I noted that archaeologists have long considered the Two Rivers Region as a northern extension of Southeast Asia, but that historians who made use of written sources in Chinese have usually treated it as the southernmost frontier country of the Chinese empires. I argue that a Southeast Asian approach—a view from the south—is actually more helpful in understanding the growth of the Li-Lao bronze drum culture than the traditional Chinese view from the north. The Li and Lao between the Two Rivers were the linguistic ancestors of the Tai-speaking peoples of Southeast Asia, and as one searches through the Chinese records of the Li and Lao it is easy to find many similarities in material culture, economic systems, and political structures with those recorded later in the lands farther to the south. The Li and Lao between the Two Rivers chewed betel, lived in stilt houses, and made bark cloth, practices that were observed in mainland and island Southeast Asia over a thousand years later.[66] The significance of the drums as ritual objects and symbols of political power is also well known among the peoples of upland Southeast Asia, and Li-Lao trade with people in the river plains followed a similar pattern to the well-known hill-to-coast upriver-downriver trade in luxury items in exchange for iron and salt in Southeast Asia.[67] In their everyday life, the Li and Lao had much more in common with the highland peoples of mainland Southeast Asia than they did with the urbanized people of the Red and Pearl River plains, whose material culture and political organization bore closer resemblance to the capital of the Southern Dynasties at Jiankang and its hinterland.

Southeast Asian approaches are valuable to the prospective historian of the Two Rivers Region because of the similar dilemmas faced by those who study upland Southeast Asian peoples of more recent times. Whereas the urban centers of premodern China are well documented, the historian of the Two Rivers Region prior to the Tang must rely on a very limited range of written sources, all of them written by people who were foreign to the cultures they described. It is only for later periods that historians have access to texts written by non-Sinitic peoples of the Two Rivers Region and can find out how people viewed themselves, but such texts are of limited use for consideration of the very distant past.[68] Whereas historians who deal with the Chinese mainstream can rely on a vast wealth of written materials for their periods, the paucity of ancient textual sources for the study of premodern Southeast Asia (particularly the history of the upland peoples) has encouraged historians to augment their philological and textual research with findings from other disciplines such as archaeology, linguistics, and anthropology. Because written records of the Li and Lao exist only in fragmentary form, the disciplinary and theoretical approaches of Southeast Asianists offer many new and useful insights for its reconstruction, but despite the many similarities between the Li and Lao and the upland people to their south, few attempts have been made thus far to study the Li and Lao in this manner.

Although the majority peoples of the nation-states of Southeast Asia have been rescued from the colonial tradition of externalist scholarship, the people in their highland territories are frequently subject to the same prejudicial treatment as the minorities of Southern China. Named and classified by outsiders, they are considered backward and isolated, in need of a good dose of civilization (now frequently referred to as "development") from the economically and culturally advanced peoples of the lowlands that form the centers of Southeast Asian nation-states. The rescue of upland peoples from this type of discourse is an ongoing enterprise, carried out by either anthropologists or by historians with a strong anthropological bent. Many of their observations of upland Southeast Asian societies in recent times correspond very closely with what can be gleaned from Chinese textual sources about the Li and Lao, and their conclusions concerning ethnic classifications, highlander-lowlander relations, and the formation of highland political structures are extremely useful concepts for discussion of the history of Li and Lao society.

Edmund Leach's *Political Systems of Highland Burma* was a detailed study of the constantly shifting linguistic and social complexities of the upland people known as Kachins and Shans. Leach's work showed how the commonly accepted ethnic categorizations applied by outsiders were not congruent with the constantly shifting situations experienced by the highlanders themselves. Members of the societies studied by Leach lived within a constantly shifting pattern of social structures, were usually multilingual, and could shift from "Kachin" to "Shan" within a single generation.[69] To become Shan one needed only to live within a Shan state, be a follower of Theravada Buddhism, and have knowledge of a Tai language; although they were recorded and classified as an ethnic group by both British and Burmese authorities, there was in fact no impermeable border between the Shan and non-Shan in the nineteenth and twentieth centuries.[70] The complexity of lived reality on the ground is something to always be kept in mind when dealing with ethnonyms in texts that seem to suggest fixed and bounded realities.

An especially influential work in the reconsideration of Southeast Asian peoples who lived outside the reaches of the lowland river plain–based states has been James Scott's history of upland Southeast Asia, *The Art of Not Being Governed*, based on Willem van Schendel's original conception of the Southeast Asian massif as a single region named Zomia.[71] Van Schendel argued that there were more commonalities in human activity within the region than between it and the lowland states to which it is now politically subject.[72] Scott elaborated on the concept with the argument that Zomia was a refuge for those who wished to escape from state-building projects in the lowlands, who would make themselves difficult to govern through living in areas difficult of access, in dispersed societies that were politically decentralized and easily moved from one area to the other. Although Scott's argument focuses on much higher ground than the heartland of the Li-Lao bronze drum culture between the Two Rivers, he also analyzes a "mini Zomia" in the Pegu-Yoma range in central Burma, which is geographically very similar to the center of the bronze drum culture in the Yunkai and Yunwu mountain ranges.[73] Both are surrounded by plains and both were forested and difficult to access for lowland armies. Although the geographical similarities of the Li and Lao to the people of this area make it tempting to speak of them as the Zomians of the extreme northeast on account of their long-term retention of political independence against an encroaching Chinese state, the resemblance between the anarchic Zomian societies described by Scott and the Li and Lao between the rivers is only obvious in the very earliest Chinese records from the middle of the fourth century.

Although the earliest descriptions of Li-Lao societies in the third century CE describe them as small, scattered societies without paramount leaders, "living in separate villages with each its own chief, without lords or sovereigns,"[74] resembling thus the highland societies described by Scott, by the sixth century they had already transformed into something quite different. By this time, the people referred to as Li and Lao lived in more complex societies known to the Chinese as *dong*, ruled by a class of hereditary clan rulers known by names such as "Li commander" (*Lishuai*) or chieftain (*qiuzhang*), who sometimes no longer ruled over single *dong* but over large confederations of smaller *dong*. These societies were involved in slave trading and wet rice cultivation in valleys, both of which Scott associates not with highland societies but with the state-building projects on the plain. By the seventh century, the Li leaders of the Ning, Feng, and Chen clans ruled over alliances of smaller chiefs and were interested in acquisition of territory and slaves. In this regard, *dong* could conceivably correspond more to Condaminas's description of the typical Tai political unit, the *mueang*, rather than Scott's anarchic Zomian societies. The aristocratic rulers of *mueang* performed the roles of chiefs of war and organizers of food production, in return for which they owned rice fields, controlled the corvée labor with which to cultivate these, and received taxes in kind from the harvest of fruit and from hunting. Most importantly, the aristocratic leaders of *mueang* (known as *taaw*) held a commercial monopoly over the export of rare commodities, which in turn gave them control over prestige goods made by craftsmen or by industry.[75] Just how closely this description fits with descriptions of the leaders of the Li and Lao will become clearer as the work progresses.

The most fitting explanation for the growth of the Li-Lao polities and the concentration of political power in the hands of the Li commanders rather than village chieftains can be found in Oscar Salemink's work on highlander-lowlander relations in Vietnam, in which he proposed that local leadership in the highlands was actually the product of economic, political, and ritual exchanges with the lowlands.[76] The historical development of the Li and Lao echoes this very closely. The Li and Lao between the Two Rivers occupied territories beyond the control of the Southern Dynasties that contained many products sought after by the people in the Chinese-controlled provinces that surrounded them. There are written records of economic exchanges with the lowlands describing trade in gold, silver, and luxury items in exchange for salt, iron, and copper, but aside from these material benefits, an additional political advantage in the form of Chinese administrative titles was received by the chieftains who provided such trade items. A side effect of the trade exchanges through which titles were obtained actually encouraged the growth of localized chiefdoms through competition among small chiefdoms for territory and manpower. The greater the territory and manpower under one's command, the easier it would have been to organize the collection of precious metals and luxury items for the trade with the river plains. The adoption of Chinese titles by the Li and Lao chieftains did not of itself lead to wholesale replacement of native leadership traditions with those derived from Chinese models of government, as bronze drums remained a symbol of prestige for local Li and Lao leaders well into the seventh century, even though such leaders bore Chinese surnames and were purportedly of Chinese ancestry.

Although unrelated to Southeast Asian highland society, another very fruitful concept for analysis of the situation between the Two Rivers is Richard White's *Middle Ground*, his term for the geographical space in the *pays d'en haut*, or the lands around the rivers that flow into the North American Great Lakes from the mid-seventeenth to the early nineteenth centuries. When looking at Native American cultural change in the area, White tries to get beyond black-and-white concepts of assimilation to European norms or cultural persistence through resistance, and instead emphasizes the compromise and creativity through which new and different political and cultural structures appeared. What created this Middle Ground was the inability of both Indians and Europeans to use force to achieve their own ends (such as territorial conquest or control of the fur trade), and what aided its growth was the need for both sides to find means other than force to gain each other's cooperation and consent. Once the balance of power shifted in favor of the Europeans, the Middle Ground soon ceased to exist. Although there is much less in the way of primary source materials to illustrate a similar point for the Li and Lao, I argue that the bronze drum culture between the Two Rivers grew under similar conditions. For centuries, the Li and Lao chieftains were not subject to military conquest, but this was due neither to the munificence of the Chinese empires, nor to their aversion to taking military action. It was because the Southern Dynasties simply were not militarily capable of taking all that they wanted in one go. The Han Empire knew of the riches of the far south and was able to conquer the Red River Plain and territories as far south as modern central Vietnam, and the successor empires to the Han were able to keep a tenuous hold on most of the region, but they became aware of the riches of the lands between the Two Rivers only when they were too weak to carry out new large-scale military conquests. Although they ate slowly away at the edges of the Li-Lao country, encroaching upon it with counties and commanderies and sending small-scale military expeditions, the military power of the Southern Dynasties was concentrated along their northern borders against the greater threat of the powerful empires to their north and they were never capable of conducting an outright military conquest of the whole area.

The Li and Lao chieftains, on the other hand, were militarily powerful and economically self-sufficient to the extent that the Southern Dynasties had to negotiate with them to acquire the desired trade items. This only further encouraged the growth and strengthening of Li-Lao political structures and the enrichment of their own leaders so that eventually it was difficult even for the stronger empires of the Sui and Tang to knock them out by military means. Once the Tang Empire had consolidated its military and political strength, the large size of the Li-Lao chiefdoms became an advantage for the Tang, as it became necessary to gain the cooperation of only a few powerful and influential leaders in order to exercise indirect control over large areas of the country.

VIỆT, YUE, AND VIETNAMESE NATIONAL HISTORIES

One corner of the Two Rivers Region that has been given exceptional treatment throughout the first millennium CE is the Red River Plain. Exceptional not only refers to the amount of academic scrutiny it has received compared to other parts of the region, but also to the tendency of this research to treat the area as a special case in isolation from its surroundings, particularly those to its north and east. The subsequent fate of the Red River Plain was to become the cultural and historical heartland of states now associated with the name Vietnam, and consequently most of the academic attention bestowed upon this region in modern times has been carried out within a context of Vietnamese national history. As such, academic treatment of the Red River Plain and its surrounds over the twentieth century can be said to have followed the trend of Southeast Asian historiography along the path from "externalism" to "autonomy" outlined above: historical developments in the

Red River Plain were scrutinized in great detail by a generation of French scholars in the colonial period, then by a generation of Vietnamese scholars who witnessed the independence of Vietnam from French rule, who were in turn followed by a generation of Japanese and Western scholars influenced by this native Vietnamese postcolonial scholarship.

French scholarship on the Han-Tang period in the Red River Plain began in the late nineteenth century and was a quintessentially "externalist" tradition heavily influenced by Sinology, promoting the view that Vietnam had developed little of its own and had been content to borrow its entire culture from China. Such a view fed into justifications for European rule of Vietnam, as the Europeans saw themselves as simply following the historical trend of bringing civilization and development to a stagnant and backward area.[77] One French scholar, Leonard Aurousseau, considered Vietnam's debt to China to have even deeper roots than simply political and cultural borrowings and suggested that the population of the Red River Delta was a result of migration from the old Kingdom of Yue on the eastern coast of China.[78] These ideas influenced a later generation of scholars outside Vietnam. Joseph Buttinger, the author of the first scholarly one-volume history of Vietnam in English, was very much reliant on French scholarship of this kind, and he also believed that the Vietnamese were forced to adopt Chinese social and cultural inventions in order to successfully fight off the Chinese.[79]

By Buttinger's time, a new school of postcolonial Vietnamese historiography on the Chinese rule of Vietnam had already emerged in North Vietnam based within a grand story of heroic resistance to foreign invaders and strongly connected to the war against contemporary invading powers such as the Americans and the French.[80] French historian Philippe Papin summed this up as "a militant, nationalistic, and very contemporary vision through which emerged a hypothetical substratum of an original Vietnam that was miraculously preserved throughout a millennium of the Chinese presence."[81] In this narrative, the Chinese empires became merely the first of the outside colonizing forces to be eventually driven out of their land, and the "Chinese" are depicted as corrupt invading colonizers, interested only in the profits they could skim off from their conquered territory.[82] One should not judge the national school of Vietnamese history writing as entirely the product of present-day nationalism and anti-colonialism. For several centuries, the literati of Đại Việt had asserted the historical continuity and cosmic legitimacy of a Southern Empire (Đại Việt) as an equal of the Northern Empire (the various incarnations of "China"), recording how the Northern Empire had ignored this repeatedly only to suffer defeat.[83] The experience of the last two centuries with powers other than the traditional enemy merely caused a rewriting of the historical tradition in a new mold. Because very few Vietnamese scholars study the Han-Tang period at present, the most detailed scholarship in Vietnamese on the subject dates from before the 1980s, and the conclusions and interpretations of this period have become the national orthodoxy. For new interpretations of the period, one must look to the work of overseas scholars.[84]

In the 1970s, Japanese scholars began to follow in the footsteps of Vietnamese postcolonial scholarship, notably Gotō Kimpei and Katakura Minoru. Gotō's *Betonamu kyūgoku kōsōshi*, although it deals entirely with the Han-Tang period, makes the connection with the contemporary resistance to foreign occupiers obvious through the photographic illustrations of protestors and peasants calmly bending over their rice fields while their rifles are stacked close at hand.[85] Katakura Minoru's two-part study *Chūgoku shihaika no betonamu* was a much less politicized study of Chinese administration and tax-collecting practices in the Red River Plain throughout the Han-Tang period, but still emphasized the unique intractability of the people there.[86]

Scholarship of this kind had a strong influence on Keith Taylor's *The Birth of Vietnam*, published in 1983. This book covered the period from the late prehistoric period until the end of Chinese rule in the tenth century and has become the standard English-language reference work on the subject. In this book, Taylor followed the line of Vietnamese nationalist scholarship and asserted the strong continuity between the pre-Chinese semi-legendary kingdoms of the Red River Plain and the formation of Đại Việt as a restoration of sovereignty one thousand years later. At this time, Taylor believed that Vietnam's independence resulted from a thousand-year struggle to throw off Chinese rule by a group of people who held a conviction "that they were not and did not want to become Chinese."[87]

Jennifer Holmgren's work *The Chinese Colonisation of Northern Vietnam*, published at the same time as Taylor's, is regrettably less well known.[88] Despite the suggestion of the title, Holmgren made a close scrutiny of the Chinese texts without interpreting the events in terms of the millennial Vietnamese struggle for independence, and unlike Taylor, she did not use different transcription systems for the Chinese characters in the original texts to make distinctions between which individuals were on the Vietnamese side and which were Chinese.[89] She did, however, refer to Vietnamese and Chinese as if these terms made sense to the people of the time and used the terms *Sinicization* and *Vietnamization* when referring to political or cultural change in one direction or another.

All of the works just quoted take the existence of some kind of Vietnamese group consciousness as given, painting the events of the distant past retrospectively according to a Chinese-Vietnamese binary, but the existence of a group consciousness as Vietnamese in later ages is no evidence for its existence during the Han-Tang period. The very terms by which the Chinese-Vietnamese binary has been expressed in modern scholarship are

fundamentally misleading for the period in question, and they have no equivalents in the texts of the time. The word *Việt/Yue*, frequently encountered in
historical writing (especially that of Vietnamese writers themselves), is often
carelessly used as if it referred to an ethnic group, when in fact the term had
had many and varied referents and nuances of use in the Han-Tang period,
very few of which had any relation to the people of the Red River Plain.[90]
No one term can be pinned down that definitely refers to a cohesive group of
people over time in the Two Rivers Region.

Aside from the basic anachronisms inherent in the writing of national history, a major problem of the works in the Vietnamese national tradition is that
their field of vision is limited only to the areas that now lie within the modern
Vietnamese national boundaries.[91] Treatment of the plain in isolation from
its surroundings has led to conclusions about the exceptional nature of the
people there. It is true that, compared to the political situation in Guangzhou,
imperial control was less than stable, and localized uprisings, the development of localized dynasties of governors, and the tendency for these to take
control of local affairs when presented with the opportunity are easily interpreted retrospectively as signs of resistance or a wish for the restoration of
long-lost national independence.

Because they lived outside the boundaries of modern Vietnam, the Li and
Lao drum makers seldom receive much more than a mention in Vietnam-
centered works about the Han-Tang period, and where they do appear they
are usually mentioned as inconsequential "tribesmen" of the hills.[92] The Li
and Lao are crucially important for an understanding of the history of the
Red River Plain during the period of Chinese rule from the first to the tenth
centuries, both as comparative examples with which to reconsider assertions
of Vietnamese uniqueness and as a contributing factor to the tendency toward
the eventual political independence of pre-Vietnamese polities in the Red
River Plain.

THE LI AND LAO AND THE RED RIVER PLAIN

Through examination of the Li and Lao, comparing their political situation
from the first to the seventh centuries CE to that of the inhabitants of the Red
River Plain, and then making comparisons back to those in the area around
the mouth of the Pearl River, the similarities between the urban centers
around the mouths of the Two Rivers become very clear. In the light of such
comparison, even the leaders of the Red River Plain, celebrated in Vietnamese national history as promoters of independence, resemble the officers of
the Son of Heaven at Canton much more closely than they do the drum-
owning chieftains of the hill country.

Historical comparison with neighboring areas is not the only challenge to the Vietnamese national story. I have argued in detail elsewhere that the growth of Li and Lao power was partly responsible for the tendency toward de facto political independence in the Red River Plain, as they helped to isolate the area from direct overland connections with the rest of the Chinese empire, discouraging new migrations of people from the north, and allowing long-term resident families to establish power bases with little competition from outsiders. These then formed localized dynasties whose members became desirous of preserving privileged positions within the imperial bureaucracy for their own members.[93] The influence of these external factors on the political life of the Red River Plain in the Han-Tang period is still greatly understudied.

Comparisons between the Red River Plain and the Li and Lao bring into question many of the claims to Vietnamese particularism that are the underlying themes of Vietnamese national history. These can be grouped roughly under the three conceptual categories of *context, cultural continuity,* and *resistance.*

The concept of *context* refers to the consideration of Vietnamese history in the background of larger regional histories, in the Vietnamese case usually as part of Southeast Asia or as part of an East Asian grouping based on the areas that adopted Chinese character writing and systems of philosophy and government. The postcolonial Vietnamese historical tradition has downplayed the commonalities with the Chinese world and emphasized Vietnam's historical commonalities with the rest of Southeast Asia. Keith Taylor once referred to this question of belonging to one area or the other as "probably one of the least enlightening in Vietnamese studies," but was still drawn to express the observation based on it, viewing Vietnam as a unique blend of East Asia and Southeast Asia, with its roots firmly in Southeast Asia, but forced into East Asian cultural norms by Chinese rule.[94] Trần Quốc Vượng believed that a study of Vietnamese history and culture should begin in the context of Southeast Asia,[95] and Phạm Đức Dương went further and described the whole of Vietnam as a "Southeast Asia in miniature" because it contained representatives of all the major Southeast Asian language families.[96] However, when the context is changed and the Two Rivers Region is included as the northernmost extension of Southeast Asia as discussed previously, comparison back to the Li and Lao country makes the Red River Plain appear all the more Chinese.

Continuity refers to the argument advanced by Vietnamese historians that the people of the Red River Plain retained a Vietnamese "cultural core" throughout one thousand years of Chinese rule, which made them different from other groups in Southern China who eventually lost their separate identities through assimilation to Chinese culture.[97] Trần Quốc Vượng called this cultural core a "Việt constant" manifest, as he said "in the substratum of water-rice culture in villages and hamlets, with a substratum of Việt culture and ancient Việt myths and legends."[98] Although the term *Việt* is an anachronism when referring to the Han-Tang period, people who dwelled in the Red River Plain did retain features throughout the long period of Chinese imperial control that marked them as different from the people of other provinces, such as their spoken languages and mythological systems. None of this, however, was specifically limited to the people of the Red River Plain. Although it is true that over the very long term the Li and Lao eventually disappeared from the lands between the Two Rivers, this was a slow process that was perhaps not complete until the seventeenth century. Although their religious beliefs and languages are unfortunately largely lost to us in the present day, the Li and Lao and their descendants long outlived the destruction of their ruling class and the division of their lands into provinces and counties in the eighth century. In the tenth century, there were still people living between the Two Rivers who were considered sufficiently different from the imperial subjects of other Chinese provinces by those who described them to warrant the use of names to indicate their "barbarous" status.

Language is also often held up as another reason for the continuity of a Vietnamese consciousness as distinct from Chinese.[99] The whole idea of linguistic continuity in the Red River Plain has been brought into question by the research of John Phan, who argued from the structure of the modern Vietnamese language that it developed from a creolized language resulting from a language shift from Middle Chinese to proto-Vietnamese after the Han-Tang period, thus indicating that a large population had been speaking some form of Sinitic language prior to this time.[100] As for the Li and Lao, there is written evidence that these people were speaking different languages between the Two Rivers as late as the eleventh century.[101]

The linguistic and cultural changes that led to the situation of the present day, whereby those who live between the Two Rivers consider themselves Chinese and those in the Red River Plain consider themselves Vietnamese, were a not a product of the first millennium CE, but rather of the millennium that followed. During the thousand years of supposed Vietnamese cultural resistance to Sinification, it was actually the Li and Lao who remained distant from Chinese norms of material and social culture. The people of the Red River Plain were by comparison much more receptive to these norms.

Because of recent historical experience, the theme of *resistance* to outside invaders is probably the most celebrated in Vietnamese national history. The effect this has had on the historical treatment of the Red River Plain is the belief that the people who dwelled there were especially intractable and rebellious compared to other peoples who came into contact with the expansion of the Chinese empires. In his history of the Vietnamese for the general

English-speaking audience, Nguyen Khac Vien described the period of Chinese rule in the Red River Plain as marked by a "steadfast popular resistance marked by armed insurrections against foreign domination."[102] However, if one observes the activities of the people of Jiaozhou during the Han-Tang period side by side with those of the Li and Lao, and in particular during the period of the Southern Dynasties, there is in fact a reversal of what one would expect to find in the light of later events, which differs markedly from what is asserted in Vietnamese nationalist historiography. The various rebellions and uprisings carried out by the inhabitants of the Red River Plain are much less convincing evidence for the inextinguishable flame of the Vietnamese nation when juxtaposed with the activities of their Li and Lao neighbors to the north; these force a reconsideration of the received notion of the Red River Plain as a hotbed of revolt against the Chinese empires.

Unlike the Red River Plain, which had been under direct control of imperially appointed (or at the very least imperially sanctioned) administrators for the centuries following Ma Yuan's defeat of the Trưng Sisters in 43 CE, there was a core of Li and Lao territory between the rivers that was not subject to direct control by *any* Chinese empire until the defeat of the local chieftains by the Tang in the seventh century. The Red River Plain in Han times was under firm imperial control, and as the administrative center of the most populous commandery of the Han Empire in the Two Rivers Region, it contained twelve closely clustered subordinate counties, whereas all the land between the Yu River and the sea could only boast only four. Within a triangle with its points at present-day Wuzhou, Hepu, and Yangjiang, the center of the Li-Lao bronze drum culture, there was only one county, and the rest of the area lay for centuries at the remote edges of the three commanderies of Cangwu, Hepu, and Yulin, its population untaxed and unregistered.

For the two centuries after Ma Yuan's campaigns, the people of the Red River Plain were fairly subdued. During this time, no rebellions against imperial rule originated in the Red River Plain, although five occurred in the adjacent commanderies.[103] The only uprising to have spread into the plain was started in 178 by the Wuhu of Jiaozhi and Hepu—the people between the Two Rivers.[104] The rebellion of 248 led by Triệu Âu (the Lady Zhao) also spread to the Red River Plain, but began in the mountains of Jiuzhen.[105] The nature of leadership in the Red River Plain in the two centuries after Ma Yuan was also significantly different from that of the Li and Lao between the rivers, based on appointments of governors from the imperial center. Later, during the politically weak Southern Dynasties, local rulers in the Red River Plain held imperial administrative titles or demanded recognition of their de facto political rule from the Southern Dynasties by use of these titles, going into open rebellion only when their efforts were frustrated or when the dynasties attempted to impinge on their local rights by appointing outsiders as the local administrators. Those who went so far as to declare themselves kings or emperors were not necessarily doing so because of resurgent national feeling; it was a common occurrence during times of political weakness at the center for disgruntled officials in all parts of the empire to try their chances for the throne, and they often adopted names of local historical importance as the name of their prospective empires. Within the Two Rivers region as a whole, the title king or emperor of Yue was a perennial favorite.[106]

This study will show that during the Southern Dynasties the people of the Red River Plain were actually more likely to accept Chinese political structures and modes of leadership than the Li and Lao. This is why the Li and Lao usually ended up with pejorative names indicating savagery and barbarity, and why their leaders were known as chieftains, whereas the people of the Red River Plain were referred to as "people" or "subjects" ruled by "governors" very similar to the people who lived around modern Canton, and it was not until the end of the sixth century that a local leader, Lý Phật Tử, was referred to as a Li person. The method with which the Southern Dynasties tried to deal with the local rulers of the Red River Plain was similar to the way they dealt with other rebellious officials and localized dynasties in their southern provinces, and the trend toward self-government in the Red River Plain has more to do with the weakness and ineffectiveness of the Southern Dynasties' rule and the constant threats to them from the Northern Dynasties, which kept military attention concentrated elsewhere.

The Li and Lao were in a different situation altogether from the people of the Red River Plain. Never having been subjected to full-scale military conquest by the Han, they remained in control of their own resources and territories throughout the Southern Dynasties, during which time their rulers consolidated such strong power bases that it was not a simple task even for the stronger successor empires of the Sui and Tang to march armies into their territory. The difference between the Red River Plain and the lands between the Two Rivers is most easily observed at the time the empires of the Sui and Tang came to conquer the Two Rivers Region. The method these empires used to gain control of the Red River Plain was significantly different from the methods they applied to the Li and Lao. Sui general Liu Fang had been able to capture the local self-appointed leader Lý Phật Tử of Jiaozhou and the Sui was able to easily install Qiu He to rule as inspector to replace him. The Tang Empire gained control of the Red River Plain when Inspector Qiu He recognized it as the new imperial authority, and thereafter the Tang court was able to appoint governors and inspectors of its own choosing and rule the people of the plain directly without needing to rely on the agreement of powerful local families.[107] In contrast, the Sui and Tang were unable to appoint officials from the center between the Two Rivers and were instead obliged to seek the cooperation and agreement of the local Li families for control of the area, sometimes appointing them as local officials. It took another fifty years for the Tang to wrest control of the lands between the rivers from the hands of these families and begin to appoint officials of their own. When viewed from the imperial capitals of China, the people of the Red River Plain may often have seemed uncontrollable, but when compared to the Li and Lao during the same period, they appear to be much more compliant with the demands of the imperial center.

BRONZE DRUMS AND THE LI AND LAO

Particularly relevant to the discussion of Vietnamese historiography is their bronze drum tradition. Vietnamese national history holds up the Đông Sơn bronze culture as an example of the authentic national culture before the Chinese conquest, and the Heger I Đông Sơn drums have been used by the Vietnamese state as a symbol of the pre-Chinese indigenous traditions, a quintessentially Vietnamese symbol that predates the forced foreign accretions of colonialism typical of later Vietnamese culture linking the Vietnamese people back to their Southeast Asian roots when they had an influential and important civilization of their own.[108] The drums are displayed as national treasures in the national museum in Hanoi, and carved miniature copies can be found in souvenir shops all over the city; the tympanum of the Ngọc Lũ drum can be found on T-shirts and postcards, and as a large transfer stuck on the windows of Vietnamese restaurants the world over. With Ma Yuan's conquest, native traditions of leadership in the Red River Plain came to an end, and the Đông Sơn bronze drum culture of the Red River Plain soon followed suit. After this came a period in which Chinese-style titles (and presumably regalia) became the symbols of governmental authority there. Just as the drum-casting tradition was being lost in the Red River Plain, a new and vigorous tradition began to blossom between the Two Rivers that would last for five centuries.

As the most important artifact that the Li and Lao left behind, the drums tell the story of the Li and Lao in a way merely hinted at in the Chinese textual records,[109] but the modern geopolitical situation in the Two Rivers Region has ensured that the Heger II drums have remained understudied. They still languish in obscurity while the famous Đông Sơn culture associated with Vietnam gets all the attention, as well as the naming rights. It is not surprising that this has occurred; at the level of Chinese national history, the Heger II drums occupy a minor position, not as a symbol of a lost national culture, but rather as features of the "nationality cultures"[110]—subsets of the greater whole that is China, and therefore hidden behind a whole raft of accomplishments of past dynasties that have been adopted as symbols of the Chinese national culture. Although they are considered important historical artifacts in Guang-dong and Guangxi, in the larger discussion of PRC national culture the drums are peripheral, a small contribution to the greater national culture, as a symbol of local diversity and "nationality history."[111]

To its great detriment, the study of bronze drums has been divided along national lines. Both Chinese and Vietnamese scholars were eager to claim credit for the invention of the bronze drum for their own nation-states. This caused a protracted academic battle in which Chinese scholars claimed that the type II drum was the original style of drum, the use of which predated the type I drums of the Red River Plain and Yunnan by centuries.[112] Even if the debate on the ultimate origins of drums is left out of the discussion, the national boundary still influences scholarship on the distribution and trans-mission of drum cultures.[113] Chinese scholars usually view the production of Heger II drums as a direct descendant of the type I drums produced by the Dian culture of Yunnan, ignoring the possibility that the drum-casting tradition may have passed through an area that is not present-day Chinese territory.[114]

The Japanese scholar Yoshikai Masato has provided a convincing argu-ment for the transmission of drums and drum-casting techniques from the lower Red River northwestward, rather than direct transmission from Yun-nan.[115] Several other pieces of evidence add weight to Yoshikai's argument: the cliff paintings at Huashan along the banks of the Zuojiang ("left-hand") River in Guangxi in which over two hundred and fifty bronze drums are depicted[116] lie along a convenient route from the Red River Plain to the Pearl River drainage area. Heger I drums have been found in Guangxi but mainly in the far northwest close to Yunnan, which suggests a stronger connection with the Dian culture.[117] Finally, the high lead content of the type II bronze drums found between the Two Rivers is similar to the lead content of Đông Son bronze but very different from that of the Heger I drums of northern Guangxi,[118] and this seems to add weight to Yoshikai's argument for a north-east flow of drum casting and the fashion of drum ownership into the Li-Lao country from the Red River Plain.

Regarding the time period of transmission, events of the later Han in par-ticular lend support to the argument for transmission of drums from the Red River Plain at that time. During the first and second centuries CE, there was some political connection between the native rulers in the Red River Plain and those to the northeast, in particular the rebellion of the Trưng Sisters in 40 CE. This began in the Red River Plain, but soon involved the indigenous peo-ples of Jiuzhen and Rinan, and most importantly those of Hepu. The uprising of 178, mentioned earlier, moved in the opposite direction, sparked off by the Wuhu of Hepu and Jiaozhi and then spreading southward as far down as what is now central Vietnam. Both of these events occurred in roughly the same period in which drum production is supposed to have begun between the Two Rivers. It was probably the gravitational pull of strong leadership in the Red River Plain that made the drums a status symbol in the eyes of surrounding peoples and gave the impetus to the local leaders of the Zuojiang River to begin producing their own drums as symbols of their own chiefly authority, and probably a similar process again that brought them to the lands between the rivers where economic circumstances and an abundant supply of copper allowed production to flourish again.

A further connection between the drum tradition of the Red River Plain and the Li-Lao drum culture is apparent from the etymology of the word used for *drum* in modern Vietnamese and the Kadai languages. The modern Vietnamese word for a drum is *trống*, but the oldest record of the pronunciation of the word is *tlóu* in de Rhodes's Vietnamese-Portuguese dictionary of 1651.[119] A clue as to how the word was pronounced even earlier is provided by the earliest written record of the word in Chữ Nôm, the old Chinese-based Vietnamese demotic script. Nguyễn Trãi's *Quốc Âm Thi Tập*, which dates from the first half of the fifteenth century, writes the word as 挂,[120] made up of two elements pronounced *cổ* 古 and *lộng* 弄 in Sino-Vietnamese and combined in a single character to convey the sound of the entire syllable *klong*, a common practice in the earliest Nôm writings.[121] The form of the character suggests very strongly that the word was originally pronounced with an initial [k-] rather than a [t-] in de Rhodes.[122] An identical Nôm character was used in the Nôm script of the Tai-speaking Tày people to represent the word *tổng*, meaning "drum."[123] The common Tai word for drum is found as *kjong*, *kong*, and *tsong* throughout the Tai languages of south China and Southeast Asia and the ancestral proto-Tai form for these variants has been reconstructed as **klɔɔŋ*.[124] Judging by the correspondence of the initial consonant cluster with other more distantly related Kadai languages, the direction of borrowing seems to have been from proto-Tai into proto-Vietic, rather than the other way around.[125] Vietnamese scholars have noted a strong proto-Tai influence on the language ancestral to modern Vietnamese. The borrowing of the word for "drum" from proto-Tai into Austroasiatic would seem at first to contradict the direction of the transmission of drum culture proposed by Yoshikai if it were not for the fact that there is also evidence of a strong proto-Tai influence on the vocabulary of proto-Vietnamese[126] and shared vocabulary relating to the production of rice.[127] No matter what the direction of these borrowings may have been, they indicate at least that speakers of proto-Tai and proto-Vietic lived in close proximity to each other and that there was a long-standing tradition of mixture and borrowing among these language families in the Two Rivers Region.

The foregoing should be reason enough to raise suspicion whenever bronze drums are claimed as the distinctive cultural property of any modern nation-state or linguistic or ethnic group. They are a common feature of material cultures of many different peoples in far-flung areas throughout mainland and island Southeast Asia and share a similar cultural significance throughout the region to widely different peoples as symbols of authority, wealth, and power. Oscar Salemink has noted that wealth in upland Southeast Asia was connected to the possession of certain ritual objects that could only be acquired through long-distance trade, and the bronze drums, although of local manufacture, seem to fulfill a similar function.[128] The many Zhou-style *ding* tripods of local manufacture found in graves predating the Han in the Pearl River drainage area show that the display of one's status through ownership of such objects was a cultural trait that long predated the drum culture in the Two Rivers Region.[129] The popularity of bronze drums for the Li and Lao who were lucky enough to live in areas rich in copper resources was most likely a continuation of the same tradition, the only difference being that the objects of desire were no longer modeled on ritual objects from the distant north, but those in possession of the neighboring (and possibly related) ruling classes of the Red River Plain. Bronze drum production in the Red River Plain did survive Ma Yuan's large-scale destruction of the indigenous ruling class for a time. A bronze drum and earthenware casting mold have been found in the remains of Luy Lâu citadel near Lũng Khê in Bắc Ninh province, a site dating from the second to the sixth centuries.[130] Even so, by the end of the third century CE, a new ruling class had developed in the Red River Plain that was content with the legitimacy conferred by imperial recognition of their position as administrators, and judging by the lack of later drum finds and written records of drum use in the central Red River Plain, they had probably begun to see bronze drum ownership as the barbaric custom of hill dwellers.[131] Among the Li and Lao between the rivers, the drum culture went on to flourish as an independent tradition of its own.

Drums were the symbols of local chiefly authority between the Two Rivers, and the number of those cast during the four centuries leading up to the foundation of the Tang Empire in the seventh century is material evidence for the autonomous power of local leaders and the lack of effective control the Southern Dynasties had over the countryside away from the coast and the main river systems. The timing of the drum-casting tradition is particularly significant: it did not begin until at least two centuries *after* the supposed conquest of the entire region of southern China by the Han Empire in 111 BCE. The heartland of drum production lay directly between the two largest Chinese cities in the region and appears to have grown and flourished even when surrounded on all sides by smaller commandery centers.

The geographical spread and number of drum finds between the rivers sheds light on many aspects of Li and Lao societies, their distribution, their complexity, and their relationships to the people of the Southern Dynasties. The extent of lands under control of the Li and Lao chieftains can be ascertained from combining the areas where there were no Chinese counties or commanderies with those areas where large numbers of bronze drums have been found. The number of drums found there suggests that there was a high level of wealth and complex social organization. Nguyen Duy Hinh estimated that, depending on the quality of copper ore, the amount required to make a single 72-kilogram drum could range from 1,000 to 7,000 kilograms. However, one person was probably only capable of extracting 10 to 20 kilograms of ore in a single day.[132] The Heger type II drums are often twice the size of their Heger I counterparts, and the casting of a single Heger II drum would therefore require double the labor. The social organization of the Li and Lao chieftains must have been sufficiently complex to support such a labor force as well, not to mention the artisans who created the drums. The growth and popularity of the culture during the Six Dynasties in an area that had been surrounded for centuries by commanderies and counties show that the drum-making tradition was not adversely affected by contact with the Chinese empires. The social prestige given by drum ownership pulled in the opposite direction from the world of bureaucratic administration and book learning associated with the Sinitic empires. Appealing to local sensibilities and local tastes, drums offered alternative symbols of authority to the administrative titles received from the Chinese empires. By their popularity from the Han to the Sui in both the copper-producing heartland and the east closer to Canton where copper was more difficult to obtain, I argue that the non-Sinitic people on the periphery of the Li-Lao country were not looking toward cities like Canton or populations of Sinitic speakers for their models of social organization, but gravitating instead to the drum-owning chiefs of the Li-Lao heartland.

METHODOLOGY AND SOURCES

Because the Li and Lao have left no written records of their own, to make some sense of their history one must rely initially on the fragmentary descriptions found in old Chinese texts. These textual sources are themselves problematic as the most detailed are still little more than outside observations of peoples peripheral and remote to the tradition that produced the written word. The writers of Chinese texts showed little interest in the internal political machinations of those they considered barbaric and, as far as is known, no attempt was made to investigate the internal histories of the Li and Lao people, and the events that were recorded were mainly connected to conflict with the Chinese. Although there are sufficient records in Chinese to arrange into a chronology for an article or chapter on the Li and Lao drum makers, studies limited to these fragmentary texts cannot help but be one-dimensional.

To gain a fuller and more nuanced picture of the Li and Lao, it is important to compare and analyze the texts through materials from outside the Chinese literary tradition, specifically the results of research from disciplines such as archaeology, historical linguistics, and historical anthropology.

Xu Songshi was the first Chinese writer to apply this combined approach to the study of the Two Rivers Region by using textual criticism based on historical linguistics and archaeology in his 1939 work *Yuejiang liuyu renmin shi* (History of the Peoples of the Yue River Drainage Area). The lack of textual materials relating to the Red River Plain and the abundance of archaeological finds have meant that Vietnamese historians have long been aware of the value of these other disciplines, with the addition of collected folklore, to provide historical answers, or as Trần Quốc Vượng put it, to put "flesh" on the mute archaeological "bones."[133] Such an approach resulted in the highly detailed (and highly imaginative) collection *Hùng Vương Dựng Nước* (The Foundation of the Country by the Hung Kings),[134] and has also become a popular approach in the study of Zhuang history.[135] The only problem is that those who have used such approaches have the unfortunate tendency toward anachronism, not only in their use of names, but also in the use of texts that were written centuries (sometimes millennia) after the period in question, quoting their contents as if they were primary sources. Historical works from Đại Việt and Ming times are particularly suspect when they deal with earlier periods because their writers were on the lookout for evidence in the distant past to explain their contemporary political situations.[136]

In my use of primary sources, I try as much as possible to follow the practice of Schafer, who used contemporary sources exclusively "in order to avoid the anachronisms which could make the characterisation of a particular era ridiculous."[137] Aside from the standard dynastic histories, the written sources I have used for this work are the "lost books," the contents of which survive only in fragmentary form (sometimes only as a single line) in encyclopedias compiled during the Tang and Song Dynasties. The only exceptions I have made to this rule are for materials that deal with distributions or descriptions of natural resources or wildlife, or linguistic material that has been transmitted unconsciously, because it is unlikely that any of these were employed for political purposes.

GENERAL ARGUMENT AND OVERVIEW OF REMAINING CHAPTERS

The story of the growth of the Li-Lao chiefdoms and their drum culture shows that geographical proximity to Chinese centers, years of Chinese military campaigns, and the long-standing Chinese practice of alliances accompanied by bestowing official titles on local rulers did not lead the Li and Lao automatically to be absorbed into the imperial administrative system or to fully adopt Chinese social and political customs. On the contrary, for most of the four centuries leading up to the Tang, Li and Lao contact with the Chinese empires actively encouraged the growth of their own political structures and their control over their own people. The final result was that even the powerful empire of the Tang was unable to rule the Li and Lao directly and was forced for the first few decades to appoint clan rulers as administrators before consolidating sufficient power in the region to replace these with appointees from the court. What we can discern here in the story of the Li and Lao is a pattern of interaction that would continue across this southern mountainous region for centuries to come, beyond the lands between the Two Rivers.

The following chapter sets the scene with a description of the larger geographical context of the Li and Lao societies. The first part is a survey of the two urban centers that lay to their east and west near the mouths of the Two Rivers, their hinterlands, the communication routes between them and other urban centers of the Southern Dynasties, and what textual and archaeological sources can tell us about post-Han changes in demography, economy, and political structures. The second part is devoted to the lands between the Two Rivers and how its population evaded direct Chinese rule even though it was firmly imposed on the people of many of the districts that surrounded them. Chapter 3 is a discussion of the difficulties involved in accepting Chinese names for foreign peoples on their periphery at face value. Here I address the varied and changing meanings of the various names used for the people who lived between the Two Rivers in Chinese texts, giving the region-specific terms *Li*, *Lao*, and *Wuhu* special attention. I argue that the ultimate etymology of these names in the native languages of the region has very little to do with the way such names were later used by Chinese writers. I also argue that rather than being the result of careful classification based on linguistic affiliation or cultural traits, it is far more likely that the use of names was based on the geographical habitat, economic activities, and modes of government of the people they referred to, coupled with a heavy reliance on older Chinese literary traditions of referring to those considered uncivilized or barbaric. It is for this reason that it is improbable that Li and Lao actually corresponded to any coherent groupings of people as has been often supposed, and once the underlying reasons for the use of names in Chinese texts are recognized, it becomes easier to understand why there are so many odd discrepancies in their use.

Chapter 4 concentrates on trends of political and social change in the Li and Lao governmental systems, beginning with the political structures of the Li and Lao, moving on to how these altered through prolonged contact with the administrative systems of the various Chinese empires from the Han onward, and finally to how they came to resemble those of the Chinese until they were almost indistinguishable from one another. Change among the Li and Lao is only part of the story, however. At the same time that Li and Lao chieftains were taking on some of the characteristics of Chinese-style governors, Chinese modes of government were changing, relying increasingly on hereditary rule over ever smaller areas of the countryside, with the result that it eventually became difficult to distinguish hereditary governors from hereditary chieftains.

Chapter 5 details the attempts of the Southern Dynasties to make inroads into the lands between the rivers through military force, and the corresponding changes in Li and Lao military technology that made this more difficult as the Southern Dynasties grew ever weaker and the Li and Lao ever more capable of causing problems for the outposts of the Chinese state.

Chapter 6 discusses the Li and Lao trade with the Chinese empires and its effects on the growth of Li-Lao political structures. I give attention to the advantageous position of the Li and Lao in this trade through their control of territories where mineral resources (gold and silver) and luxury items sought after by the Chinese (such as ivory and kingfisher feathers) were abundant, proposing that the growth of larger autonomous Li-Lao polities was due to their internal competition for the monopoly of trade in such resources. I also argue that through this trade, the Chinese acquired knowledge of the uses of certain plants and animals between the Two Rivers, and give a few examples of cultural borrowings that moved in a south-to-north direction.

The seventh and final chapter discusses the larger Li-Lao–based political structures that had developed between the Two Rivers by the late sixth and early seventh centuries, singling out three of the most well-known ruling families between the Two Rivers as examples of a type who had an ambiguous status in Chinese texts, constantly shifting between the categories of uncivilized foreigner and ordinary imperial subject, between the role of chieftain and governor. This chapter ends with the destruction of their leaders' monopoly on power between the Two Rivers and the final disappearance of the Li-Lao chieftains.

NOTES

1. The seat of government of Gongzhou is today's Pingnan County in east central Guangxi.

2. The seat of Gaozhou lay to the northwest of present-day Maoming in Guangdong province. The source for these two records is Liu Xun's tenth-century miscellany *Lingbiao luyi*, LBLY ch. 1: 4.

3. LWDD ch. 7: 254.

4. GHYHZ 14.

5. GXTZ 229: 1a.

6. Wang Jia 王佳, "Zhouheng tonggu nishen bao guojia yiji wenwu—shen gaodu guan quanguo" 周亨銅鼓擬申報國家一級文物身高度冠全國, Huaxia.com news article sourced from *Nanfang ribao* 南方日報, August 7, 2009, http://big5. huaxia.com/zhwh/whbh/2009/08/1525896.html.

7. Li Minzhan 李明湛, "Jiangmen Enping jingxian daxing Donghan tonggu gumian zhijing chao yi mi" 江門恩平驚現大型東漢銅鼓 鼓面直徑超一米, *Jiangmen ribao* 江門日報, September 15, 2009, http://news.china.com/zh_cn/history/all/11025807/20090915/15639778.html.

8. Zhang Zhoulai 張周來, "Guangxi rongxian faxian liangqian nian qian datonggu—tixing shuoda wenshi jingzhi" 廣西容縣發現兩千年前大銅鼓一體型碩大紋飾精緻, *Xinhuawang guangxi pindao* 新華網廣西頻道, December 13, 2010, http://www.gx.xinhuanet.com/dtzx/2010-12/13/content_21621008.html.

9. Xu Haiou 許海鷗, "Wachu tonggu bei er wumai cunmin qianyuan shuhui jiao guojia" 挖出銅鼓被兒誤賣村民千元贖回交國家, *Nanguo ribao* 南國日報, April 9, 2011, 9.

10. Zhou Ruyu 周如雨, "Wuming xian luobo zhen cunmin wa chu qiannian tonggu" 武鳴縣羅波鎮村民挖出千年銅鼓, *Nanguo zaobao* 南國早報, June 17, 2014, 11.

11. For a useful overview of the typologies adopted by Chinese and Vietnamese scholars and their relationship to each other, see Han Xiaorong, "Who Invented the Bronze Drum? Nationalism, Politics, and a Sino-Vietnamese Archaeological Debate of the 1970s and 1980s," *Asian Perspectives* 43, no. 1 (2004): 7–33.

12. Some authors refer to many different types of bronze drums indiscriminately as Đông Sơn, even those not found at the Đông Sơn site, for example, Ambra Calò, *The Distribution of Bronze Drums in Early Southeast Asia: Trade Routes and Cultural Spheres* (Oxford: Archaeopress, 2004); Nishimura Masanari 西村昌也, "Hokubu vietonamu dōko wo meguru minzokushiteki shiten kara no rikai" 北部ヴィエトナム銅鼓をめぐる民族史的視点からの理解, *Tōnan ajia kenkyū* 東南アジア研究 46 no. 1 (2008): 3–42. The authors of *Dong Son Drums in Vietnam* state that Heger II drums should not be referred to as Đông Sơn drums; see Pham Huy Tong, ed., *Dong Son Drums in Vietnam* (Hanoi: Vietnam Social Science Publishing House, 1990), 268.

13. The largest bronze drum ever found is the "king of bronze drums" (*tonggu wang*), 1.65 meters across the tympanum, unearthed in Beiliu in 1955. See Yao Shun'an 姚舜安, Wan Fubin 萬輔彬, and Jiang Tingyu 蔣廷瑜, eds., *Beiliu xing tonggu tanmi* 北流型銅鼓探秘 (Nanning: Guangxi renmin chubanshe, 1990), 4, 8.

14. The largest bronze drum of Heger type I ever found is the Ngọc Lũ I drum unearthed in Lý Nhân prefecture in Hà Nam province, with a tympanum 79 cm in diameter (Pham, *Dong Son Drums*, 4–5).

15. Ibid., 170.

16. This number is a total of the two subsets of Heger II drums used at present in China, the 164 examples of Beiliu style drums recorded in Yao Shun'an, *Beiliu xing tonggu tanmi*, 8–23, and the seventy-one examples of the Lingshan style recorded in Yao Shun'an 姚舜安, Jiang Tingyu 蔣廷瑜, and Wan Fubin 萬輔彬, "Lun lingshan xing tonggu" 論靈山型銅鼓, *Kaogu* no. 10 (1990): 929–43.

17. Pham, *Dong Son Drums* is a comprehensive catalogue of all drums found in Vietnam by that date.

18. Even though Chinese researchers have determined that the period of drum casting only began during the Eastern Han Dynasty (23–220 CE), it is common for Chinese museums and media to attach the longest possible pedigree to the drums and uncritically report or display newly found drums as relics from the Han Dynasty, ignoring the possibility that they could have been cast over five centuries later. For dating of the Heger II type drums, see Jiang Tingyu 蔣廷瑜, "Yueshi tonggu de chubu yanjiu" 粵式銅鼓的初步研究, in *Gudai tonggu xueshu taolunhui lunwenji* 古代銅鼓學術討論會論文集 (Beijing: Wenwu chubanshe, 1982), 143–47, and Zhongguo gudai tonggu yanjiuhui 中國古代銅鼓研究會, *Zhongguo gudai tonggu* 中國古代銅鼓 (Beijing: Wenwu chubanshe, 1988), 117–22.

19. The term *Northern and Southern Dynasties* is now preferred in Chinese, however, because it recognizes the legitimacy of the Northern Dynasties, which traditional Chinese histories frequently did not. The term *Six Dynasties* refers to the empires of the Wei, Jin, Liu-Song, Qi, Liang, and Chen, and the Southern Dynasties only to the last four.

20. Geoff Wade, "The Lady Sinn and the Southward Expansion of China in the Sixth Century," in *Guangdong: Archaeology and Early Texts*, ed. Shing Muller, Thomas Hollmann, and Putao Gui, South China and Maritime Asia Series vol. 13 (Wiesbaden: Harrassowitz Verlag, 2004), 140–41.

21. Particularly common are place names beginning in *na* 那, which is Tai for a paddy field. For a discussion of this and additional evidence for the former use of Tai languages in this area in the toponyms of this region, see Xu Songshi 徐松石, *Yuejiang liuyu renmin shi* 粵江流域人民史 (Shanghai: Zhonghua shuju, 1939), 192–209, and Li Jinfang 李錦芳, *Dongtai yuyan yu wenhua* 侗台語言與文化 (Beijing: Minzu chubanshe, 2002), 288–301. Note that both of these works are to be used with caution when dealing with place names found in texts prior to the Tang.

22. Note that this is only done when speaking about the Li and Lao in a general sense; when translating from a primary source I give the name exactly as it appears in the text.

23. River terminology is extremely confusing, as rivers not only change their names over time, but different stretches of the same river have different names. The modern term *Pearl River* refers properly to the whole river system that enters the sea at Canton, and *West River* (*Xi Jiang*) refers to the river only as far west as Wuzhou. The very handy Southern Dynasties term *Yu River* referred to the entire stretch of river from Canton to present-day Nanning. Because it has no equivalent shorthand term in present-day usage, I have revived its use in this book, retaining Pearl River only when referring to the entire river system that drains into the sea in Guangdong.

24. When they are mentioned at all in national histories, Tai groups are cast in a supporting role as a sideline to the important events of the centers. In "nationality history" *minzushi* they receive detailed treatment, but are depicted as eternal minorities, as ancestors to the Chinese Zhuang or Vietnamese Tày-Nùng and the other classifications popularized in the 1950s for the Tai-speaking peoples in both countries.

25. O. W. Wolters, *History, Culture and Region in Southeast Asian Perspectives*, rev. ed. (Ithaca, NY: Southeast Asia Program, Cornell University, 1999), 17.

26. There are already several names for this region that have been used in other studies: the Tang Dynasty circuit of Lingnan "The Land South of the Passes" included the coast and river plains of the northern half of modern Vietnam, whereas the modern sense of the term in Chinese refers only to the region that is the territory of the People's Republic. The use of *Southern China* is not only an encouragement to think of the area as having always been Chinese, but also excludes the Red River Plain. Terms used during the Six Dynasties include *Southern Yue* (Nanyue or Nam Việt). Schafer's use of Nam Việt fits the geographical area covered in this work, but names containing Việt/Yue suggest too strongly a continuity between the people called Yue in the past and those who refer to themselves as Yue or Việt today, that is, the Vietnamese and Cantonese. In addition, Yue is often overused in Chinese and English works to refer to the people of times and periods in which the term was rarely employed.

27. Xu Songshi, *Yuejiang liuyu renmin shi*; Luo Xianglin 羅香林, *Baiyue yuanliu yu wenhua* 百越源流與文化 (Taipei: Zhonghua shuju, 1955); Matsumoto Nobuhiro 松本信廣, *Indoshina no minzoku to bunka* 印度支那の民族と文化 (Tokyo: Iwanami shoten, 1942).

28. Wang Gungwu, "The Nan-Hai Trade: A Study of the Early History of Chinese Trade on the South China Sea," in *Southeast Asia-China Interactions*, ed. Geoff Wade (Singapore: National University of Singapore Press, 2007, originally 1957), 57.

29. Donn Bayard, "North China, South China, Southeast Asia, or Simply Far East?" *Journal of the Hong Kong Archaeological Society* 6 (1975): 71–79.

30. William Meacham, "On Chang's Interpretation of South China Prehistory," *Journal of the Hong Kong Archaeological Society* no. 7 (1976–1978): 101–9.

31. Wilhelm J. Solheim II, "Prehistoric South China: Chinese or Southeast Asian?"*Computational Analyses of Asian and African Languages* (Tokyo) no. 22 (1984): 13–20.

32. Charles Higham, *The Bronze Age of Southeast Asia* (New York: Cambridge University Press, 1999), 73–135.

33. This is not a universal trend, however, and it is not shared by the majority of Vietnamese and Chinese archaeologists, who have until recently tended to work within the boundaries of their respective nation-states.

34. Denys Lombard, "Another 'Mediterranean' in Southeast Asia," trans. Nola Cooke, *Chinese Southern Diaspora Studies* 1 (2007): 3–9, http://csds.anu.edu.au/volume_1_2007/Lombard.pdf.

35. This is on account of its recurring tendency toward political consolidation. He has, however, declined to give the region a name and refers to it as "northern Vietnam and southern China." Yoshikai Masato吉開將人, "Rekishi sekai to shite no ryōnan—hokubu betonamu; sono kanōsci to kadai" 歴史世界としての嶺南　北部ベトナム―その可能性と課題, *Tōnan ajia rekishi to bunka* 東南アジア歴史と文化 no. 31 (2002): 79–95.

36. Two particularly good sources in English are de Crespigny's discussion of the region as a whole during the later Han and under the Three Kingdoms state of Wu, and Michael Loewe's overarching survey from the Han to the Sui from the information contained in the standard histories, ostensibly for the Guangzhou region, but actually inclusive of the entire region: Rafe de Crespigny, *Generals of the South: The Foundation and Early History of the Three Kingdoms State of Wu* (Canberra: Faculty of Asian

Studies, 1990), 29–43; Michael Loewe, "Guangzhou: The Evidence of the Standard Histories from the Shi ji to the Chen shu, a Preliminary Survey," in *Guangdong, Archaeology and Early Texts*, ed. Shing Müller, Thomas O. Hollman, and Putao Gui (Wiesbaden: Harrassowitz Verlag, 2004), 59–80. In Chinese, Hu Shouwei has written an excellent one-volume history of the region before the Tang, covering such diverse subjects as administrative change, famous products, and migration. Hu Shouwei 胡守為, *Lingnan gushi* 嶺南古史 (Shaoguan: Guangdong renmin chubanshe, 1999).

37. Edward Hetzel Schafer, *The Vermilion Bird: T'ang Images of the South* (Berkeley: University of California Press, 1967).

38. Ibid., 155–247.

39. Charles Holcombe, "Early Imperial China's Deep South: The Viet Regions through Tang Times," *T'ang Studies* nos. 15–16 (1999): 125–56. See also by the same author *The Genesis of East Asia: 221 B.C.–A.D. 907* (Honolulu: University of Hawai'i Press, 2001), 145–54.

40. Meng Wentong is a notable exception in Chinese scholarship, noting that Yue was a general term for all non-Sinitic southerners during Han times, just as the name *Hu* was applied indiscriminately to all non-Sinitic northerners. Meng Wentong 蒙文通, *Yueshi congkao* 越史叢考 (Beijing: Renmin chubanshe, 1983), 24. Heather Peters and William Meacham have made two excellent surveys and criticisms of Chinese scholarship on the Hundred Yue people that are illustrative of many of the assumptions inherent in Chinese-language ethnohistorical scholarship: Heather Peters, *Tattooed Faces and Stilt Houses: Who Were the Ancient Yue?* Sino-Platonic Papers no. 17 (Philadelphia: Department of Oriental Studies, University of Pennsylvania, 1990); William Meacham, "Is an Anthropological Definition of the Ancient Yue Possible?" in *Lingnan gu yuezu wenhua lunwenji* 嶺南古越族文化論文集 (Collected Essays on the Culture of the Ancient Yue People in South China), ed. Chau Hing-wa (Hong Kong: Urban Council, 1993), 140–54.

41. Wang Wenguang 王文光, ed., *Zhongguo nanfang minzu shi* 中國南方民族史 (Beijing: Minzu chubanshe, 1999), 103–39; Wang Wenguang 王文光 and Li Xiaobin 李曉斌, *Baiyue minzu fazhan yanbian shi: cong yue, lao dao zhuangdong yuzu ge minzu* 百越民族發展演變史:從越,僚到壯侗語族各民族 (Beijing: Minzu chubanshe, 1999); Fang Zhiqin 方志欽 and Jiang Zuyuan 蔣祖緣, eds., *Guangdong tongshi (Gudai shangce)* 廣東通史 (古代上冊) (Guangzhou: Guangdong Gaodeng jiaoyu chubanshe, 1996), 399–401.

42. See Zhang Shengzhen 張聲震, ed., *Zhuangzu tongshi* 壯族通史 (3 vols.) (Beijing: Minzu chubanshe, 1997), 1: 284–92, 317–21. I refer to Zhuang as "recently created" because no group corresponding to the Zhuang of the present day existed in southern China before its creation in the 1950s.

43. See James Axtell, "Ethnohistory: An Historian's Viewpoint," *Ethnohistory* 26, no. 1 (1979): 1–13; the technique is presented as a valid methodology for the study of ethnohistory, but the use of twentieth-century materials and concepts to reconstruct the history of two millennia previous, such as is found in the *Zhuangzu Tongshi*, is highly questionable.

44. Ruey Yih-fu 芮逸夫, "Laoren kao" 僚人考, *Guoli zhongyang yanjiuyuan, lishi yuyan yanjiusuo qikan* 國立中央研究院歷史語言研究所期刊 28 (1957): 727–71.

45. See Wolfram Eberhard, *The Local Cultures of South and East China*, trans. A. Eberhard (Leiden: E. J. Brill, 1968), 439–55, for Eberhard's conclusions about the "Liao" culture and its characteristics.

46. Inez de Beauclair, "The Keh Lao of Kweichow and Their History According to the Chinese Records," *Studia Serica* no. 5 (1946): 1–44.

47. Schafer, *Vermilion Bird*, 48.

48. Ibid., 276.

49. Ibid., 53.

50. Xu Hengbin 徐恆彬, "Liren ji qi tonggu kao" 俚人及其銅鼓考, in *Gudai tonggu xueshu taolunhui lunwenji* 古代銅鼓學術討論會論文集 (Beijing: Wenwu chubanshe, 1982), 152–58.

51. See Liao Youhua 廖幼華, *Lishi dilixue de yingyong: Lingnan diqu zaoqi fazhan zhi tantao* 歷史地理學的應用: 嶺南地區早期發展之探討 (Taipei: Wenjin chubanshe, 2004), 247–76; Zheng Chaoxiong 鄭超雄 and Tan Fang 覃芳, *Zhuangzu lishi wenhua de kaoguxue yanjiu* 壯族歷史文化的考古學研究 (Beijing: Minzu chubanshe, 2006), 477–83.

52. Edwin G. Pulleyblank, "The Chinese and Their Neighbours in Prehistoric and Early Historic Times," in *The Origins of Chinese Civilization*, ed. David N. Keightley (Berkeley: University of California Press, 1993), 431–33.

53. The term *Han* was already employed in Six Dynasties texts, but only in a historical sense to refer to people who had lived during the time of the Han Empire (206 BCE–220 CE). The term was employed in a pejorative sense by the Turkic rulers of the Northern Qi (550–577 CE), but does not appear to have been used in the empires of the Southern Dynasties.

54. The term *German* in English is similarly problematic, but not so in present-day usage in German-language scholarship, where a distinction is now made between the ancient *Germanen* and the modern *Deutsche*.

55. See Victor Lieberman, *Strange Parallels: Southeast Asia in a Global Context, c. 800–1830* (Cambridge: Cambridge University Press, 2003), 6–15, for a summary of the externalist and autonomous traditions of scholarship as these relate to the historiography of Southeast Asia.

56. Nicolas Tapp, *The Hmong of China: Context, Agency, and the Imaginary* (Leiden: Brill, 2001), 40.

57. Harold J. Wiens, *China's March toward the Tropics* (Hamden: Shoe String Press, 1954).

58. Charles Patrick FitzGerald, *The Southern Expansion of the Chinese People* (Canberra: Australian National University Press, 1972).

59. Stevan Harrell, "Civilizing Projects and the Reaction to Them," in *Cultural Encounters on China's Ethnic Frontiers*, ed. Stevan Harrell (Seattle: University of Washington Press, 2001), 3–36.

60. For a highly politicized account according to the narratives of "development and mixture," see Zhu Dawei 朱大渭, "Nanchao shaoshu minzu gailun ji qi yu hanzu de ronghe" 南朝少數民族概況及其與漢族的融合, *Zhongguo shi yanjiu* 中國史研究 no. 1 (1980): 57–76.

61. Zhang Shengzhen, *Zhuangzu tongshi*, 303–6; Fang Zhiqin and Jiang Zuyuan, *Guangdong tongshi*, 370–3. Another scholar, Huang Xingqiu, notes that his

explanation of warfare as the primary reason for the movement of Tai peoples out of the south "would not be accepted by some scholars," which suggests that interethnic warfare in Chinese history is still an unacceptable subject in some quarters. See Huang Xingqiu 黃興球, *Zhuangtaizu fenhua shijian kao* 壯泰族分化時間考 (Beijing: Minzu chubanshe, 2008), 252. Records of the brutalities of warfare are plentiful in the original sources, and non-Chinese scholars have not been so guarded in their use; see, for example, Schafer, *Vermilion Bird*, 61–69.

62. Wu Yongzhang 吳永章, "Nanchao Lingnan li lao kai lun" 南朝嶺南俚獠概論, in *Baiyue minzu yanjiu* 百越民族研究, ed. Peng Shifan 彭適凡 (Nanchang: Jiangxi jiaoyu chubanshe, 1992), 234–42.

63. Peng Fengwen 彭豐文, "Nanchao lingnan minzu zhengce xintan" 南朝嶺南民族政策新探, *Minzu yanjiu* 民族研究 5 (2004): 95; "Xijiang duhu yu Nanchao Lingnan kaifa" 西江督護與南朝嶺南開發, *Guangxi minzu yanjiu* 廣西民族研究 2, no. 76 (2004): 62–67.

64. For a detailed discussion of the Lady Xian's story in English, see Wade, *The Lady Sinn*.

65. Liao Youhua, *Lishi dilixue*, 247–78.

66. For an overview of premodern Southeast Asian material culture as observed by Europeans from the fifteenth century onward, the best source in English is Anthony Reid, *Southeast Asia in the Age of Commerce 1450–1680: Volume One—The Lands below the Winds* (New Haven, CT: Yale University Press, 1988), especially 64–115.

67. Kenneth R. Hall, "Economic History of Early Times," in *Cambridge History of Southeast Asia, Volume One, Part One,* ed. Nicholas Tarling (Cambridge: Cambridge University Press, 2008), 190.

68. Two examples are John E. Herman, *Amid the Clouds and Mist: China's Colonization of Guizhou 1200–1700*, Harvard East Asian Monographs 293 (Cambridge, MA: Harvard University Press, 2007), and David Holm, *Killing a Buffalo for the Ancestors: A Zhuang Cosmological Text from Southwest China* (DeKalb: Southeast Asia Publications, Center for Southeast Asian Studies, Northern Illinois University, 2003). Both are analyses of texts written in the vernacular languages of the people studied. The only extant texts (discussed in chapter 7 of this work) made by those referred to as Li or Lao that date from the time period covered in this work are two stelae from Qinzhou detailing the ancestry of the Ning clan that ruled over what are now the Sino-Vietnamese borderlands on the Gulf of Tongking.

69. Edmund Leach, *Political Systems of Highland Burma: A Study of Kachin Social Structure* (London: Athlone Press, 1970). Leach also observed that the societies of those known as Kachin oscillated between an anarchistic and egalitarian system he called *gumlao* and the *gumsa* system, which was closer to the hierarchical and autocratic society typical of the Shans, the (mainly) Tai-speaking peoples of the valleys who cultivated wet rice. Due to lack of records, it is difficult to know whether anything resembling a *gumlao* system, devoid of autocratic chiefs or hierarchy and living off slash-and-burn agriculture, was widely practiced among the Li and Lao between the Two Rivers during the main period under discussion in this work, but the general trend of social change observable among the Li and Lao was toward an increasingly hierarchical system.

70. Andrew Turton also observed this generally in Tai societies. Andrew Turton, "Introduction to *Civility and Savagery*," in *Civility and Savagery: Social Identity in Tai States*, ed. Andrew Turton (Richmond, Surrey: Curzon, 2000), 1–29.

71. James Scott, *The Art of Not Being Governed: An Anarchist History of Upland Southeast Asia* (New Haven, CT: Yale University Press, 2009).

72. Willem van Schendel, "Geographies of Knowing, Geographies of Ignorance: Jumping Scale in Southeast Asia," in *Locating Southeast Asia: Geographies of Knowledge and Politics of Space*, ed. Paul Kratoska, Remco Raben, and Henk Schulte Nordholt (Singapore: Singapore University Press, 2005), 275–307.

73. Scott, *Art of Not Being Governed*, 167–72.

74. NZYWZ of the third century CE quoted in the tenth-century encyclopedia TPYL 785: 8a. The earliest record of Lao social structure in the *Wei shu* (WS 101: 30b) describes the Lao as selecting a leader as king (*wang* 王). The same passage in the ninth-century encyclopedia *Tongdian* (ch. 187, 999) records the word as lord (*zhu* 主), but both of these descriptions of Lao refer to people who lived in what are now Yunnan and Sichuan, not those of the region between the Two Rivers, and may therefore be a reference to entirely unrelated groups.

75. Georges Condaminas, *From Lawa to Mon, from Saa' to Thai: Historical and Anthropological Aspects of Southeast Asian Social Spaces*, trans. Stephenie Anderson, Maria Magannon, and Gehan Wijeyewardene, ed. Gehan Wijeyewardene (Canberra: Department of Anthropology, Research School of Pacific Studies, 1990), 54.

76. Oscar Salemink, "A View from the Mountains: A Critical History of Lowlander-Highlander Relations in Vietnam," in *Opening Boundaries: Upland Transformations in Vietnam*, ed. Thomas Sikor, Nghiem Phuong Tuyen, Jennifer Sowerwine, and Jeff Romm (Singapore: National University of Singapore Press, 2011), 27–50.

77. For a deeper discussion of this trend of scholarship and its political implications with regard to Vietnam, see Nola Cooke, *Colonial Political Myth and the Problem of the Other: French and Vietnamese in the Protectorate of Annam* (PhD thesis, Australian National University, 1991).

78. Leonard Aurousseau, "La première conquête chinoise des pays annamites (IIIe siècle avant notre ère)," *Bulletin de l'École française d'Extrême-Orient* 23 (1923): 245–64.

79. Joseph Buttinger, *The Smaller Dragon: A Political History of Vietnam* (New York: Praeger, 1958), 11: "In order to fight off the Chinese successfully, Vietnam had to adopt many of the Chinese social and technical inventions."

80. Patricia Pelley has made an in-depth study of the growth in the twentieth century of a narrative of Vietnamese history built on resistance to outside invaders: Patricia Pelley, *Postcolonial Vietnam: New Histories of the National Past* (Durham, NC: Duke University Press, 2002).

81. Philippe Papin, "Géographie et politique dans le Việt-Nam ancien," *Bulletin de l'École française d'Extrême-Orient* 87, no. 2 (2000): 609.

82. For examples of this style of scholarship, see Đào Duy Anh, *Lịch Sử Việt Nam từ Nguồn Gốc đến Thế Kỷ XIX* (Hanoi: Nhà Xuất Bản Văn Hoá Thông Thin, 2006, originally published in 1957), and Trần Quốc Vượng and Hà Văn Tấn, eds., *Lịch Sử Chế Độ Phong Kiến Việt-Nam*, vol. 1 (Hanoi: Nhà xuất bản giáo dục, 1960).

83. The development of a historiographical tradition in Đại Việt is an entire subject in itself. Esta Ungar provides a useful outline of its development in the earliest texts in Esta S. Ungar, "From Myth to History: Imagined Polities in 14th Century Vietnam," in *Southeast Asia in the 9th to 14th Centuries*, ed. David Marr and Tony Milner (Singapore: Institute of Southeast Asian Studies, 1986), 117–38.

84. For the national orthodoxy, no clearer text exists than the treatment of the Han-Tang period in the sixth-grade national school textbook published by the Vietnamese Ministry of Education: Bộ Giáo Dục and Đào Tạo, Lịch Sử 6 (Hanoi: Nhà Xuất Bản Giáo Dục, 2006), 35–76.

85. Gotō Kimpei 後藤均平, *Betonamu kyūgoku kōsōshi* ベトナム救国抗争史 (Tokyo: Shin jinbutsu ōraisha, 1975).

86. Katakura Minoru 片倉穣, "Chūgoku shihaika no betonamu—Chūgoku shoōchō no shūdatsu ni kansuru shironteki kōsatsu" 中国支配下のベトナム—中国諸王朝の収奪に関する試論的考察, *Rekishigaku kenkyū* 歴史学研究 380 (1972): 17–26; 381 (1972): 28–35.

87. Keith W. Taylor, *The Birth of Vietnam* (Berkeley: University of California Press, 1983), xviii. Taylor later retreated from the nationalist position. Keith W. Taylor, "The Early Kingdoms," in *Cambridge History of Southeast Asia, Volume One, Part One*, ed. Nicholas Tarling (Cambridge: Cambridge University Press, 2008), 137. The introductory paragraph to this article reflects his later view that "by the end of the third century [CE] the efforts of Chinese frontier administrators and leading local clans had produced a relatively stable provincial polity, sensitive to Chinese imperial interests while at the same time representing a local system of power capable of taking initiative on behalf of its own interests when Chinese dynastic power was weak or in transition."

88. Jennifer Holmgren, *Chinese Colonisation of Northern Vietnam: Administrative Geography and Political Development in the Tongking Delta, First to Sixth Centuries A.D.* (Canberra: Australian National University Press, 1980).

89. For the implications of such spelling choices, see Michael Churchman, "Before Chinese and Vietnamese in the Red River Plain: The Han–Tang Period," *Chinese Southern Diaspora Studies* 4 (2010): 25–37, http://csds.anu.edu.au/volume_4_2010/04-2_Churchman_2010.pdf25-6.

90. Việt and Yue are merely two different transcriptions of the same Chinese character: 越. For an examination of the various uses of the term and their relation to peoples of the Two Rivers Region, see ibid., 27–31.

91. Even areas such as the northern coast of the Gulf of Tongking are not usually included, even though they were ruled directly from the Red River Plain as part of the province of Jiaozhou for more than two centuries.

92. Taylor, *Birth of Vietnam*, 67, calls them "tribal peoples"; Holcombe, *Genesis*, 154, refers to them as "tribesmen" and the districts they inhabited he calls "tribal enclaves" (*Early Imperial China's Deep South*, 140–44).

93. Michael Churchman, "The People in Between, the Li and Lao from the Han to the Sui," in *The Tongking Gulf through History*, ed. Nola Cooke, Li Tana, and James A. Anderson (Philadelphia: University of Pennsylvania Press, 2011), 67–86.

94. Taylor, *Birth of Vietnam*, xxi. The author's later views on the subject are expressed in Keith W. Taylor, "Surface Orientations in Vietnam: Beyond Histories of

Nation and Region," *Journal of Asian Studies* 8, no. 4 (1998): 949–78, in which he emphasizes a division between southern and northern Vietnam, with the south more strongly resembling its Southeast Asian neighbors.

95. Trần Quốc Vượng, "Truyền thống văn hóa Việt Nam trong Bối Cảnh Đông Nam Á và Đông Á," in *Văn Hóa Việt Nam Tìm Tòi và Suy Ngẫm* (Hanoi: Nhà Xuất Bản Văn Học, 2003), 7–16.

96. Phạm Đức Dương, *Văn hóa Việt Nam trong Bối Cảnh Đông Nam Á* (Hanoi: Nhà Xuất Bản Khoa Học Xã Hội, 2000), 124–46. This is also true of the modern provinces of Guangxi, Guangdong, and Hainan, where there are populations of Austronesian (Utsat) and Austroasiatic (Vietnamese and Lai) speakers, in addition to the many groups speaking Kadai and Miao-Yao languages.

97. FitzGerald, *Southern Expansion*, 1, notes that in contrast to the Yue of Vietnam, "The more northerly Yue were annexed to the Han Empire and lost their separate national identity." On page 22 he refers to the Cantonese as the "more assimilated cousins" of the Vietnamese.

98. Trần Quốc Vượng, "Traditions, Acculturation, Renovation: The Evolutional Pattern of Vietnamese Culture," in *Southeast Asia in the 9th to 14th Centuries*, ed. David G. Marr and A. C. Milner (Singapore: Institute of Southeast Asian Studies, 1986), 217–18.

99. Taylor, *Birth of Vietnam*, 300: "The survival of the Vietnamese language was very significant, for it means that whatever the Chinese did in Vietnam was conditioned by a cultural realm that remained distinct and separate from the Chinese sphere of thought."

100. John D. Phan, "Re-Imagining 'Annam': A New Analysis of Sino–Viet–Muong Linguistic Contact," *Chinese Southern Diaspora Studies* 4 (2010): 3–24, http://csds.anu.edu.au/volume_4_2010/03-1_Phan_2010.pdf.

101. The linguistic situation between the Two Rivers at this time is hinted at by descriptions of customs collected by Le Shi in his geography *Taiping huanyuji* of the late tenth century. This work describes the Li people of Qinzhou "not understanding how to speak," inferring that they do not speak a Sinitic language (TPHYJ 167: 13b). It also notes that the people of Rongzhou (present-day Rong County in Guangxi) spoke three mutually unintelligible kinds of language (TPHYJ 167: 4b), and that the Tiyi Lao of Yongzhou (districts surrounding present-day Nanning) had four discrete kinds of language, all of which had to be translated if communication was to be possible (TPHYJ 166: 5a).

102. Nguyen Khac Vien, *Vietnam: A Long History* (Hanoi: Foreign Languages Publishing House, 1987), 21. Like many authors, Nguyen chooses to skip over the period of Chinese rule rather than going into any detail about it.

103. For details, see Holmgren, *Chinese Colonisation*, 66–71. Ascribing uprisings that originated in the southern commanderies of Jiuzhen and Rinan to a Vietnamese consciousness ascribes a unity to these people for which there is no evidence other than the fact that the areas where they dwelled are now Vietnamese territory. It also begs the question of why the Wuhu uprising of 178, originating in an area that was much closer to the Red River Plain than Rinan and Jiuzhen, is never described as an act of Vietnamese resistance.

104. HHS 8: 10b; 13a.

105. TPYL 371: 3b.

106. Those who did so included Lý Bôn, "Emperor of Yue" from the Red River Plain in the mid-sixth century, Feng Lin "King of Nanyue" from west of Canton in the eighth, and Liu Yan of Canton, who originally gave himself the title "King of Great Yue" (*Dayue*), later changing it to "Emperor of Great Han" (*Dahan*). For the background reasons for the attraction of the name Yue, see Churchman, "Before Chinese and Vietnamese," 29–30.

107. For the Lý Phật Tử period in the Red River Plain, see Taylor, *Birth of Vietnam*, 158–62, which gives an excellent, well-translated summary, as he does for the transitional period from the Sui to the Tang period on pages 166–69.

108. See, for example, the explanation of the significance of the drums in Pham, *Dong son Drums in Vietnam*, 262–67.

109. Unfortunately, aside from the bronze drums, very little attention has been paid to other aspects of Li-Lao archaeology. A notable exception is Feng Mengqin 馮孟欽, "Guangdong liren yicun de kaoguxue guancha" 廣東俚人遺存的考古學觀察, in *Baiyue yanjiu* 百越研究, ed., Baiyue minzu shi yanjiuhui 百越民族史研究會 (Nanning: Guangxi kexue jishu chubanshe, 2007), 1: 216–30, which discusses finds of tiles, burial urns, and pottery.

110. In recent years, it has become popular to translate *minzu* into English as "ethnic group" or "ethnicity," but this is a distortion of the Chinese sense of the term and disguises its connections. In most PRC works, use of the term *minzu* ostensibly follows Stalin's definition of a group of people who share a common territory, common language, common economic life, and common psychological makeup; however, Jacques Lemoine has argued that the term *minzu* is actually an untranslatable term unique to PRC political discourse. Jacques Lemoine, "What Is the Actual Number of the (H)mong in the World?" *Hmong Studies Journal* 6 (2005): 1–8, http://hmongstudies.org/LemoineHSJ6.pdf. The use and connotations of the cognate term *dân tộc* in Vietnamese are almost identical to those in Chinese, however. I prefer to use the English translation "nationality," as it preserves more of the political and ideological connotations of the term that are absent from "ethnicity."

111. It is only in the Guangxi Zhuang Autonomous Region that the drums are in evidence, in the regional museum in Nanning, and the recently built National Museum of Nationalities is built in the shape of an enormous bronze drum. Manhole covers in the central city are also decorated to look like the tympana of bronze drums.

112. Han Xiaorong, "Who Invented the Bronze Drum?" goes into detail about this debate and its origins.

113. Some of this may be due to the fact that Vietnamese and Chinese archaeologists seldom study one another's language, and are as a consequence unaware of each other's findings and opinions. This has created a division into two schools of drum scholarship that are confined by national or regional boundaries. This division has also carried over into the works of outsiders. Bernet Kempers devotes only a single page to the Heger II drums of southern China (Bernet Kempers, *The Kettledrums of Southeast Asia: A Bronze Age World and Its Aftermath* [Rotterdam: A. A. Balkema, 1988], 32). Nishimura Masanari's recent study similarly gives scant attention to any drums but those found in the territories that now lie within Vietnamese territory

(Nishimura Masanari 西村昌也, "Hokubu vietonamu dōko wo meguru minzokushi-teki shiten kara no rikai" 北部ヴィエトナム銅鼓をめぐる民族史的視点からの理解, *Tōnan ajia kenkyū* 東南アジア研究 46, no. 1 (2008): 3–42.

114. Yao, Wan, and Jiang, *Beiliu xing tonggu*, 24–27.

115. Yoshikai Masato 吉開將人, "Dōko saihen no jidai—issennenki no beto-namu, minamichūgoku" 銅鼓"再編"の時代——千年期のベトナム、南中國, *Tōyō Bunka* 東洋文化 78 (1998): 199–218. He bases this claim on the appearance of the innovation of incorporating decoration into the drum molds before casting, rather than the old practice of incising decorations on to finished drums. One group of Chinese scholars has begun to investigate the possibility that the Heger I drums of the Đông Sơn had an influence on later types of drum while continuing to maintain that the Heger II drums of Guangxi are direct descendants of the Heger I drums of the Dian culture (see Wan Fubin 萬輔彬, Fang Minghui 房明惠, and Wei Dongping 韋冬蘋, "Yuenan tonggu zai renshi yu tonggu fenlei xinshuo" 越南東山銅鼓再認識與銅鼓分類新說, *Guangxi minzu xueyuan xuebao [zhexue shehui kexueban]* 廣西民族學院學報 [哲學社會科學版] 25, no. 6 [2003]: 77–83).

116. Wang Kerong 王克榮, Qiu Zhonglun 邱鍾侖, and Chen Yuanzhang 陳遠璋, *Guangxi zuo jiang yanhua* 廣西左江巖畫 (Beijing: Wenwu chubanshe, 1988), 193. On page 204 the authors suggest that these are depictions of Heger I drums.

117. However, only two Heger I drums have been found in the vicinity of the Li-Lao country, both from the same site in Gui County to the east of Nanning, in the Boluowan tomb that dates from the time of the Nanyue kingdom. For an analysis of these, see Li Longzhang 李龍章, *Lingnan diqu chutu jingtongqi yanjiu* 嶺南地區出土青銅器研究 (Beijing: Wenwu chubanshe, 2006), 119; for the geographical distribution of different drum types, see Yoshikai, *Dōko saihen no jidai*, figures VIII and IX.

118. Đào, *Lịch Sử Cổ Đại Việt Nam*, 284, states that the high lead content of Đong Sơn bronze (around 16 percent) is what makes it distinct from Chinese bronzes. The high lead content is also typical of the Heger type II drums of the central Li-Lao country, which usually have around 15 percent lead content, but is not typical of the Heger I drums found in northern Guangxi or Yunnan. For the metal content of the various types of drum in Guangxi, see Huang Zengqing 黃增慶, "Zhuangzu gudai tonggu de zhuzao gongyi" 壯族古代銅鼓的鑄造工藝, *Guangxi minzu xueyuan xuebao* 1 (1984): 41–47. For the type I drums typical of the Dian culture, see Zhang Zengqi 張增祺, *Dianguo yu dian wenhua* 滇國與滇文化 (Kunming: Yunnan meishu chubanshe, 1997), 90.

119. Alexandre de Rhodes, *Dictionarium Annamiticum Lusitanum, et Latinum ope Sacrae Congregationis de propaganda fide* (Rome, 1651), 813.

120. Paul Schneider, *Dictionnaire historique des idéogrammes Vietnamiens* (Nice: Université de Nice-Sophia Antipolis, Unité de recherches interdisciplinaires sur l'Asie du sud-est, Madagascar et les îles de l'océan Indien, 1992), 2: 94.

121. Lê Văn Quán, *Nghiên Cứu về Chữ Nôm* (Hanoi: Nhà Xuất Bản Khoa Học Xã Hội, 1981), 88. Lê notes that this style of compounding characters fell out of use in the seventeenth century.

122. This initial is still pronounced *kl-* in some Vietnamese and Muong dialects, such as in the Thạch Bi Mường *klống* (ibid., 109).

123. Hoàng Triều Ân, ed., *Từ Điên Chữ Nôm Tày* (Hanoi: Nhà Xuất Bản Khoa Học Xã Hội, 2003), 545–46.

124. Proto-Tai reconstructions are based on Li Fang-kuei, *A Handbook of Comparative Tai* (Honolulu: University Press of Hawai'i, 1977), 221–26, for examination of the initial cluster *kl-.

125. Two cognates in the Hloi language of Hainan exhibit the same correspondence: the words for "fish scales" and "far" have an initial l- that corresponds to an initial *[kl-] in proto-Tai, and [tɕ-] in the Tai spoken northwest of modern Nanning. See Wang Jun 王均, ed., *Zhuangdong yuzu yuyan jianzhi* 壯侗語族語言簡志 (Beijing: Minzu chubanshe, 1984), 808, 858. Harry Shorto reconstructed its proto-Austroasiatic form as [*jtuuŋ]; Harry Shorto, *A Mon-Khmer Comparative Dictionary*, ed. Paul Sidwell (Canberra: Pacific Linguistics, Research School of Pacific and Asian Studies, 2006), 190.

126. Nguyễn Ngọc San, *Tìm Hiểu Tiếng Việt Lịch Sử* (Hanoi: Nhả Xuất Bản Đại Học Sư Phạm, 2000), 135–40.

127. Phạm, *Văn hóa Việt Nam*, 183–228.

128. Salemink, *A View from the Mountains*, 31.

129. See Lothar von Falkenhausen, "The Use and Significance of Ritual Bronzes in the Lingnan Region during the Eastern Zhou Period," *Journal of East Asian Archaeology* 3, nos. 1–2 (2001): 193–236.

130. Nishimura Masanari 西村昌也, "Kōka deruta no jōkaku iseki, Lũng Khê jōshi wo meguru shin ninshiki to mondai" 紅河デルタの城郭遺跡, Lũng Khê城址をめぐる新認識と問題, *Tōnan ajia rekishi to bunka* 東南アジア歴史と文化 30 (2001): 46–69.

131. It is interesting to note that the social significance of the drums for the people of the Red River Delta was not discovered by the Vietnamese until the twentieth century. The oldest Đại Việt texts, such as the *Lingnan zheguai liezhuan* (Vietnamese: *Linh Nam Chịch Quái liệt truyện* 嶺南摭怪列傳) and *Yueshi lue* (Vietnamese: *Việt Sử Lược* 越史略), do not even mention them, let alone associate them with the legendary past of the pre-Han period.

132. Nguyen Duy Hinh, "The Birth of the First State in Vietnam," in *Southeast Asian Archaeology at the XV Pacific Science Congress,* ed. Donn Bayard (Dunedin: University of Otago Studies in Prehistoric Anthropology, 1984), 183–87.

133. Trần Quốc Vượng, "Từ Truyền Thuyết Ngôn Ngữ đến Lịch Sử," in *Hùng Vương Dựng Nước,* ed. Viên Khảo Cổ Học (Hanoi: Nhà Xuất Bản Khoa Học Xã Hội, 1970), 1: 148–49. Trần called for a "synthesised approach" (*phương pháp vận dụng tổng hợp*) of these disciplines.

134. Viện khảo cổ học, ed., *Hùng Vương Dựng Nước* (4 vols.) (Hanoi: Nhà Xuất Bản Khoa Học Xã Hội, 1970–1974).

135. It forms the basis, for instance, of Zheng and Tan's *Zhuangzu lishi wenhua* (Zhuang History and Culture) and much of the first volume of Zhang Shengzhen's *Zhuangzu tongshi* (Comprehensive History of the Zhuang).

136. Researching origin myths of Medieval Europe, Susan Reynolds has argued that this was not so much a deliberately deceptive process for the justification of the political ideology of the present, but more the result of a scientific search for

explanation about how the present came to pass, based on the writers' assumption that it was natural that a political or linguistic unit would have a single ancestor. See Susan Reynolds, "Medieval *Origines Gentium* and the Community of the Realm," *History* 68, no. 224 (1983): 375–90.

137. Schafer, *Vermilion Bird*, 2.

Chapter 2

The Two Rivers and
the Lands Between

A Geographical Outline

Near the entrances of the two great rivers to the sea lay the two metropolitan centers of Guangzhou and Jiaozhou. Known by various names over the centuries, these centers correspond to the present-day cities of Canton and Hanoi. The *Sui shu* compiled in the 630s described them in the following manner:

> In the twenty or more commanderies south of the passes the ground is mostly damp, there are many miasmas and people die at a very young age. Nanhai and Jiaozhi are the two great cities and they are both situated close to the sea. In that place there is an abundance of rhinoceros, elephants, tortoiseshell, pearls, and strange and precious things. That is why so many merchants go to those places to become wealthy.[1]

From the description of Nanhai (Canton) and Jiaozhi (Hanoi area) as "great cities," it appears that the author still considered both to be of considerable commercial importance. However, by the time of this description Jiaozhi was not the important commercial center it had been under earlier empires. At the time this text was written, it had only recently been reconquered after a century of local political autonomy, and in the seventh century under the Tang it was given the special status of Protectorate of the Pacified South (*Annan duhu fu*) under a protector general (*duhu*), an administrative unit defined by Charles Hucker as "a military duty assignment to preside over submitted alien peoples."[2] The special administrative status given to Jiaozhi indicated that it required military protection as a newly conquered region and was no longer counted as an ordinary province of the Tang Empire.

Seven centuries previously, the city of Jiaozhi had been the capital of a well-integrated province of the Han imperial administration that covered the Red River Plain, and for a short period of five years after the conquest of the kingdom of Nanyue by the Han Empire (111 BCE), the citadel of Luy Lâu in the Red River Plain to the northeast of modern Hanoi had been the administrative center of the entire Two Rivers Region, a single large unit that also went by the name of Jiaozhi (and later Jiaozhou). The initial choice of the Red River Plain as the seat of government was presumably to keep the new administrative center a safe distance from the remnants of loyalists to the recently conquered Nanyue kingdom in its old capital of Panyu (present-day Canton), but it also indicates that there was little risk of local resistance to Han rule in the plain at this time, or indeed, in the lands between the two river plains. In 106 BCE, the administrative center of this Jiaozhou was then moved to Guangxin (near present-day Wuzhou in eastern Guangxi). This was conveniently located near the upriver connection to the Han capital at Luoyang through the Ling Qu, or "Magic Trench," canal, dug on the orders of the First Emperor of the Qin in 214 BCE to provide a route for food and military supplies for his armies as they fought their way into the Two Rivers Region. Guangxin was also conveniently connected to Panyu by water and by several overland routes to Jiaozhi. Just over a century after the move to Guangxin, in 226 CE, the large province of Jiaozhou was divided into two smaller provinces named Jiaozhou and Guangzhou, a division that was sub-sequently abandoned but then reinstated in 264 by the Three Kingdoms state of Wu.[3] For the following two centuries, Chinese imperial administration of the Two Rivers Region was based around the two centers of Jiaozhou and Guangzhou. The smaller province of Jiaozhou was administered from Long Biên, near the present-day city of Hanoi. Long Biên oversaw a network of subordinate centers of population concentrated around the mouths of minor river systems on the coast stretching between what is now central Vietnam northward along the coast to the east of the Leizhou Peninsula.[4] The province of Guangzhou controlled population centers along the tributaries of the Pearl River system and the smaller rivers east of the Leizhou Peninsula that drained into the South China Sea. The administrative reach of these two provinces was not significantly altered until the foundation of Yuezhou in 474, which removed the Hepu area from the jurisdiction of Jiaozhou.[5]

By the seventh century, the Red River Plain had fallen from its preeminent position as the trade and political center of the south, and even required a special status under the Tang as a frontier region with a protector-general appointed to ensure its security. In contrast, the center at Nanhai that in Han times had been considered too politically volatile to use as an administrative center had become a well-integrated part of the Sui and Tang Empires. Over the seven centuries between the extension of Han power into the Two Rivers Region and the foundation of the Tang, the balance of Chinese power in the Two Rivers Region had shifted markedly, and many of the changes that led to this occurred over the two centuries when these two urban centers at Jiaozhi

(Hanoi) and Nanhai (Canton) controlled the two provinces of Jiaozhou and Guangzhou. To examine why this happened, we must compare the economic and political changes in the two provinces from their foundation to the end of the fifth century, when the new province of Yuezhou was founded.

THE DECLINE OF JIAOZHOU AS A CENTER FOR MARITIME TRADE

Long Biên on the Red River Plain was the administrative center of the province of Jiaozhou from 264 until the beginning of the Daye period of the Sui (605–617).[6] Written records and the geographical layout of administrative units suggest that during this period communications between this center and its subordinate commanderies were mainly by sea rather than over land. Tao Huang, who was appointed in 269 as regional inspector and governed Jiaozhou in the last decades of the third century, noted that the southern commanderies of Jiaozhou were "Over a thousand *li* [approximately three hundred kilometers] distant by sea."[7] The locations of the commandery seats of Jiude, Jiuzhen, and Hepu also suggest the primacy of maritime communications; these were all a short distance from the sea along river courses and the majority of their subordinate counties were clustered closely around them. In addition, calculations of distance from the provincial center at Jiaozhi in the *Song shu* were made over water rather than over land.[8] The maritime route to the south from Jiaozhi was also the favored communication line for trade between the Han Empire and Southeast Asia, as the southern commanderies of Rinan and Jiuzhen received ships from the south, which would then carry on northward to Jiaozhi or Hepu. The geographical treatise of the *Jiu Tang shu* (Old book of the Tang) recorded: "All of the countries in the sea to the south, mostly situated to the south and south-east of Jiaozhou have sent tribute from the time of Emperor Wu of the Han, and have had to go by way of Jiaozhi."[9] At first, ships that continued from Jiaozhi on to Panyu probably used the sea route through the Qiongzhou strait between Hainan Island and Xuwen on the southern tip of the Leizhou Peninsula, but this was known to be a dangerous route to navigate and the directions of wind and currents varied depending on the time of the year.[10] The small size of the ships involved in trade with the far south made it dangerous for them to stray too far from the coast, which meant that the commanderies of Jiaozhou were of great commercial importance as the first ports of call in the Han Empire for foreign shipping. By the end of the third century CE, shipping routes shifted eastward as improvements in ship-building technology had made it possible to build larger craft that were capable of sailing over the open sea directly from Guangzhou to lands far to the south of Jiaozhi. No longer dependent on staying close to the coast, they began to bypass the Gulf of Tongking and the commanderies of Jiaozhou altogether.[11] The effect of this was that Jiaozhou lost its strategic importance as the gateway for commerce. The sea ports at Xuwen and Hepu lost their economic importance as fewer ships passed through them on their way to Guangzhou, and Jiaozhou slowly ceased to be the gateway to the north for the trade from Southeast Asia.[12] Jiaozhou did, however, retain an economic significance of its own as a producer of luxury goods and was still considered in the seventh century to be equal to Nanhai at least in this regard, as can be seen from the description in the *Sui shu*. The status of Jiaozhou as a trade center was further eroded by the expansion of the kingdom of Linyi (or Lâm Áp in Sino-Vietnamese) to its south, a precursor to the Champa polities of later centuries, that from 340 onward began to encroach on the southernmost commandery of Rinan, which it eventually occupied along with large parts of Jiuzhen. Another reason for the decline of trade through Jiaozhi was constant warfare over these areas with Linyi in the mid-fourth century.[13] The eventual loss of Rinan meant a loss of trade revenue for the province of Jiaozhou, as Rinan had once been the gateway to the Han Empire and had received traders of luxury goods who came from places as far afield as Daqin (the Eastern Roman Empire). The trade there had previously been so lucrative that corrupt inspectors of the province of Jiaozhou and the governor of Rinan Commandery had been able to skim off 20 to 30 percent of the value of the goods traded there into their own pockets.[14] Once the Rinan area was taken by Linyi, it could no longer provide trade revenue for Jiaozhou province, and as Jiaozhou declined in importance as a commercial center for maritime trade, so Guangzhou grew. This is reflected in the proliferation of complaints regarding official corruption related to the trade in luxury goods in the latter province after the fourth century and the corresponding lack of such reports in connection with Jiaozhou.

JIAOZHOU AND ITS OVERLAND CONNECTIONS WITH THE NORTH

Aside from the maritime route between Hainan and the Leizhou Peninsula, Jiaozhou was connected to other parts of the empire along a small number of overland river routes.

The Red River Valley connected Jiaozhou to Ningzhou in the northwest. This was a province in which the imperial presence was rather tenuous and was ruled from the present-day city of Kunming. Han general Ma Yuan was said to have traveled up the river from Mê Linh in the Red River Plain to Xinggu Commandery (close to present-day Wenshan in Yunnan), passing through the lands of a former kingdom named Jinsang, which had been conquered and turned into a county.[15] This lay somewhere near present-day Lào Cai on the Sino-Vietnamese border,[16] and from the time of the Han possessed a customs gate on the river that indicates the use of the waterway as a trade route.[17] A more recent source states that the Red River was not easy to navigate, but that junks could sail it up to around the modern Sino-Vietnamese border,[18] so this customs gate was probably situated at the highest navigable point where junks would have needed to offload their goods for land transport. This was the route by which Yang Ji, the first prefect to Jiaozhou appointed by the Jin Empire, arrived with his army from Shu (present-day Sichuan) around 266–268.[19] Other records from the pre-Tang period also indicate the continued use of the Red River as a communication route with Ningzhou,[20] but Ningzhou itself was remote from the capital of the Southern Dynasties at Jiankang (Nanjing) and this would have made the Red River route too long and circuitous to be of great importance as a means of communication between Jiaozhou and the capital.

The two most significant (and most direct) routes of overland communication between the Red River Plain and the rest of the empire were those that passed over the watershed between rivers that flowed north and west into the Yu River and those that flowed southward into the Red River or the Gulf of Tongking. Detailed records of these can be found in the *Zhu pu*, or "Manual of Bamboo," a fifth-century treatise on species of bamboo attributed to Tai Kaizhi, purportedly a Jin (265–420) author,[21] who claimed to have traveled to Jiaozhou. Tai recorded two passes, one at Ningpu and the other at Linzhang in the southwest of Guangzhou, that gave access to Jiaozhou, noting that some attributed the construction of these passes to Zhao Tuo, king of Nanyue, and others to the Han general Ma Yuan.[22]

The most celebrated land route to Jiaozhou was that which traversed the "Ghost Gate Pass" (*Guimen Guan*); this is almost certainly identical to the Linzhang pass referred to by Tai Kaizhi. The Ghost Gate Pass route followed the tributary of the Yu River, now known as the Beiliu River, to its source southwestward from Cangwu, and then from the source of what is now called the Nanliu (also known at the time as the Lian River or *Lianjiang*) down to Linzhang Commandery, where it finally drains into the Gulf of Tongking at Hepu. The tradition attributing the creation of the pass to Ma Yuan dates back to the *Hou Han shu* (Book of the Later Han), even though this book does not explicitly state Ma Yuan's expedition of 40 CE to subdue the Trung Sisters had used this pass. His biography states only that his army arrived at Hepu and cut a road overland along the coast from there;[23] however, a clue to his use of the Ghost Gate Pass route is to be found in another account of his expedition from the same work, which describes him as having constructed roads and bridges, opening blocked valleys and leading soldiers from four regions to the north (Changsha, Guiyang, Lingling, and Cangwu) southward.[24] Cangwu refers to a commandery centered on Guangxin, now the city of Wuzhou, and indicates the strong likelihood of an overland expedition to Hepu through Linzhang as the most direct route, as a maritime route from Cangwu to Hepu would have involved doubling back to make a naval transport from Nanhai (Canton). This route was considered to be of considerable age already by Tang times;[25] it was noted as the main route to the Red River Plain under the Jin Empire in a tenth-century geography,[26] and even into the twentieth century it remained an important local trade route from the Gulf of Tongking to Wuzhou.[27] The road was described as first opened to the Tang upon the surrender of the Ning family, who lived to the west of Hepu in 622, to Tang general Li Jing,[28] suggesting that they had made it inaccessible for many years. Hepu almost always rates a mention in descriptions of the route to Jiaozhi, which indicates that the way through the Ghost Gate Pass was the most important and most frequently traveled land route there. What remains unclear is how travelers departed from Hepu to Jiaozhou, whether they went by ship or followed a land route along the coast instead. For instance, in 410, Jin Dynasty rebel Lu Xun was recorded as having come from Hepu to attack the seat of Jiaozhou, but by what means he and his troops traveled between these two cities is not mentioned.[29]

As for Tai Kaizhi's Ningpu Pass, this probably referred to the open country between the south bank of the Yu River near present-day Heng County and the headwaters of the Qin River (*Qin Jiang*), which flows south into the Gulf of Tongking at Qinzhou. A record of the use of the Ningpu Pass dating from the fourth century is provided in the unfortunate story of Ruan Fang, appointed as inspector of Jiaozhou in the sixth month of 323, who was ambushed and killed there by a general named Gao Bao on his way to take up office.[30] The fact that there was no recorded administrative outpost at the mouth of the Qin River until the foundation of Songshou Commandery in the late fifth century suggests that this route to Jiaozhi was not nearly as important as the Ghost Gate Pass route connecting Hepu to Cangwu.[31]

Another overland route not mentioned by Tai Kaizhi lay further to the west from Ningpu along the *Zuojiang* (Left-Hand River)[32] through what is now the district of Lạng Sơn in northeastern Vietnam. This route appears to have been little used during the Southern Dynasties, but had been important for the Han Dynasty. Noting two Han outposts along the Left-Hand River, Hans Bielenstein argued that settlement of the Red River Plain by northerners had followed this route.[33] The two outposts were named Linchen and Yongji; the second was close to the present-day Sino-Vietnamese border and had a customs gate, indicating that the river was also used as a trade route. The outpost at Linchen was abandoned in 76 CE, and the fate of Yongji is unclear. Writing at the beginning of the sixth century in his *Commentary on the River Classic* (*Shui jing zhu*), Li Daoyuan noted that the source of the river was in

Long Biên County in Jiaozhi,[34] which at least shows that it was known to connect through to Jiaozhou. The lack of other records about it and the absence of administrative units along the river for several centuries suggest that this route, while still known, was only of minor importance. It was also apparently neglected for a long time, as Sui general Liu Fang was credited with reopening the same route to Jiaozhi five centuries later. In 637, local leader Ning Shijing was recorded as having followed Liu Fang's road there while "opening up" (*kaituo*) the lands of the Yi and Lao to found a new province named Rangzhou.[35] This was the first administrative unit to be established along the river since Han times.[36]

Overall, direct overland routes from the Red River Plain to the northeast were few in number and it was easy to block them if one wished to cut off Jiaozhou from the rest of the empire. This occurred in 380, when Lý Tốn, governor of Jiuzhen, instructed his two sons to "cut off and block the fords and narrow passes on the water and land routes" to prevent the arrival of a new governor into the province.[37]

MIGRATION AND LEADERSHIP STRUCTURES IN JIAOZHOU—FIRST TO SIXTH CENTURIES CE

During Han times, the commandery of Jiaozhi in the Red River Plain and the two commanderies of Jiuzhen and Rinan farther south possessed particularly good agricultural land and all of them supported large populations of taxable individuals. In the Han census of 2 CE, Jiaozhi Commandery boasted a greater population than all the other commanderies in the Two Rivers Region combined.[38]

Migration to these areas and to the commercial port of Hepu from the north during Han times is also attested by the number of Han-style brick tombs (over 120) found in the Red River Plain and the low hill country to its southwest. These were built either by migrants or by locals influenced by the material culture of a migrant population, either possibility confirming the presence of a significant number of Chinese migrants to the area from the north. It is also worth noting that no bronze drums have been found in any of these tombs,[39] and if these are burials of locals rather than migrants, this indicates a switch from the pre-Han Đông Sơn practices and material culture in a relatively short period of time. Even the commandery centers far to the south, such as Jiuzhen and Rinan Commanderies, were home to communities of Han migrants from the north. Yu Yiqi, a sojourner down the coast in the latter half of the fourth century, gave an account of a migrant community in a letter to his friend Han Kangbo of people whom he called Ma liu, the "Ma wanderers." This was a group of about two hundred households who lived to the north of Linyi (that is, the far southernmost limits of the empire along the central Vietnamese coast), all of them with the surname Ma, which they shared with general Ma Yuan. They were said to have been the descendants of ten families of soldiers who had accompanied him three hundred years previously, and Yu noted that their language and eating habits were said to have remained the same as other "Hua" people.[40] Although Yu Yiqi's record of these people does contain some less credible elements,[41] recent excavations at Trà Kiệu near Hội An in central Vietnam indicate that there were indeed settled communities of northerners living far down the coast of what is now central Vietnam who made Han-style roof tiles and pottery and owned seals written in Chinese characters.[42] The attractions of the Jiaozhi area during the first two centuries CE were probably mainly commercial, but as the Han Empire disintegrated, people began to flee the political chaos in northern China to seek the relative peace and safety that the area afforded. The *San guo zhi* (Records of the Three Kingdoms) recorded that, during the rule of Shi Xie in the last two decades of the second century, Jiaozhi was a popular place of refuge; it was reported that "gentlefolk fled there in hundreds."[43]

Two censuses from the post-Han and pre-Tang period are useful sources of information about the government and population of the Red River Plain. First, there is the census contained in the *Jin shu* (Book of the Jin), which has been identified as an inventory of taxable households made around 280.[44] The next population census to have been preserved dates from the mid-fifth century at the height of power of the Liu-Song Empire, which was probably carried out in 464.[45] The two censuses show a marked decline in the registered populations of the Jiaozhou area: at the time of the Jin census, Jiaozhou still counted more taxable households than any other commandery in the Two Rivers Region.[46] The number of these fell sharply in the almost two centuries between the Jin census and the Liu-Song census. Between these two censuses, figures for Jiaozhi Commandery fell by over half, and the commanderies upriver (Xinchang and Wuping) had only a fifth of their Jin total.[47] Comparing the results of the Jin census with those in the Han census, Hans Bielenstein's opinion on the Jin census was that "the district officials had control only over the areas in the immediate vicinity of their residential towns, or that they did not care to carry out a correct census."[48] Katakura Minoru suggested an additional reason for the low figures for Jiaozhou in the Jin and Liu-Song censuses: that the local administrators were deliberately underestimating the taxable population in the areas under their control because they were retaining a proportion of the tax revenue they had been employed to collect for themselves.[49]

The decline in registered population between the Jin and Liu-Song censuses goes hand in hand with a downturn in migration from the north into Jiaozhou. This is reflected in the archaeological record through a sharp reduction in the number of Chinese-style brick tombs dating from after the end of the Han, and the distribution of such tombs becomes restricted to the area around modern Hanoi and Bắc Ninh.[50] A similar reduction has been noted for Hepu and seems to indicate a decline in settler numbers from the north in all of the commanderies subordinate to Jiaozhou, as the construction of brick tombs in the Pearl River drainage area continued well into the Southern Dynasties.[51] Migration to the area did not dry up altogether, however. Zhang Hua's *Bowu zhi* (Record of Wide Gleanings), written in the late third century, recorded that there were constantly people taking their families and crossing over the sea to Jiaozhi,[52] and even though subsequent records of constant large-scale flight to Jiaozhi after this time are less frequent, the area remained a haven for groups of northerners over the following few centuries as a relatively peaceful refuge from the chaos north of the Yangtze River caused by the disintegration of empires, warfare between rival empires, and the invasion of steppe peoples from the north and west. In 306, crowds of officials and commoners from Ningzhou fled to Jiaozhou (presumably along the Red River) to escape a famine and pestilence that had killed tens of thousands and the depredations of the Yi people of Wuling (*Wuling yi*) who, it was said, had become so strong they had defeated the imperial troops on several occasions.[53] Another clue to the continued existence of populations of refugees from the north residing in Jiaozhou comes from the first few decades of the fifth century, when Du Huidu served as both assistant magistrate (*zhubu*) and protector general of refugees (*liumin duhu*) of Jiaozhou.[54] The latter administrative title occurs only twice in the Chinese standard histories and was borne only by Huidu and his son Du Hongwen, to whom he passed the title. Although the origins of the refugees whom these two were commissioned to protect are unknown, there must have been a significant number of them at the time if a special administrative post was required for their supervision. Liao Youhua has proposed that these were actually migrants from the southern commanderies escaping from areas that had suffered raids from Linyi or had been conquered and occupied by their armies.[55] The last reference to migration to Jiaozhou comes from the third month of 468, upon the occasion of the death of the inspector of Jiaozhou, Liu Mu, when a local named Lý Trương Nhân is recorded to have rebelled and subsequently killed either a group of refugees from the north or troops who had been under Liu Mu's command.[56] This also shows that even at this late period, whether there for military purposes or as refugees, there was still a population of recent migrants from the north residing in Jiaozhou.

As far as the leadership structures of Jiaozhou were concerned, until the end of the fifth century these more or less resembled those of other provinces of the Six Dynasties. Following Ma Yuan's defeat of the Trưng Sisters, there were no more large-scale uprisings against Chinese imperial rule originating

from the Red River Plain, and for the next four centuries the area became
a fairly well-integrated part of the Han Empire and its successor empires,
the Wu and the Jin. Holmgren describes this as the end of an era, which
began the "slow but inevitable formation of a new type of Vietnamese elite
educated by, and working within, the social codes and structures of Chinese
society" who aspired to "positions of wealth and influence within the established system."[57] This is certainly how the writers of the Chinese standard
histories perceived the ruling class of Jiaozhou; when they rebelled, they
were referred to in the terms applied to disobedient officials elsewhere in
the empire, and their rebellious deeds differed little from those in provinces
closer to the capital, such as people without official titles who attempted to
usurp political power through self-declaration as governor or inspector. Even
those celebrated in Vietnamese national histories as leaders of the Vietnamese independence movements, such as Lý Trương Nhân and Lý Thúc Hiến
who declared themselves kings and Lý Bốn who declared himself emperor,
were merely following the practice of disgruntled officials known in other
parts of the empire.

The emergence of families who held hereditary administrative posts in a
single locality for several generations was not a peculiarity of the Red River
Plain; it was common throughout the Six Dynasties period even in areas close
to the imperial capital at Jiankang. Where the Red River Plain differed from
other areas is that localized dynasties continued to hold power over Jiaozhou
during and after the Liu-Song, when the governors and inspectors of other
provinces and commanderies were usually members of the royal household
appointed to the area. In other parts of the empire, regional upstarts and those
who supported them risked attack and punishment by those who professed to
act out of loyalty to the emperor. But the same geographical isolation that had
made the Red River Plain an attractive place of refuge also made it easy for
members of powerful families there to retain power over their own localities
or disobey outright the commands of the imperial capital, especially during
periods of political chaos or disunity. The end of the Six Dynasties period
was characterized by military and governmental turmoil in the rest of the
empire, a time in which the courts had trouble controlling even areas close
to the capital at Jiankang ruled by members of their own royal houses. The
de facto independence of the Red River Plain in the first half of the sixth
century needs to be seen in the light of the general weakness of the Southern
Dynasties and the geographical isolation of the region from other parts of
the Chinese empires. The causes of this isolation were not merely a result of
physical distance; they were also attributable to the activities of the people
who lived between Jiaozhi and the neighboring province of Guangzhou, but
before moving on to the people in between, let us compare Jiaozhou with the
province of Guangzhou.

GUANGZHOU'S GEOGRAPHY AND LINKS
TO THE REST OF THE EMPIRE

Just as the name of the province Jiaozhou was derived from its initial seat of government in Jiaozhi, so the province of Guangzhou was named after its earliest administrative seat at Guangxin, and the name of the province remained even though its administrative center was soon shifted to Panyu (modern Canton) at the mouth of the Pearl River. Panyu also did service as the seat of Nanhai Commandery and the two names Nanhai and Panyu were often used interchangeably, with Nanhai tending to replace Panyu as the name of the city in post-Han usage. The city of Panyu had previously been the capital of the Nanyue kingdom, and many of the remains of the large-scale constructions carried out during the time of this kingdom (204–111 BCE), such as the palace, shipyards, and sluice gates, show that it was already a significant urban and commercial center even in that period. From the time of the (re) foundation of Guangzhou in 246 until the inclusion of Shian Commandery and most of the settlements along the Li River into the province of Xiangzhou in 424, the province of Guangzhou was responsible for all the lands along the western and eastern tributaries of the Pearl River drainage system, and Chinese settlement and administrative expansion in the province over this period moved northeastward and westward from the center at Canton along these major waterways. The main administrative centers subordinate to Guangzhou lay at the confluences of the main tributaries of the Yu River,[58] the most important of these being Guangxin, situated at the confluence of the Li and Yu Rivers. This was the seat of Cangwu Commandery, but for a short time it had been both the capital of the Han province of greater Jiaozhou and of Guangzhou. Along the stretch of the coast to the southwest as far as the Leizhou Peninsula, there were also a few larger settlements subordinate to Guangzhou, such as Gaoliang.

As the aforementioned improvements in shipping technology allowed trade from the south to bypass the Gulf of Tongking and sail directly to Nanhai (Canton) over the open sea from Southeast Asia, the city was frequented by foreign traders and trading ships. As the focal point of trade between the Chinese empires and Southeast Asia shifted to the area, the type of officials inclined to take advantage of this trade for their own personal benefit also began to gravitate to Guangzhou instead of Jiaozhou. In the early fifth century, it was mentioned that a single box of the treasures to be acquired at Guangzhou could support a family for several generations,[59] and around the turn of the sixth century it was well known that the officials there became very rich. It was said proverbially that simply by passing through the city gate of Nanhai as inspector of Guangzhou one could obtain thirty million coins.[60] The *Liang shu* (Book of the Liang) described the situation as follows:

In Nanhai there are slaves from Gaoliang, ships arrive there several times a year, and foreign merchants come to trade and exchange. In former times the provincial and commandery leaders would go to purchase goods for half price and then sell them again for several times the profit. This was never considered abnormal.[61]

This sort of corruption was so common that governors who did not try to monopolize the trade to enrich themselves were considered exceptionally virtuous. It was even said that a "Spring of Greed" (*tan quan*) lay close to the Dayu Pass on the road south into Guangzhou. Legend had it that newly appointed administrators who drank from this spring on their way to take up office in Guangzhou would forget their morals and become greedy for the riches that they could gain at their new post.[62]

During the Southern Dynasties, the provincial seat of Guangzhou in Nanhai Commandery was well connected to the capital at Jiankang and the provinces to the north. Tai Kaizhi named the three land routes to Guangzhou as passing through the commanderies of Nankang, Shian (through the "Magic Trench" canal), and Linhe.[63] Easy access to the north through Shian and Linhe is also suggested by the inclusion of these last two commanderies in 424 into the new province of Xiangzhou.[64] Both of these commanderies had their centers on northern tributaries of the Pearl River, but the new provincial capital of Xiangzhou to which they were subordinate was at what is now Changsha on a tributary of the Yangtze River. Their incorporation into this province indicates that there were few barriers to communication between the two commanderies and their provincial capital.

These two routes were used less once the imperial capital of the Jin was shifted from Luoyang in the north to Jiankang in the northeast in 317; from this time onward the northeastern route through Nankang became the most direct overland route to the capital. The Nankang route passed from the commandery of Shixing (near present-day Shaoguan) on a tributary of the Pearl River, past the "Spring of Greed" through the Dayu Pass to Nankang (now Ganzhou on the Gan River). Aside from Tai Kaizhi's descriptions, there are other records that indicate its regular use as the main route connecting Guangzhou with the capital. In 410, the rebel Lu Xun organized the transportation of timber across the pass from Nankang to Shixing to sell as a ruse to secretly collect materials to build his own fleet of warships,[65] and judging from the description of his journey, Xiao Mai, the inspector of Guangzhou,[66] almost certainly used this route to return to Jiankang when summoned back to the capital from his post during the 530s.[67]

The maritime route to the capital eastward over the sea from Guangzhou seems also to have been commonly used and was once the main method of communication between Panyu/Nanhai and the heartland of the empire in the north. In Han times, it was recorded that tribute from Jiaozhou had been taken over sea to Houguan (Fuzhou) and transported overland from there, but that so many ships had been lost on this route in storms and rough seas that the roads were put in good repair and the tribute was taken overland instead.[68] The renewed importance of the shipping route later under the Southern Dynasties can be seen from the increase in new administrative units along the coast to the east of the mouth of the Pearl River, namely the counties of Haifeng, Haining, and Chaoyang, which were all subordinate to the new Yian Commandery (now Chaozhou) founded in 413.[69] Prior to this, under the Western Jin, there had been no administrative unit on the coast between the mouth of the Pearl River and Tongan (present-day Quanzhou in Fujian). A story concerning the Lu family of Gusu (present-day Suzhou) shows that even small boat traffic went to the capital by sea from Guangzhou. This family had a huge stone by their front gate, said to have been brought back from Yulin by their ancestor Lu Ji, who had been governor of the commandery of Yulin under the Wu. Unlike other officials, he had not made use of his position to accumulate the riches that were to be obtained in the commandery, so as he returned to the north, his ship was too light and was rocked about by the waves. He had taken this large stone from the riverbank to use as ballast, and the famous stone later became a symbol of his incorruptibility.[70]

POPULATION, MIGRATION, AND LEADERSHIP STRUCTURES IN GUANGZHOU—FIRST TO SIXTH CENTURIES CE

Unlike Jiaozhou, Guangzhou and its subordinate commanderies had a choice of many well-trodden paths to connect them to the northern provinces of the Southern Dynasties and their imperial capital, and the ease of communications with the north helped to integrate the provincial capital and its surrounding area more firmly into the rest of the empire than was possible for Jiaozhou. This was reflected in the growth of Guangzhou's registered population and the proliferation of new subordinate commanderies during the Six Dynasties period. Like the Red River Plain, Nanhai and Cangwu Commanderies did not only attract migrants seeking benefits from its trade economy, but also attracted refugees fleeing post-Han warfare and political upheaval in the north as the Han Empire began to crumble. As in the Red River Plain, large numbers of Han-style brick tombs have been found in the lower Pearl River drainage area, concentrated along the major waterways that connected Guangzhou to the north along the main inland watercourses that meet at Canton and, significantly, in the city of Canton itself, where over eight hundred tombs had been excavated by the mid-1990s.[71] Despite the greater number of Han tombs found here compared to those excavated in the Red River Plain, the registered populations of the commanderies in the Pearl River drainage area in the Han census of 2 CE were only a fifth of those of the Red River Plain, which suggests that a greater proportion of the registered population of the area around Nanhai (Canton) were of recent northern extraction origin than was the case in Jiaozhou.[72] Even in the Jin census of 280, the number of registered households of the two commanderies of Nanhai and Cangwu still did not significantly outweigh those of Jiaozhi Commandery. The events of the fourth century altered this markedly, the most important change coming with the last major southward movement of Chinese population into the Guangzhou area. The period of most intense migration from the north began in the early fourth century in the Yongjia period (307–313), after which the Jin Empire lost its territory to the north of the Yangtze River. From this time until the foundation of the Wei Empire in 386, refugees from the north streamed southward into what was left of the Jin Empire in the south to escape the warfare and chaos that had engulfed their homelands.[73]

There are a few written records relating to this population shift as it relates to the Guangzhou area. Shen Huaiyuan's *Nanyue zhi* (Annals of Nanyue), written in the 470s or 480s, records that there was once a refugee encampment (*liuren ying*) in the commandery of Yian that was made into a county (Yi County) in 405.[74] The same book records another encampment in the far southwest nearer to Hepu, from which Zhaoyi County was founded in 405 but which was subsequently abandoned.[75] The place of origin of these refugees is unfortunately unclear, but the mention of encampments suggests that these were especially organized by the imperial administration as settlements, and their subsequent upgrade to county status suggests that they were organized projects of colonization. A record from the early decades of the fifth century notes that a certain Xu Daoqi of Donghai (the political heartland of the Eastern Jin Empire) took refuge in the Canton area but was ridiculed for his ungentlemanly conduct by those who had sojourned there for a long time, showing that there was a community of longtime refugees or sojourners in the provincial seat of Guangzhou as well.[76]

Migration was not limited to a north-to-south movement; significant numbers of people from southern Jiaozhou also sought refuge close to Canton, and a special commandery was founded for them in 441 with four subordinate counties named Songxi Commandery, subsequently renamed Songlong nine years later. In the Liu-Song census of 464, this commandery boasted 6,450 households and seven counties.[77] The foundation of this commandery for refugees from Jiaozhou corresponds with the records of regular attacks by Linyi on the southern commanderies of Jiaozhou in the 430s and early 440s.[78] It is not known by which route these refugees arrived in Guangzhou, but the location of the county close to the coast at Nanhai suggests that it was by sea.

Comparison of the results of the Jin and Liu-Song censuses taken before and after this population shift shows that registered populations in the various commanderies of the Two Rivers Region grew most in areas adjacent to the Pearl River Delta and the confluences of the tributaries of the Yu River in Cangwu. The number of administrative units in this area also increased substantially over this time, the most significant changes occurring around Nanhai and Cangwu. Nanhai Commandery around Canton was split into five new commanderies and the number of registered households in these had increased 73 percent from what it was previously. Cangwu was split into seven new commanderies and the registered population of these commanderies combined almost tripled. Household numbers in Linhe Commandery increased by almost half again from the Jin total, and those of Shixing Commandery more than doubled. All of the commanderies that showed a rise in registered populations between the censuses lay in the east of the Two Rivers Region and were conveniently connected by river traffic to the Canton area and the major inland transportation routes from the north and the imperial capital at Jiankang. Even so, neither the Jin nor the Liu-Song Empire could claim half as many registered households for the area around Nanhai and Cangwu as had been counted by the Eastern Han census.

The archaeological record also shows that the construction of brick tombs continued in Guangzhou throughout the Jin and Southern Dynasties. The tombs from these periods are concentrated mainly in areas close to the main waterways and their confluences, especially on the river routes from the north. Tombs dating from the post-Jin period are found further away from the main waterways, and this corresponds to the administrative expansion of the Eastern Jin and Liu-Song into previously unoccupied areas of the Two Rivers Region.[79]

As in Jiaozhou, there was a shift in the formation of the local administrative leadership of Guangzhou. At the beginning of the fifth century CE, regional inspectors of Guangzhou were appointees from outside the province and often natives of the area around the imperial heartland of Jiankang. By the middle of the century, some of these appointees had put down roots in Guangzhou and the imperial authorities began to employ members of their families as governors and inspectors rather than employing outsiders, in parallel development to Jiaozhou. This had begun under the Jin Empire when governorships and inspectorates of the area were held by various members of the Wang, Xiu, and Teng families,[80] and the practice continued with the Chang and Liu families during the Liu-Song.[81] In the latter half of Liu-Song rule from the mid-fifth century onward, imperial policy changed and the court began instead to appoint members of the imperial household as officials to the Guangzhou area; the Qi and Liang Empires followed suit. The Liang was especially fond of this tactic, appointing four of Emperor Wu's cousins or nephews at different times to the inspectorate of Guangzhou; Inspector Xiao Mai, mentioned previously, was one of these.[82] The appointment of officials from the imperial household rather than reliance on local families is an indicator of the increased importance the Liu-Song, Qi, and Liang Empires attached to central control of the area. The same dynasties were unable to carry out a similar policy in the Red River Plain, where instead they were increasingly reliant on the compliance of local families to supply local administrators. In summary, from the beginning of the fourth century onward, the lower Pearl River drainage area saw an increase in migration from the north, resulting in the growth of registered population and the number of administrative units. Although there was a trend toward localized gubernatorial dynasties, from the mid-fifth century the imperial households had an increased say over who held the most important administrative positions.

JIAOZHOU AND THE LANDS BETWEEN

If one compares the political and economic developments in Guangzhou and Jiaozhou over the period of the Southern Dynasties, it is clear that the latter province was losing its appeal as a destination for migrants and was developing a trend of political autonomy, whereas in Guangzhou the opposite was happening. Registered populations fell sharply in Jiaozhou, few new administrative units were founded, and local families became de facto holders of political power whom it was increasingly difficult to unseat. The one attempt the Liang made to appoint a nephew of Emperor Wu as inspector of Jiaozhou had dire consequences for Liang rule in the Red River Plain, which will be discussed in chapter 4.

Through this comparison of the two provinces, it is easy to find evidence of the development toward localized rule in Jiaozhou that lends weight toward interpretation of events as part of a national independence struggle against Chinese rule. However, an examination of the situation in the lands between Jiaozhou and Guangzhou offers an alternative explanation of why changes in migration, administrative structure, and local leadership that occurred in Guangzhou during the Southern Dynasties did not occur in parallel in Jiaozhou. If one compares changes in the two provinces over this time, Guangzhou and Jiaozhou look very different. If, however, a comparison of Jiaozhou is made with the lands directly to its northeast that separated it from Guangzhou, Jiaozhou appears in contrast to be a well-integrated part of the imperial administrative system.

The trends in Jiaozhou toward localized rule in this period were not merely a result of internal resistance to outside forces; they were also due in large part to the isolation of the Red River Plain from the rest of the Southern Dynasties empires. Descriptions of Jiaozhou in the *Nan Qi shu* (Book of the

Southern Qi) emphasize its isolation, referring to the area in one case as an "island": "Jiaozhou is a completely isolated island which controls the outer lands and as a consequence of this it frequently relies on its strategic position to not submit to authority."[83] "Jiaozhou is a far distant borderland. In fact it ought to be classed as the wild circuit, and it relies on this distance to be the last to submit to authority; indeed, this a constant occurrence."[84] "Jiaozhou is controlled from Jiaozhi, it lies among the islands of the Boiling Sea . . . it borders on the lands of the southern Man and produces many precious goods. For rare treasures of the mountains and seas it is incomparable. Relying on their strategic position and distance the citizens are fond of rebellion."[85] The use of the word *island* is especially significant for its implication that maritime routes were the most important mode of transport to Jiaozhou and that the land route was either blocked or at least difficult to utilize.

What isolated the Red River Plain from easy overland contact with the rest of the empire was the expanse of hilly country to its northeast that cut it off from the commanderies belonging to Guangzhou. This country and the people who dwelled there were quite unlike those of the two administrative centers described above, and even though later geographical works insisted that the area had been part of imperial administrative units since the Han, until the beginning of the sixth century vast areas of this country still lay outside the effective reach of imperial administrations. Chinese settlement of the Two Rivers Region up until the latter half of the fifth century was a slow administrative encroachment confined to areas along the major waterways or the sea coast, and this area lay far from both. If the limited nature of the Chinese presence here in the past is not immediately obvious from historical records, it is because compilers of Chinese geographies had the habit of including contemporary administrative units retrospectively into older administrative units, implying that they had always been part of imperial territory and giving the impression that administrative units in previously unoccupied areas represented new divisions of existing structures rather than an expansion into new territory.[86] The compilers of historical maps such as the *Zhongguo lishi dituji* (Historical Atlas of China) constructed their maps according to a similar principle and chose to depict administrative units in large blocks of color within tidy boundaries,[87] whereas more accurate indicators of imperial control in such maps are the concentrations of names written in black, indicating administrative centers.[88] Map 3 depicts the location of commandery centers according to the geography contained in the *Jin shu*, and shows an obvious absence of imperial control south of the Yu River, west of modern Nanning, west of Hepu to the modern Sino-Vietnamese border, east of Hepu to Gaoxing (near the present-day city of Yangjiang), and north of Hanoi. These represent areas that were bypassed by the Han on their way south to the Red River Plain and remained beyond the control of subsequent empires.

One reason for the isolation of Jiaozhou was that the physical environment was a danger for outside visitors to the lands between the Two Rivers. "The ground has miasmic vapours that can kill people," says the *Nan Qi shu* in its description of the lands adjacent to Hepu, going on to note that in Han times the inspector of Jiaozhou would always go somewhere high to avoid these in the summer months, and that even though the land of Jiaozhou was at peace, the miasmas of Yuezhou (the Hepu region) remained formidable.[89] This "miasmic gas" probably referred to the visible steamy haze from the moist jungle in the summer months, but what actually killed people is more likely to have been malaria, endemic throughout the Two Rivers Region and especially dangerous in the foothills further south than 26° latitude (roughly anything to the south of a line through Kunming). The most dangerous time for malarial diseases was during the late summer months, and this corresponds neatly to Chinese records of the times when miasmas were most potent.[90] The lands between Jiaozhou and Guangzhou, and especially the lands south of the Ghost Gate Pass, were notorious for miasmas; Ma Yuan was said to have seen the miasma from a river kill a bird in midflight,[91] and the miasmas were held responsible for the deaths of four or five out of every ten soldiers who attempted to pass through the area with him.[92] There was even a "Miasma River" (*Zhang jiang*), which was a tributary of the Nanliu River, and a Linzhang Commandery, the name of which meant "near the miasma," founded close by under the Liu-Song.[93] Spring miasmas were said to have killed six or seven out of every ten soldiers who were on their way to Hepu to fight Lý Bốn in the mid-sixth century.[94] The Chinese chroniclers noted that locals had strategies for dealing with this, either living in stilt houses to avoid miasmas and pestilences[95] or making an annual migration on rafts to a safe area during the hottest season from the sixth to the tenth month in a manner similar to that of the Han inspector described above.[96]

In addition to the physical difficulties of passing through the lands between the Two Rivers, there was the difficulty of dealing with the people who lived there, for although this area was empty from the point of view of the imperial administration, it was no uninhabited wilderness. On the contrary, it was populated by groups of people who were hostile both to their neighbors and to passersby, and both of the main land routes to Jiaozhou from Guangzhou, over the Ghost Gate Pass and the Ningpu Pass, passed through their territory. Chinese written records of this area suggest that travelers considered this country and its inhabitants to be wild and dangerous, and indicate that firsthand knowledge of them was difficult to come by. What did make it to the ears of writers were exaggerations and travelers' tales; some of the more frightening descriptions spoke of the Wuhu people who lived there as savage cannibals, who ate their first child at birth and who considered human palms and feet as a great delicacy.[97] The Li people of the area were said to have to fend off huge swarms of carnivorous beetles that consumed the flesh of human corpses when attempting to bury their dead,[98] and were purportedly fond of shooting outsiders with poisoned arrows that could make living flesh rot on the bone.[99] There were also reports of fantastic serpents and centipedes so large that their skins could be used to cover drums.[100]

The manner in which this region had been bypassed by the administrative and military machines of the Chinese empires is made clear in the following two descriptions by officials who had both served long terms in the Red River Plain. Over fifty years after a great Wuhu uprising in the region in 178 CE, Xue Zong, governor of Jiaozhi, wrote a memorial to the throne in 231 describing the situation in Jiaozhou as follows:

> Now although it is said that Jiaozhou is more or less settled, there are still the incorrigible bandits of the area around the boundaries of Nanhai, Cangwu, Yulin and Zhuguan [Hepu] commanderies who are still not under control. They rely on banditry and stealing, and have become a lair of refuge for rebels and escapees.[101]

The area he describes was one of the biggest empty areas in terms of the absence of Chinese administrative units, and the Ghost Gate Pass route—the main thoroughfare to Jiaozhou—cut right through the middle of it. Several decades later, a letter from Tao Huang, inspector of Jiaozhou under Emperor Wu of the Jin (reigned 265–290), is quite specific about the location and population of peoples beyond effective control of the Jin Empire:

> On the South Bank of Guangzhou for an area six thousand *li* around there are over fifty-thousand households who will not submit to authority, as well as about ten thousand households in Guilin who are of an uncontrollable type, as for those who follow the official orders there are just about over five thousand families. The two provinces [Jiaozhou and Guangzhou] are connected as lips and teeth, and can only be held by military force.[102]

The "South Bank" of Guangzhou referred to the lands south and west of the Yu River through which all the overland traffic to Jiaozhou was obliged to pass. Tao Huang would have known these areas well because they lay between the province he ruled and the rest of the Jin Empire. The value of his description is its estimate of the population that lived outside the Jin administration. The taxable households counted in the Jin census for the entire Two Rivers Region numbered only 66,720, and yet on the south bank of the Yu and in Guilin Commandery alone Tao Huang estimated almost double that number of households beyond the reach of Jin administration. Another description of the people of the area from the geography of the *Nan Qi Shu*, written around two centuries later, reveals that little had changed:

Guangzhou is controlled from Nanhai, control of the coasts and corners of the sea is given to Jiao[-zhou], although there are a few families of subjects (*min*), there are numerous Li and Lao scattered about. They all live in towers in mountainous and inaccessible places and are unwilling to submit to authority. The sources of the two rivers to the south and west are remote and distant. A protectorate was established especially for the purposes of attacking them.[103]

The protectorate mentioned here was the protectorate of the Western Rivers, the foundation of which was an important step in the process of the military subjugation of the Li and Lao and will be discussed in more detail in chapter 5.

In addition to the terms *Li* and *Lao*, which are value judgments in themselves, all of the foregoing records describe the people between Jiaozhou and Guangzhou as stubborn, recalcitrant, and uncontrolled, refusing to accept the authority of what the writers considered the civilized world. In addition to these general complaints, there is also a concrete record of how they affected the travel plans of an individual sent to Jiaozhou, who passed through this country in the mid-fifth century:

Emperor Xiaowu [reigned 454–465] of the [Liu-]Song had wished to build a Pagoda, and Zhang Rong had donated only a hundred cash, so the Emperor said "Since Rong is especially poor we should organise a good job for him," and he was sent off to serve as magistrate of Fengxi County [in the Red River Plain]. On his way to take up office, he had to pass through the hilly and inaccessible terrain between Guangzhou and Yuezhou where he was caught by Lao bandits who were going to kill and eat him, but Rong's spirit and countenance remained firm, and he then sang them a *luosheng* chant. The bandits marvelled at this and did not harm him. He then sailed over the sea to Jiaozhou, composing the "Sea Rhapsody" on the way.[104]

This text is specific about where Zhang Rong was caught: the mountainous region between the spheres of influence of Guangzhou and Yuezhou, a province founded in the mid-sixth century and ruled from close by Hepu. The description of this area fits the location of the Ghost Gate Pass route and shows that there were very real dangers posed by the people of the Li-Lao country to those who dared pass through their territory.

The records above indicate a fairly stable situation in the lands between the Two Rivers from the third to the fifth centuries in which Li and Lao societies of significant size dwelled on the fringes of Chinese knowledge and beyond the reach of direct imperial control. The decline of what imperial presence there was is reflected in a comparison of the Jin and Liu-Song taxation censuses of 280 and 464: although there was a small increase in administrative units in these lands between the Two Rivers between the censuses, the census results for the commanderies lying between Jiaozhou and Guangzhou show the sharpest falls in imperial taxation (and therefore imperial administrative control) of any area in the Two Rivers Region. An analysis of the Jin and Liu-Song census by individual command-ery results for the Two Rivers shows that the decline in registered populations was not confined merely to the area that now constitutes part of modern Viet-nam.[105] The highest falls in registered household numbers were in the large commanderies of Yulin and Wuping,[106] which both fell by over 80 percent. Guilin and Jiaozhi commanderies dropped by 72 and 64 percent, respectively, followed by the Hepu area, which lost either 70 percent or 53 percent of its registered population.[107] These statistics indicate that the revenue gathering and organizing abilities of the Southern Dynasties in the area were minimal overall, but that they had declined most and were weakest of all in the lands between the Red River Plain and Cangwu that the Li and Lao inhabited.

Table 1   Registered Population Change in the Two Rivers Region, 280–464

Commandery	Number of Households (Jin) 280	Number of Households Liu-Song–464 AD	Percentage of Change
Nanhai	9,500	Nanhai 8,574 Xinhui 1,739 Dongguan 1,332 Yian 1,119 Tuojian 3,764 (total 16,528)	+73.9
Linhe	2,500	(to Xiangzhou, renamed Linqing) 3,715	+48.6
Shian (Shijian)	6,000	(to Xiangzhou) 3,830	−36.2
Shixing (Guangxing)	5,000	(to Xiangzhou) 1,1756	+135.2
Cangwu	7,700	Xinning 2,653 Jinkang 4,547 Yongping 1,609 Cangwu 6,593 Haichang 1,724 Songkang 1,513 Songxi 2,814 (total 21,453)	+178.6
Yulin	6,000	1,121	−81.3
Guilin	2,000	558	−72.1
Gaoliang	2,000	1,429	−55.3 (incl. Gaoxing)
Gaoxing	1,200		−28.6 (excl. Gaoxing)
Ningpu	1,220	No data	
Hepu	2,000	938	−70.7 (incl. Gaoxing) −53.1 (excl. Gaoxing)
Jiaozhi	12,000	4,233	−64.7
Xinchang	3,000	to Wuping 1,490	−81.4
Wuping	5,000		
Jiuzhen	3,000	2,328	−22.4
Jiude	No data	809	
Rinan	600	402	−33

Comparing Jiaozhou with the lands that lay between them and the rest of the empire in the early fifth century, it is clear that much of the rebellious nature of the people of Jiaozhou was a result of their isolation rather than their status as recalcitrant indigenes. The isolation of the Red River Plain from its surroundings also explains why rebellions and uprisings in the post-Han period remained localized in the plain and no longer spread over a wide area in the manner of the Trưng Sisters' uprising. Unlike the Trưng Sisters, the post-Han ruling class in the Red River Plain resembled the semi-aristocratic families in Guangzhou and had little in common with the Li and Lao chieftains, or for that matter the people in the hill country that surrounded the plain to the north and west. It was difficult to involve these Li and Lao in warfare against the Chinese empires because to them, the rulers of Jiaozhou and the people of the plain would have appeared as representatives of the empires themselves. This is reflected in the name for the ethnic Kinh of the Red River Plain, *kon kɛɛu* or "people of Jiao," based on their belonging to the Chinese province. This term is still current in many of the Tai languages and retains the Early Middle Chinese pronunciation of the character for *jiao*, reconstructed as **kɛɛw*, indicating that is was borrowed into the ancestors of these languages sometime between the third and sixth centuries CE. To the writers of Chinese texts during the Southern Dynasties, the societies of Li and Lao people who lived between Jiaozhou and the rest of the empire were perceived as markedly different and as a consequence their rulers were referred to as uncontrollable native chieftains rather than rebellious officials.

The existence of these societies around all the major routes to Jiaozhou from the northeast created an added complication for those fleeing from the far north who sought refuge in the south. It was easy enough for them to come overland to reach the commanderies of Nanhai or Cangwu, but if they had no access to a ship to travel farther along the coast to Jiaozhou it was necessary for them to pass through the lands of the Li and Lao, which by the fourth century were dangerous for lone travelers. In this way, Li and Lao societies acted as a filter through which only officials or those who were armed or could afford an armed guard could easily pass, and the result of this filtering was that the Red River Plain received minimal outside migration from the north after the mid-fourth century. With no large influx of new migrants from the other cities of the empire to alter the linguistic and political situation in the Red River Plain, the end result was that the Jiaozhou area became a pressure cooker for localized loyalties in which a small number of localized families could consolidate de facto independent rule there in relative isolation from the jurisdiction of the Southern Dynasties. After the foundation of a state in the Red River Plain in the tenth century, these early moves toward autonomy were later retrospectively interpreted as Vietnamese resistance to Chinese rule, but in the texts that survive from before that period, the deeds of officials in the Red River Plain look fairly tame in comparison with the activities of the people who cushioned them from direct contact with the rest of the Southern Dynasties empires.

The Li and Lao were surely not the only reason that migration to Jiaozhou dried up after the fourth century. Other factors already mentioned, such as the danger of tropical disease, the economic downturn caused by changes in shipping technology, and the intermittent wars with Linyi in the south, were probably also significant. All of these would have encouraged migrants fleeing the chaos in northern China to end their journey in relatively safe areas such as Nanhai, Cangwu, and Shixing. As these areas around the Pearl River Delta filled with northern migrants and flourished economically at the expense of Jiaozhou, they also became more closely integrated with the other provinces of the Southern Dynasties. Denied these new migrants by geography, economic change, and the activities of the Li and Lao, the Red River Plain began to develop in relative isolation in its own direction. But who exactly were these Li and Lao people who prevented easy communication between Jiaozhou and the rest of the empires? That is the subject of the following chapter.

NOTES

1. SuS 31: 14b.
2. Charles O. Hucker, *A Dictionary of Official Titles in Imperial China* (Stanford, CA: Stanford University Press, 1986), 539–40.
3. The early history of this division is confusing. At some time between 226 and 264, the division between Guangzhou and Jiaozhou had been abandoned, hence the need for the reinstatement of both provinces. For details, see Loewe, "Guangzhou: Evidence of the Standard Histories," 60.
4. The main administrative centers (Jiuzhen and Jiude) lay on the Lei River (*Leishui*) and the Jiudejiu River. The upper reaches of most of the rivers that flow into the Gulf of Tongking and south lie outside imperial administration.
5. The name *Jiaozhi* changed meaning several times before becoming restricted to the commandery on the Red River Plain. In texts from the Han, Jiaozhi can mean either the commandery of Jiaozhi or the larger area, including later Guangzhou and Jiaozhou. Jiaozhou can mean the same. After the foundation of Guangzhou, this is no longer a problem. Because this work deals with the period after the foundation of Guangzhou, from here onward the term *Jiaozhou* (unless stated otherwise) will be used only in reference to the smaller, post-264 province, and *Jiaozhi* applied only to the commandery in the Red River Plain.
6. SuS 31: 12b.
7. JS 57: 5b.
8. SS 37: 39a–43b.
9. JTS 41: 43a.

10. Roderich Ptak, "The Gulf of Tongking: A Mini-Mediterranean?" in *The East Asian "Mediterranean": Maritime Crossroads of Culture, Commerce and Human Migration,* ed. Angela Schottenhammer (Wiesbaden: Harrassowitz Verlag, 2008), 60–62, 70.

11. See Yang Shaoxiang 楊少祥, "Shilun hepu xuwengang de xingshuai" 試論合浦徐聞港的興衰, in *Zhongguo kaogu jicheng (Huanan juan)* 中國考古集成 (華南卷) (Zhengzhou: Zhongzhou guji chubanshe, 2005), 2: 1498–501.

12. Nishimura Masanari, "Settlement Patterns on the Red River Plain from the Late Prehistoric Period to the Tenth Century AD," *Indo-Pacific Prehistory Association Bulletin* no. 25 (2007): 106.

13. Wang Gungwu, "The Nan-Hai Trade," 91.

14. JS 97: 9b.

15. SJZ ch. 37: 1154.

16. For the location of Jinsang, see Fang Guoyu 方國瑜, *Zhongguo xinan lishi dili kaoshi* 中國西南歷史地理考釋 (Taipei: Taiwan shangwu yinshu guan, 1987), 79–80.

17. Defined by Loewe, "Guangzhou, Evidence of the Standard Histories," 66–67, as "a point of control where incoming and outgoing travellers and goods could be checked."

18. An early-twentieth-century geography of China describes it thus: "Throughout nearly the whole of Yunnan it is but a torrent, running in deep gorges and intersected with rapids." L. Richards, *Comprehensive Geography of the Chinese Empire and Dependencies, translated into English, revised, and enlarged by M. Kennelly* (Shanghai: T'usewei Press, 1908), 179.

19. JS 57: 4b.

20. In particular, the attention paid to the description of its tributaries in SJZ ch. 37: 1152–59. Tao Huang noted that land and water routes from Xinggu in Ningzhou were both passable from Jiaozhou at a distance of 1600 *li* (JS 57: 6a). ZZTJ ch. 81: 2575 has a similar text with the additional detail "the Man occupy the upper river."

21. There is a problem with the dating of this work, as it mentions Linzhang Commandery, not founded until the foundation of Yuezhou in 471. The names of administrative units seem to suggest a date in the late fifth century.

22. ZP 2a–b.

23. HHS 24: 12a.

24. HHS 86: 10a.

25. JTS 41: 40a notes that all the traffic to Jiaozhi in ancient times passed through this Ghost Gate Pass.

26. TPHYJ 167: 3b. "All traffic going to Jiaozhi in the time of the Jin would pass through this gate."

27. "Another but less important tributary, the Yung Kiang [Beiliu River] which joins the Si Kiang [Yu River] above Wuchow Fu, establishes easy connection with Pakhoi [Beihai]. Goods coming by the Lien Kiang [Nanliu] as far as Fomien Fohwei-k'ü to the S.W. of Yuhlin Chow are transported thence upon the backs of carriers to the Yung Kiang, which is navigable from Pehliu Hsien and beyond." Richards, *Comprehensive Geography*, 198.

28. ZZTJ ch. 190: 5949.

29. JS 92: 5a.

30. JS 49: 5b; ZZTJ ch. 92: 2912 provides the date.

31. NQS 14: 25b notes that Songshou was founded by being detached from Yuezhou in 480. This was already the second year of the Southern Qi Dynasty, but it is extremely unlikely that the Qi would found a commandery with a name meaning "longevity of Song" and the commandery was probably founded in the last years of the Liu-Song (420–479).

32. At the time this river went by the name Jinnan River (*Jinnan Jiang*) or Jin River (*Jin Jiang*).

33. Hans Bielenstein, "The Census of China during the Period 2–742 A.D.," *Bulletin of the Museum of Far Eastern Antiquities* 19 (1947): 137.

34. SJZ ch. 40: 1269.

35. TPHYJ 167: 14b–15a; JTS 41: 42a. Rangzhou lay somewhere in the vicinity of the present-day county of Longzhou in Guangxi.

36. A Chinese historical atlas (Tan Qixiang 譚其驤, ed., *Zhongguo lishi dituji* 中國歷史地圖集 [Beijing: Zhongguo ditu chubanshe, 1982–1987], vol. 4, plate 31) notes a county with the name of Jincheng to the southwest of what is now Nanning in a map of the Two Rivers Region under the Southern Qi (479–501). The name suggests that it was founded some time during the Jin and was mentioned in the geographies of the Qi and the Song, but it had disappeared by the Sui. I have been unable to find any record of it in this location.

37. SS 92: 4a.

38. HS 28a: 10a–11b. The numbers are 746,237 individuals for Jiaozhi Commandery compared to a total of 626,053 in the six other commanderies in the circuit.

39. See Gotō, *Betonamu kyūgoku kōsōshi*, 131–35, for a discussion of the tombs in the Vietnam area in general, and Olov Robert Thule Janse, *Archaeological Research in Indo-China* (Cambridge, MA: Harvard University Press, 1947–1958), for a detailed report on a group of tombs in Thanh Hóa and Nghệ An provinces.

40. SJZ ch. 36: 1146. This is the one occurrence in an Early Medieval text I have found of a term that comes anywhere close to the meaning of the modern term *Chinese*.

41. For instance, he states that the bronze pillars planted by Ma Yuan once stood beside the settlement of the Maliu but that they had since sunk beneath the sea, and that there were originally only ten families of soldiers but they had married only among themselves to increase their number to two hundred families.

42. Nguyen Kim Dung, I. C. Glover, and M. Yamagata, "Excavations at Tra Kieu and Go Cam, Quang Nam Province, Central Viet Nam," in *Uncovering Southeast Asia's Past—Selected Papers from the 10th Conference of the European Association of Southeast Asian Archaeologists*, ed. E. A. Bacus, I. C. Glover, and V. C. Pigott (Singapore: National University of Singapore Press, 2006), 216–31.

43. SGZ 49: 9b.

44. Hans Bielenstein, "Chinese Historical Demography A.D. 2–1982," *Bulletin of the Museum of Far Eastern Antiquities* 59 (1967): 16–17.

45. SS 35: 2b.

46. Hans Bielenstein, "Census," 125–30, describes the Jin census as a "list of taxable households" made in the Taikang era (280–290) as an inventory of the newly reunified empire. This was also due to the fact that Shixing was detached from Nanhai

Commandery. By this time the combined household count for these two commanderies that made up the territory of the old Nanhai Commandery was 14,500, but for the old territory of Jiaozhi, including the then detached Wuping and Xinchang Commanderies, the combined household count was still 20,000.

47. The commandery of Xinchang was omitted from the Liu-Song census.

48. Bielenstein, "Census," 145.

49. Katakura, "Chūgoku shihaika no betonamu," 33; Lü Shipeng 呂士朋, *Beishu shidai de Yuenan* 北屬時代的越南 (Hong Kong: New Asia Research Institute, Chinese University of Hong Kong, 1964), 97.

50. Nishimura, "Settlement Patterns," 106, notes a decline in numbers of Chinese-style brick tombs, attributing it to a shift in trade patterns and cultural change among the Jiaozhou elite, which led them to abandon the practice.

51. Annette Kieser, "Nur Guangdong ist ruhig und friedlich; Grabkult und Migration während der Sechs Dynastien im heutigen Guangdong," in *Guangdong Archaeology and Early Texts (Zhou-Tang)*, ed. Shing Müller, Thomas O. Höllmann, and Putao Gui, South China and Maritime Asia Series vol. 13 (Wiesbaden: Harrassowitz Verlag, 2004), 101–24. Kieser (p. 105) also mentioned the possibility that in the area that is now Vietnam a lack of finds may be indicative of the reluctance of Vietnamese archaeologists to pay attention to the archaeology of the period. For an idea of the extreme paucity of Vietnamese scholarship on the period, one need only compare the amount of space given to it in the collections of archaeological reports in the annual volumes produced by the Vietnamese Institute of Archaeology (Viện khảo cổ học, *Những Phát Hiện Mới về Khảo Cổ Học* [Hanoi: Nhà Xuất Bản Khoa Học Xã Hội, 1972–2009]). These volumes run to 800 pages or more for each issue, but until recently the millennium between the end of the Đong Sơn culture and the foundation of Đại Việt was passed over in silence.

52. BWZ ch. 1: 11.

53. ZZTJ ch. 86: 2718–19.

54. SS 92: 4b, 6a.

55. Liao, *Lishi dilixue*, 63–64.

56. NQS 58: 15b, refers to those who were punished as "troops" (*buqu*). SS 94: 15a, records the same event but refers to them as "refugees" (*liuyu*). ZZTJ ch. 132: 4144, provides the date and follows the NCS, naming them "troops."

57. Holmgren, *Chinese Colonisation,* 136.

58. Others were Yulin at the confluence of the Zangke and Tan Rivers, Jinxing at the confluence of the Youjiang and Zuojiang Rivers, and Sihui or "four meetings," so named because it lay at the confluence of four rivers.

59. This is from a description of Guangzhou from around the beginning of the fifth century: "Guangzhou embraces the mountains and the seas, and rare and unusual things are produced there, one box of them can support several generations, but there are many miasmas and pestilences, and people's natures are fearful because of these." JS 90: 9b.

60. NCS 32: 2a.

61. LS 33: 2b–3a.

62. JS 90: 9b.

63. ZP 2a–b.

64. SS 37: 21a–23b.

65. ZZTJ ch. 115: 3628, says that wood for a fleet of ships was collected in the mountains of Nankang and shipped four hundred *li* across to Shixing.

66. Xiao Mai's name sometimes appears as Xiao Li due to a graphical mistake based on the similarity of the characters.

67. NS 51: 3b–4a. It is recorded that he was crowded by boats on his departure from Guangzhou and that he eventually passed through the county of Xinjin, where a local woman presented him with fish and local boys swam out to his boat to welcome him.

68. HHS 33: 20b–21a. Because this record dates from the Han, Jiaozhou probably refers to the larger province that encompassed later Jiaozhou and Guangzhou, rather than the smaller province centered on the Red River Plain.

69. SS 38: 34b.

70. XTS 196: 11b. The fact the Lu Ji had to use a stone as ballast was symbolic of his unusual virtue as an official, in that he did not use his time as an official in Yulin to avail himself of the riches that corruption could bring.

71. Francis Allard, "Frontiers and Boundaries: The Han Empire from Its Southern Periphery," in *Archaeology of Asia,* ed. Miriam T. Stark (Malden, MA: Blackwell Publishing, 2006), 240. Allard's total of two thousand tombs found in Guangxi includes those excavated in Hepu, which would be better discussed separately in the context of Jiaozhou and the Red River Plain.

72. HS 28b, 10a–11b: Jiaozhi, Jiuzhen, Jinnan, and Hepu Commanderies counted a combined total of 159,041 households, whereas Nanhai, Yulin, and Cangwu Commanderies counted only 56,407; Jiaozhi Commandery alone had 92,440 households, compared to 19,613 for Nanhai and 24,379 for Cangwu.

73. Zhou Yiliang 周一良, "Nanchao jingnei zhi gezhong ren ji zhengfu duidai zhi zhengce" 南朝境內之各種人及政府對待之政策, in *Weijin nanbei chao shilunji* 魏晉南北朝史論集 (Beijing: Zhonghua shuju, 1963), 32–39.

74. NYZ, quoted in TPHYJ 158: 3b–4a.

75. NYZ, quoted in TPHYJ 167: 9b.

76. SS 50: 5a. This is mentioned in conjunction with events that occurred in 419.

77. SS 38: 33a.

78. Holmgren, *Chinese Colonisation,* 125–26; Taylor, *Birth of Vietnam,* 115–18.

79. See Kieser, "Nur Guangdong ist ruhig," 121–22, for an overview and map of the graves within the boundaries of modern Guangdong Province.

80. Hu Shouwei, *Lingnan gushi,* 130–49, lists a Xiu family, a Wang family, and two Liu families, the members of which inherited positions in the Pearl River drainage area.

81. Ibid., 131–32, 139–42.

82. The others were Xiao Yuanjian, who served in 514 (LS 23: 7b), Xiao Ang, who served in the late 510s (LS 9: 4a), and Xiao Yu (CS 17: 5b). For a discussion of these people, see Hu, *Lingnan gushi,* 176–91.

83. NCS 58: 15a–b.

84. NCS 40: 6b.

85. NCS 14: 24b. The ellipsis replaces a short quote from a geographical work by Han author Yang Xiong (53 BCE–26 CE) called "Probings into the Twelve Provinces" (*Shier zhou jian* 十二州箴), as these are not relevant to the fifth century.

86. For example, a thirteenth-century geographical work (YDJS 117: 1a) records that the Gaozhou area (close to the present-day city of Gaozhou) was a part of Nanhai Commandery under the Qin and Gaoliang Commandery under the Han, but not a single county was founded in the area for six centuries until the foundation of Haichang Commandery in 439 under the Liu-Song. Similarly, Songshou Commandery was recorded as having been split off from Yuezhou in one source (NCS 14: 25b, footnote 31), whereas another source says it formerly belonged to the jurisdiction of Jiaozhou (SS 38: 44b). Because there was not even a county founded in the area prior to 480, it was probably split from neither and represents an expansion of the administration into a previously ungoverned area.

87. This habit has also been discussed in Geoff Wade, "The Southern Chinese Borders in History," in *Where China Meets Southeast Asia: Social and Cultural Change in the Border Region*, ed. G. Evans, C. Hutton, and K. E. Kuah (Singapore: Institute of Southeast Asian Studies, 2000), 28–50.

88. See, for instance, Tan Qixiang 譚其驤, ed., *Zhongguo lishi dituji* 中國歷史地圖集 (Beijing: Zhongguo ditu chubanshe, 1982–1987), 3: 57–58; 4: 31–33, where there are large empty blocks of territory between a few concentrations of counties and commanderies along the river banks and coast.

89. NCS 14: 26a. The first "Jiao" here refers to the Han province of Jiaozhou that encompassed the entire Two Rivers Region, and the second only to the area around the Red River Delta, as this was the extent of Jiaozhou at the time the book was written.

90. See Joseph Earle Spencer, *Asia, East by South: A Cultural Geography* (New York: J. Wiley, 1954), 108–9.

91. TPHYJ 167: 3a, associates the story with Rongzhou, on the northern side of the Ghost Gate Pass. The original story is from HHS 24: 13a–b.

92. HHS 24: 14a.

93. TPHYJ 169: 2b.

94. CS 8: 1b.

95. TPHYJ 169: 6a; TPHYJ 161: 2a.

96. WLDLZ, quoted in TPYL 771: 2a. The safe area was at Gaoyao (present-day Zhaoqing).

97. NZYWZ, quoted in HHS 86: 7b.

98. BWZ ch. 2: 25.

99. Ibid.

100. JZJ, quoted in TPYL 946: 7b.

101. SGZ 53: 10b. Taylor's version of this letter (*Birth of Vietnam*, 75–76) is garbled and omits this important passage.

102. JS 57: 6a.

103. NQS 14: 20a–b.

104. NQS 41: 1a–b.

105. Keith Taylor (*Birth of Vietnam*, 120) provides this only for the commanderies that are now part of Vietnamese territory, leading him to the conclusion that the

decline of imperial influence in the Vietnam area was a peculiarity of that area alone. On page 121, he draws the conclusion that "the fifth century was a time of phenomenal growth and in population and administration; yet this growth was confined to Guang and the new province of Yue." On page 122 he states: "In 471 Yue Province was organised from portions of Guang and Jiao. The immediate reason for this was to recognise those portions of Jiao that were still under imperial authority. . . . Yue Province, in effect became the new frontier of the Empire." If all the population statistics for the Two Rivers Region are calculated commandery by commandery, the picture is rather different. (Pinyin altered from original.)

106. The percentage of decline for Wuping is calculated from the Jin statistics for both Wuping and Xinchang because the latter was close to Wuping but was not recorded in the Liu-Song census.

107. The number depends on whether or not the household count of the area of the former Gaoxing Commandery of the Jin census was included. Similarly, depending on whether Gaoxing was included, the registered population of Gaoliang Commandery fell by either 55 or 29 percent.

Chapter 3

Why Are the Li and Lao?

The Shifting Meanings of Ethnonyms

From the beginning of the first millennium CE onward, Chinese descriptions of the lands between the Two Rivers used various names to refer to the local inhabitants who were not under direct Chinese rule. Sometimes they would call them bandits or brigands, but usually they would use generalized terms for foreigners based on their relative position in regard to what was considered the center of China, such as *Yi* and *Man*, or more specific terms, such as *Li*, *Lao*, and *Wuhu*, which were geographically bound to specific areas.

The different Chinese terms for "foreigner" have often been referred to uncritically in English-language scholarship as types of "barbarian," a habit that historian Christopher Beckwith has recently criticized on account of the associations of the word with a European mindset that stemmed from Greek and Roman perceptions of nomadic peoples, and had little to do with the way Chinese perceived and wrote about foreigners.[1] Although this is a reasonable argument, even if we desist from the practice of using the European concept of "barbarian," simply replacing the term with "foreign" does not sufficiently express the level of contempt Chinese writers held for the foreigners whom they so named. The word *Man*, referring to the non-Chinese peoples to the south, definitely indicated something less than human from the Chinese perspective; the character's radical was a symbol indicating snakes, worms, and bugs, and the influential second-century etymological dictionary *Shuowen jiezi* claimed that this was because Man were in fact descended from snakes.[2] From Chinese writers' descriptions of those they perceived as foreign, it is obvious that they saw this type of foreignness as something undesirable, uncultured, and inferior, and that the application of the names by Chinese writers such as those mentioned earlier to certain people of the Two Rivers Region indicates that they perceived them as uncultured and barbaric, distinct from the ordinary "people" (*ren*) or "subjects" (*min*) among whose ranks they counted themselves.

With the foregoing in mind, even without translating these terms as "barbarian," the names Man, Yi, Li, Lao, and Wuhu that appear in Chinese texts in relation to the Two Rivers Region should still at least be read with a similar subtext of contempt for their referents. This is best expressed perhaps through the terminology of the European colonialist mindset rather than that of ancient Greece and Rome, by means of vocabulary such as "savage" and "native" (the latter in a pejorative sense). If no general term like *barbarian* can be applied to all of these people, then at the very least we might distinguish grades of *barbarism* or *savagery* perceived by the Chinese observers among the people they wrote about, in contrast to their own perceived superior and civilized behaviors. These are evident in the different connotations of all the names used in reference to the Two Rivers Region.

The two terms *Yi* and *Man* were very widely employed in Chinese texts; they were half of a set of four traditional terms for foreign peoples found in pre-Qin texts based on the four cardinal points of the compass—the Rong of the west, Di of the north, Yi of the east, and Man of the south—and it was only natural that the words for the southern and eastern foreigners should end up being used for people of the Two Rivers Region. Although Man referred specifically to the inhabitants in and beyond the southern boundaries of the empire, the semantic range of Yi had become so diluted through wide usage that it could refer to foreign peoples on points of the compass ranging from the northeast (Korea and Japan) to the southwest (Yunnan and the Two Rivers Region) of the Chinese imperial center. By the second half of the first millennium CE it ended up as the default term for foreigner by which all others were defined.[3] The wide semantic range of the terms *Yi* and *Man* has led to general scholarly recognition that these were general terms for foreigners and did not refer to specific groups of people, whereas in regard to names with more geographically bound usage such as Li, Lao, and Wuhu, there still exists a widely held belief that they must have been based on a concrete reality of coherent ethnic groupings.

The disparity between ethnonyms and lived realities on the ground has long been recognized in other fields of history, particularly in Southeast Asian studies where it is well known that ethnonyms applied by outsiders often have very little relationship to how the referents consider themselves. Some names that were eventually defined as those of ethnic groups in relatively recent times have been exposed as based on little more than people's geographical location,[4] their administrative status in the eyes of the state,[5] or the pejorative terms applied to them by their neighbors.[6] Even in southern China of the present day, there are many groups of people whose language usage and self-identity do not fit the nationality (*minzu*) to which they have been officially assigned by the Chinese state. These include speakers of Tai-Kadai and Austroasiatic languages who have ended up classified officially into groups of Han or Miao,[7] and people who are officially designated as belonging to the Zhuang nationality even though they actually refer to themselves by various names such as Yay, Nung, Tu, and Sha and are unable to understand the radio broadcasts made in the standardized official version of their designated mother tongue.[8] It is highly unlikely that the writers of ancient Chinese texts were armed with superior ethnographic knowledge to those in modern times, and it is therefore also equally unlikely that ancient Chinese names for foreigners and indigenous peoples reflect categories perceived by their referents. Any ethnonym recorded in a premodern Chinese text needs to be approached with a certain amount of suspicion.

Because the people designated Li and Lao in ancient Chinese texts have left no records of their own aside from a few stelae dating from the seventh century CE, how they actually referred to themselves in earlier periods is a question that cannot be answered with any certainty. That they probably did not use the terms *Li* and *Lao* is suggested by the nature of the many references to the Li and Lao, used over many centuries and often inconsistently, for widely scattered and disparate groups of people. These groups almost certainly spoke unrelated languages,[9] shared little in the way of material culture, and were never politically unified. The oft-repeated refrain that "it is their custom to enjoy attacking one other"[10] indicates that it was unlikely that they considered themselves to be a single unified group. Although is highly doubtful that they had any meaning for those to whom they were applied, the names *Li* and *Lao* did have meaning and significance for those who used them. Rather than answering the question "who were the Li and Lao?" it is better to extend the question, and ask in imitation of F. K. Lehman's query concerning the Karen of Burma, "who were the Li and Lao, and if so, why?"[11]

The most important criterion for the application of the names *Li* and *Lao* to groups of people was that those who wrote about them considered them to be inferior. A characteristic shared by both names is that the characters used to write them carry negative connotations. Wuhu is a slightly different case that will be discussed shortly. Li is written with a character that has the original meaning "bumpkin" or "rustic" and Lao is written with the "dog" radical, implying savagery. But within this general application based on perceived rusticity or barbarity, it is also possible to determine distinct patterns of usage in these names, particularly in the context of the Two Rivers Region, and these patterns can perhaps answer the question of why certain names were employed for certain people and not for others.

In his study of Chinese interactions with peoples to the north and west, Nicola di Cosmo noted that during Han times there was a shift in the Chinese naming of peoples in those areas from names based on the points of the compass, such as Di and Rong, to the name Hu based on an "anthropological type," but that this new name still did not imply that its referents were ethnically or linguistically similar.[12] Other than a vague connection to peoples of the west and south, the compass-point terms *Man* and *Yi* were not fixed geographically, and they continued to be used very generally for non-Sinitic peoples throughout the Two Rivers Region alongside the three new terms *Li*, *Lao*, and *Wuhu* that came into use around the same time as the term *Hu*. Like the name *Hu*, the first two terms seem to have a connection with anthropological types perceived by the Chinese, whereas the name *Wuhu* had a more localized and specific meaning. Li and Lao had divergent meanings over time and space that are difficult to pin down to specific cultural characteristics other than differences in political and social organizations from those who described them.[13] All three terms differed from the compass point terms *Man* and *Yi*, as these were more or less fixed for direction and referred over time to peoples ever more distant from the Chinese center, first to the peoples of Chu in the first millennium BCE, then to the peoples of the Two Rivers Region during Han times, and finally expanded to a general term referring to all foreigners living in a vaguely southerly direction. Li, Lao, and Wuhu were never used in such a generalized sense and referred only to peoples within specific geographical contexts. Of the three terms, *Wuhu* was the most geographically and temporally specific, and *Lao* the least so and used over the widest area for the longest time. As for the term *Li*, this had a fairly localized use, but was often inconsistently applied over time.

THE DERIVATION AND DISTRIBUTION OF THE NAMES *WUHU, LAO,* AND *LI*

The earliest work to mention the term *Wuhu* was the *Nanzhou yiwu zhi* (Annals of Oddities from the Southern Provinces) by Wan Zhen, governor of Danyang during the time of the Three Kingdoms state of Wu (222–278). Wan Zhen noted that Wuhu had originally been a toponym referring to the area "South of Guangzhou and North of Jiaozhou" and that the people of that area took the name *Wuhu* from the area by that name where they lived.[14] This may well have been the case, as subsequent records of the Wuhu people are mainly limited to a district in the vicinity of the Yu River. The meaning of the characters wu 烏 and hu 滸 ("black" and "riverbank") makes little sense as the name of an entire district, and it may be that the term derives from a transliteration into Chinese of a name in an indigenous language. Another quote from the same work, preserved as a commentary to the *Hou Han shu* (Book of the Later Han), records them as living in or to the "west of Jiaozhi."[15] The *Hou Han shu* elsewhere refers to Wuhu living in Yulin Commandery and in Hepu and Jiaozhi. Under the Han, Yulin was a large commandery that contained twelve counties and controlled the territories along the Yu, Tan, and Zangke Rivers, so the Wuhu recorded in the *Hou Han shu* were probably the inhabitants of the areas adjacent to the Tan and Yu Rivers where these joined at the seat of Yulin Commandery.[16] In Jiaozhi and Hepu dwelled the Wuhu who were responsible for setting off the great 178 uprising,[17] and Pei Yuan's *Guangzhou ji* of the Eastern Jin records them in Jinxing (in the vicinity of present-day Nanning). A single outlier record exists in a fifth-century work that records Wuhu living in Wuyang County, an area in the mountains northwest of Shixing (present-day Guilin), distant from the Chinese administrative presence.[18] Without this outlier record, the rather limited geographical and temporal distribution of the name suggests that it might actually have corresponded to a specific ethnolinguistic group. Although common in texts before the fourth century CE, the term *Wuhu* soon passed out of use; Tang and post-Tang texts mention them either only in historical context when quoting older books or replace them with the terms *Li* and *Lao* when recording the contemporary activities of the people in the same area.

The term *Lao* 獠 first appears paired with Yi in a passage in the *Hou Han shu*. In texts that predate this, the character stood for an unrelated word pronounced *liao*, meaning "to hunt at night with torches."[19] Like the characters for Wuhu, the character used to write Lao was probably employed as a transliteration of a native term. It has been suggested that the name *Lao* was probably a shortening of two character combinations pronounced in Mandarin as *Ge-Lao*, standing for a name pronounced *Klao* with a complex initial cluster,[20] which seems highly likely because examples exist elsewhere of the first consonant in an initial consonant cluster being dropped when vocabulary was borrowed into Sinitic languages.[21] The earliest record of the name to indicate the presence of a complex initial consonant is found in the *Huayang guo zhi* (Records of the Lands to the South of Mt. Hua), written in the mid-fourth century, with characters pronounced *Jiu-Lao* 鳩獠 referring to people in the commanderies of Xinggu and Yongchang, both of which lay in the mountains upriver northwest from Jiaozhou.[22] The next mentions were connected to events of the fifth and sixth centuries: the *Song shu* recorded that the people of Nanxuzhou (on the south bank of the Yangtze River just east of the capital Jiankang) had heard old tales of the cannibal *Hu-Lao* 狐獠 people, and were therefore terrified by the strange appearance of a few hundred soldiers from Shu (Szechwan) who wore rhinoceros-skin armor.[23] The *Liang shu* and *Chen Shu* both recorded the name of *Qu-Lao* 屈獠, who inhabited a valley[24] in Jiaozhi near the confluence of the Black River and the Red River.[25] These were the people who beheaded Yue emperor Lý Bốn when he attempted to take refuge among them after his defeat in 546.[26] The characters given for these three names *Jiu-Lao*, *Hu-Lao*, and *Qu-Lao* would have been pronounced something like *kɔ-lawʔ*, *ɣɔ-lawʔ*, and *k'ut-lawʔ* in Early Middle Chinese, all of which could easily stand for an original *klao*.[27] Names such as these that indicate a complex initial do not reappear until late Tang times.[28] If *klao* was the original form of the name, it seems unusual that it occurs in later works than the first records of *Lao*, but the stability of the second graph in these names indicates perhaps that the monosyllable was the older borrowing and that those who wrote of the *Ge-Lao* were in fact already conscious of the name *Lao*. It is possible that the authors assumed that the first syllables in these names were actually a description for different types of Lao peoples, due to the meanings of the characters *jiu* 鳩 ("dove") and *hu* 狐 ("fox"), but the similarity in the sounds of the first syllable of the different versions of the name suggests that in each case there was an attempt to transcribe a name heard in a spoken language rather than a name picked up from reading a text, and it is most likely related to the word *klao*, meaning "person," found in languages of the Kra branch of the Kadai language family.[29] If these terms were in fact picked up from speech, it suggests that people speaking these languages were once widespread throughout the mountains where the Two Rivers have their source. An alternative etymology suggested by Li Jinfang was that the word *lao* was a transliteration of the pronoun "we" or "us," *rao* (proto-Tai *rəu*) common to many Tai languages, with the initial *k-* deriving from a word meaning "people," so that the many written variations of *klao* were in fact transliterations of a term meaning "our people."[30]

The term *Lao* in its monosyllabic form was applied to people over a wide geographical area over a long period of time. The first record of the term occurs in Chen Shou's *San guo zhi* and Zhang Hua's *Bowu zhi*, both written in the last decades of the third century, and it was still being employed to refer to hill people in southern China in the seventeenth century. The *San guo zhi* record refers to Yi and Lao people living in Yongchang Commandery in what is now Western Yunnan along the upper reaches of the Mekong: "The Yi and Lao occupy the strategic spots, constantly commit banditry, and will not submit."[31] Zhang Hua refers to them as *Laozi* and notes their distribution from the far southwestern boundary south of Jingzhou to Shu,[32] an area that encompassed a wide swath of country stretching from present-day Guangdong up into Sichuan. The *Hou Han shu* contains a reference to the Lao in a passage concerning a former ruler known as the "Bamboo King" (*Zhu Wang*), who was said to have been born from inside a section of bamboo and ruled over the Yi and Lao of the Zangke and Yelang area (northern Guangxi and southern Guizhou).[33] The *Shuijing zhu* associates this story with the Zangke River (known at the time as the *Tun shui*), a northern tributary of the Yu River.[34] The *Jin shu* recorded Lao far to the south of these regions in the hill country of Wuping, Jiude, and Xinchang around the Red River Plain, where the land was steep and inaccessible.[35]

The *Guangzhou ji*, composed sometime during the Eastern Jin (317–420), has a record of Li and Lao in reference to their bronze drums, which in this case limits the referents to people who lived in the area to the west of Canton and south of the Yu River.[36] The *Song shu* noted numerous kinds of Li and Lao in "The Mountains of Guangzhou,"[37] a record of Li and Lao at a place called Shiqi, which lay somewhere between Hepu and Jiaozhou,[38] and the Man and Lao in the south in general.[39] The majority of the records of Lao in the *Nan Qi shu* refer to people from the Yizhou area (present-day Sichuan) and Ningzhou (now Yunnan),[40] but there were also Li and Lao recorded in Yuezhou and Guangzhou.[41] The *Chen shu* noted the presence of Yi and Lao in Jiaozhi who would "join forces to carry out banditry,"[42] and also Yi and Lao in Xiangzhou, Hengzhou, Gùizhou, and Wuzhou (present-day Hunan and northern Guangdong and Guangxi), who were attacked by the Prince of Shixing, the second son of the first emperor of the Chen.[43] In the *Sui shu*, Lao were mentioned mostly in connection with areas to the north of the Two Rivers Region, but occasionally further to the south. Li and Lao were said to have rebelled against a greedy and cruel regional governor in Panzhou,[44] north of Canton, before they were placated by the Lady Xian[45] and together with Yi as partners in banditry in Panyu (Canton).[46] All of the mentions of Lao people before the seventh century are used in reference to people inhabiting a very wide area, stretching from Canton in the far east to the region of present-day Thanh Hóa in the south and west, but the earliest and most concentrated use of the term was far to the northwest of the Two Rivers Region, in the area where the water drains into the Yangtze River rather than the Pearl or Red Rivers. It is highly doubtful that these widely scattered people belonged to a single ethnic or linguistic grouping.

During the Southern Dynasties period, the name *Li* was used over a much smaller geographical region than *Lao*, and only in reference to people who dwelled within the Two Rivers Region. Like Lao, the character used to write Li (俚) had an alternate meaning in pre-Han texts, in this case "vulgar" or "bumpkin," before it was applied to people in the Two Rivers Region. The etymology of the name is uncertain, but like Lao it may also have derived from a transcription of a term in an indigenous language.[47] Most Chinese scholarship regards the earliest record of this name as dating from 43 CE in reference to people in the hills of what is now central Vietnam, but this is uncertain, as it is written with the character 里 in the original text and could just as easily stand for the word "village."[48]

Because the terms *Li* and *Lao* are often put together in a compound *Li and Lao*, many of the locations noted above for the Lao also applied to the Li. The earliest definitive record of Li people using the character 俚 is Wan Zhen's *Nanzhou yiwu zhi*, in which he refers to them as the "Li bandits of Guangzhou," but does not go into further detail as to the districts they inhabited.[49]

More specific records of the geographical distribution of Li people date from
the Liu-Song (420–479) and can be found in the *Song shu* and in Shen Huaiyuan's *Nanyue zhi*. The *Song shu* recorded Man and Li in Shixing Commandery to the north of Canton at the beginning of the Yuanjia period (424–454)[50]
and Li in one of the commandery's subordinate counties known as Zhongsu.[51]
The same book also recorded the governor of Jinkang Commandery attacking the Li, who presumably lived close to his territory,[52] and some Li also
lived closer to Jiaozhou.[53] The *Nanyue zhi* mentions Li living at Duanxi[54]
and Fuchun,[55] both in Jinkang Commandery, in Gaozhou to the southwest of
Nanhai,[56] as well as further to the northwest in Gùizhou,[57] and far to the south
in Songchang County in Jiude Commandery (north central Vietnam).[58] The
term was also used for those who lived on the coast; *Nan Qi shu* recorded
that a Li fisherman of the Gaoliang area on the coast southwest of Canton
had fished up an odd-looking bronze sculpture of an animal in his net.[59] The
Liang shu has several records of Li but mentions their specific locations only
twice, on the borders of Shixing, to the north of Canton where they were said
to be especially fond of banditry so that before the 470s, administrators of
the area were obliged to carry swords for protection.[60] The *Nan Shi* notes Li
involved in piracy along the coast of Guangzhou.[61] There were many records
of armed attacks against the Li in the sixth century, mostly concentrated south
of the Yu River to the southwest of Canton, and it is only in Tang texts that
the term was applied to people living to the east of Canton.[62] By the tenth
century, records of Li people are again confined to the Pearl River drainage
area to the west of Canton.[63]

WHAT LI AND LAO ACTUALLY MEANT

The distribution of the use of the terms *Lao* and *Li* in pre-Tang texts can be
summarized as follows: *Lao* was used for people throughout the Two Rivers
Region, mainly in the hill country or areas more distant from the Chinese
administrative centers. It was also used further afield to refer to people of the
mountainous country of modern Yunnan, Guizhou, and Sichuan far to the
north and northwest of the Two Rivers Region. *Li* was used mainly to the
north and west of Canton, but also in the Red River area in both the hills and
the plains. However, inconsistencies in the use of the terms abound; in some
cases, the same events are recounted in different works, or even within a
single work, employing different names for the same groups of people. In one
case, in two early texts Wuhu and Li are interchanged.[64] On another occasion
the names *Li* and *Lao* are confused: in the *Chen Shu*, a military expedition
that leads to the capture of a certain Chen Wenche (about whom more will
be said later) is recorded as "against the Yi and Lao,"[65] but the reference to

the same expedition in the *Liang shu* refers to Chen Wenche personally as a "Li leader" (*Lishuai*), and the *Nan shi* identifies him as a "Li leader from west of the river."[66] In addition, many Chinese writers also had the habit of compounding terms such as *Yi and Lao* and *Man and Lao*; all of these usages suggest that writers named the people of the south with whatever terminology they had at their disposal and not because they had done enough research into their culture or customs to distinguish discrete groups among them.

As previously mentioned, Pulleyblank speculated that the names had a connection with speakers of Tai languages, and this was probably true of the first recorded Lao and Gelao, from whose speech the name *Lao* was most likely borrowed, but the etymology of the name does not necessarily equal its later usage, and the later more widespread use of the term over southwest China probably had very little to do with Chinese identification of linguistic groups and was based on other factors. Taylor proposes that the distinction between Lao and Li was related to their habitat, and that Lao referred to mountain dwellers in contrast to Li, which referred to "non-Chinese peoples living a settled existence in the lowlands."[67] This is a reasonable observation made from the respective geographical distributions of the two names, but further investigation shows that the distinction between Li and Lao went beyond differences in their geographical habitat. In sixth- and seventh-century texts, it is more likely that the authors were making distinctions loosely based on people's political organization and their relationships to the Chinese administrative system. The geography of the areas inhabited by Li or Lao merely encouraged different patterns of settlement and social organization on which the distinction was based.

The general pattern of usage through the Six Dynasties is that Li was increasingly applied to people who lived close to imperially controlled urban centers and were culturally close to what the writers of Chinese texts considered the norms of civilized behavior. Those called Lao, on the other hand, tended to live in mountainous areas remote from Chinese centers, suggesting that the term referred to people not only more geographically distant, but also those more culturally divergent from the norms of those who wrote about them. This distinction between Li and Lao becomes more apparent in the light of the ambiguous status of some Li individuals in Chinese texts, particularly those recorded in the period from the sixth to the eighth centuries. From the sixth century onward it is not uncommon to find the term *Li* interchanged with *person* (*ren*). For example, Wang Zhongxuan, who lived in the Canton area in the 590s, is referred to in four different ways in the same book, as a Yi of Panyu, as a Lingnan chief (*Lingnan qiuzhang*), as a Li commander (*li shuai*), and as a man of Panyu (*Panyu ren*).[68] Similarly, Lý Phật Tử of Jiaozhou, who was influential in the local politics of the area in the second half of the sixth century and led an uprising there in 602, is called a "man of

Jiaozhou" (*Jiaozhou ren*) in one chapter, a "Li man of Jiaozhou" (*Jiaozhou li ren*) in another, and a "great leader of Jiaozhou" (*Jiaozhou jushuai*) in yet another.[69]

The cases of Wang Zhongxuan and Lý Phật Tử are examples of individuals sometimes referred to as Li, and at other times as ordinary people, an increasingly common occurrence in the seventh century in references to members of the great ruling clans between the Two Rivers such as the Ning, Feng, and Chen. In Chinese texts, those who were considered "people" were usually inhabitants of urbanized areas close to the sea or to large rivers who paid taxes and carried out corvée labor, or the holders of imperial titles who administered them. The reason why Li individuals are often confused with the *ren* or unnamed groups of people is that they often resembled these people so closely in their administrative status and social habits that they lost their barbaric status altogether in the eyes of some Chinese writers and entered the realm of *ren* as ordinary citizens and administrators.

By the late seventh century, those named Li also had an administrative status in the Tang Empire; there were households classified as "Li households" (*Li hu*) who only paid half the taxes of ordinary citizens,[70] and when the protector-general of Annam, Liu Yanyou, decided in 687 to levy full tax on the Li households there, a member of their faction named Lý Tư Thận joined with others to attack and sack the seat of the protectorate to try to kill him.[71] In this case, Li refers to people who were involved with the imperial administrative system and is obviously approaching the meaning of an administrative category. The case of the taxation of Li households in the Tang is additional evidence for the proximity of the Li to Chinese administrative and cultural norms. In the context of the Two Rivers Region, there are very few equivalent examples of ambiguous usage between the terms *Lao* and ordinary *people*; the Lao are usually referred to as an unnamed collective, whereas the Li are usually recorded individuals bearing Chinese-style names. In the few cases where a certain individual is referred to as "Lao" and as a "person," the same individual will almost certainly be referred to as a "Li" in some other text. Lao was also frequently collocated together as a compound word with classical pejorative terms for uncivilized people, such as Yi or Man as Yi-Lao and Man-Lao, suggesting that the term was more indicative of perceived barbaric behavior than Li, which could be compounded with Lao as Li-Lao, but was never compounded with either Yi or Man.

The contexts in which the two terms were used suggests that the general distinction between Li and Lao was neither based on linguistic categories nor on locality, but was more similar to the later categorization of peoples into two different grades of foreigner, the savage and recalcitrant "raw" foreigners (*sheng fan*) and tamer, submissive "cooked" foreigners (*shu fan*).[72] Characteristic of the "raw" type was that they lived under their own autonomous (and often intractable) rulers and had customs that deviated widely from the habits of those who wrote about them. In contrast, the "cooked" type were still recognizable as different people but had adopted Chinese customs. Their leaders were incorporated to some extent into the imperial system and were usually obedient to imperial authority.[73] The usage of the terms *Li* and *Lao* in the Two Rivers Region, particularly from the sixth century onward, corresponds better to the later concepts of "raw" and "cooked" barbarity than it does to any possible differences in language, material culture, or group identity.[74]

What is even more interesting about the case of Lý Phật Tử's status as a Li is that he was said to be a kinsman of Lý Bốn, who was never described as a foreigner/indigene of any kind. This shows that it was possible for whole families as well as individuals to slip back and forth between the categories of uncivilized foreigner/indigene and civilized person or subject depending on their political behavior. From the Sui onward there are several examples of purportedly "Chinese" lineages that had a long association with the lands between the Two Rivers (such as the Ning and Feng clans discussed in chapter 7), but had been attributed uncivilized foreigner status in the eyes of Tang writers. At one point, the entire Red River Plain, usually treated as nothing more than a province, acquired the status of foreign region when it was included in the section on uncivilized foreigners in the last chapters of the *Nan Qi shu*.[75] The *Nan Qi shu* was compiled sometime in the first decades of the sixth century, a time in which the great local families of Jiaozhou began to assert their autonomy from imperial rule.[76] It is likely that the treatment of Jiaozhou in the *Nan Qi shu* is closely connected to the political behavior of the local rulers and to the tenuous grip the Liang Empire had over the area during these years.

When Chinese descriptions of people cease to use terminology that marks their referents as uncivilized foreigners, it usually indicates that the referents had become outwardly close enough in their day-to-day habits and political structures to the people of other parts of the empire to be considered nothing more than regional variations on a larger theme. When people and their leaders began to deviate from what was considered the norm, through political activity or through social or material culture, it was easy for them to slip back into the categories of uncivilized foreigners. These various ambiguities between Li people and those people or subjects without marked ethnonyms were not only due to the uncivilized foreigners/indigenes coming to resemble the ordinary "people" or "subjects," but also due to the "people" approaching (or moving away from) behavior thought to be characteristic of the uncivilized foreigner/indigene. In addition, because the norms of Chinese "civilized" behavior were constantly shifting, certain types of political structure considered typical of uncivilized Li people in one era were regarded as quite normal in another. With this in mind, it is more accurate to speak of a kind of meeting in the middle between the two than an absorption or acculturation of Li to Chinese behavior. That the descendants of Li chieftains eventually came to look like localized great families in other parts of the empire was as much a result of change in the way Chinese administered themselves and how they chose local administrators as it was of Li or Lao acculturation to Chinese administrative practices and political norms. It is to these processes of change and the political context of the Li and Lao that we now turn.

NOTES

1. Christopher I. Beckwith, *Empires of the Silk Road: A History of Central Eurasia from the Bronze Age to the Present* (Princeton, NJ: Princeton University Press, 2009), 356–60.

2. SWJZ 13a, 25a.

3. The 760 CE dictionary *Yupian* 玉篇 and the later *Guangyun* 廣韻 (1008) define Man as "a name of the Yi in the south" (*nan Yi ming* 南夷名).

4. For instance, Keith W. Taylor, "On Being Muonged," *Asian Ethnicity* 2, no. 1 (2001): 25–34.

5. It has been argued, for instance, that "Yao" in Ming texts was originally an administrative category rather than an ethnic group and that the division between Yao and ordinary subjects arose from a distinction in Ming local administration—the Yao lived on land that was registered under native officials, in contrast to those who lived on land registered under transferable officials appointed through the imperial administrative system. See David Faure, "The Yao Wars in the Mid-Ming and Their Impact on Yao Ethnicity," in *Empire at the Margins: Culture, Ethnicity and Frontier in Early Modern China*, ed. Pamela Kyle Crossley et al. (Berkeley: University of California Press, 2006), 187–89.

6. See the case of the Katu people of upland Vietnam in Oscar Salemink, *The Ethnography of Vietnam's Central Highlanders: A Historical Contextualization 1850–1990* (Honolulu: University of Hawai'i Press, 2003), 30–31. Their present ethnonym was a word meaning "savage" used by their neighbors for people living farther up in the mountains than those who referred to them.

7. These are the Pao or Peu (written in Chinese with the character *Biao*) people of northwestern Guangdong and the Lai 倈 of western Guangxi. See Liang Min 梁敏 and Zhang Junru 張均如, *Biaohua yanjiu* 標話研究 (Beijing: Zhongyang minzu daxue chubanshe, 2002), 1, and Li Xulian 李旭練, *Laiyu yanjiu* 倈語研究 (Beijing: Zhongyang minzu daxue chubanshe, 1999), 2.

8. This is mainly from my own observations traveling around Guangxi. A map of what the people officially classified as Zhuang actually call themselves can be found in Zhang Junru 張均如 et al., *Zhuangyu fangyan yanjiu* 壯語方言研究 (Chengdu: Sichuan minzu chubanshe, 1999), 318.

9. It is highly unlikely that any single language or even language family was spread over the wide areas where Li and Lao people were recorded. Jerry Norman and

Tsu-lin Mei, "The Austroasiatics in Ancient South China, Some Lexical Evidence," *Monumenta Serica* 32 (1976): 274–301, once suggested a very wide spread of Austroasiatic (the family to which Vietnamese belongs) as far north as the Yangtze River, but this theory has been refuted by Laurent Sagart, "The Expansion of Setaria Farmers in East Asia—A Linguistic and Archaeological Model," in *Past Human Migrations in East Asia: Matching Archaeology, Linguistics and Genetics*, ed. Alicia Sanchez-Mazas, Routledge Studies in the Early History of Asia vol. 5 (London: Routledge, 2008), 133–81.

10. CS 23: 3b; TPYL 785: 8b; Sus 80: 4b.

11. F. K. Lehman, "Who Are the Karen, and If So, Why? Karen Ethnohistory and a Formal Theory of Ethnicity," in *Ethnic Adaptation and Identity: The Karen on the Thai Frontier with Burma*, ed. Charles F. Keyes (Philadelphia: Institute for the Study of Human Issues, 1979), 215–53.

12. See Nicola Di Cosmo, *Ancient China and Its Enemies: The Rise of Nomadic Power in East Asian History* (Cambridge: Cambridge University Press, 2002), 102, for the use of Rong and Di, and p. 129 for Hu, which Di Cosmo explains as "a blanket term that included mounted bowmen who practised pastoral nomadism as their main economic activity."

13. Ruey, *Laoren kao*, proposed cultural characteristics such as bronze drums and stilt houses, but none of these were spread over the entire geographical region as that for which the names *Li* and *Lao* were recorded.

14. TPYL 786: 3b.

15. NZYWZ, quoted in HHS 86: 7b. This could mean either west of Jiaozhi Commandery (meaning west of the Red River Delta) or west of the later Han capital of Jiaozhi Circuit at Canton.

16. I base this assumption on the locations of new counties founded between the Han and the Jin. HHS 86: 14a refers to the foundation of seven new counties on the territory of over 100,000 surrendered Wuhu. A Qing commentator (DSFYJY ch. 108: 4438) says this later became Yuping County (present-day Gui County).

17. HHS 86: 14a.

18. JZJ in TPHYJ 122: 12a.

19. In "The Chinese and Their Neighbours," Pulleyblank has already given a detailed analysis of the term *Lao*, also noting the way in which its character 獠 has been erroneously transcribed as *Liao* rather than *Lao* and that it was sometimes also written as 姥 or 狫. The transcription error *Liao* originates in the alternative pronunciation of the character that stood for the phrase "to hunt at night with torches," and further confusion has arisen from the simplification of the character for Lao in PRC texts whereby the "dog radical" of the character was replaced with the "man radical," making it identical to the written form of the very common word *liao*, meaning "colleague" or "companion," that is, 僚, even retrospectively in traditional character reprints of classical texts. *Liao* and *Lao* correspond to Sino-Vietnamese *Liêu* and *Lão*, respectively.

20. Pulleyblank, "The Chinese and Their Neighbours," 431. Unfortunately, Hanyu Pinyin Romanization obscures the sound of the characters in Mandarin, which according to the International Phonetic Alphabet would be [kɤ lau].

21. Compare the Chinese word for betel leaf, *Piper betle*, originally recorded as *fuliuteng* in Early Medieval texts. The first syllable was eventually dropped and the word became *lou* 蔞 or *lao* 茗 in modern varieties of Chinese. See Li Hui-lin, *Nan-fang ts'ao-mu chuang—A Fourth Century Flora of Southeast Asia* (Hong Kong: Hong Kong University Press, 1979), 112–13.

22. HYGZ ch. 4: 57.

23. SS 84: 43a deals with a period in the second half of the fifth century. This may have been an error for the graphically similar Gu-Lao 孤獠. See also note 33.

24. LS 3: 33b; CS 1: 3b–4a. In the same chapter, the *Liang shu* (LS 3: 29a) refers to them as simply "Lao."

25. This was the location arrived at by Đào Duy Anh, *Đất nước Việt Nam qua các đời nghiên cứu địa lý học lịch sử Việt Nam* (Huế: Thuận Hóa, 1994), 68.

26. Taylor, *Birth of Vietnam*, 143, calls this the "Khuất Liệu Valley," the first part of the name being the Sino-Vietnamese transcription of Qu-Lao. This should in fact be Sino-Vietnamese "Khuất Lão."

27. All Early Middle Chinese reconstructions are from Pulleyblank, "Chinese and Their Neighbours."

28. Other records of similar forms of the name occur in later works in reference to the people in the area that is now Kweichow: XTS 222c: 19a and TPHYJ 120: 12b. Both refer to *Ge-Lao* 葛獠; TPHYJ 108L: 6a uses an alternative spelling for the same sound 葛姥. Buddhist patriarch Huineng of Xinzhou was also said to be of "Ge-Lao" origin, in this case written with the characters 獦獠; LZTJJC ch. 1: 4.

29. See Weera Ostapirat, "Proto Kra," *Linguistics of the Tibeto-Burman Area*, 23, no. 1 (2000): 13–18. The words for "head" and "house" show a similar sound change across Tai-Kadai languages.

30. See Li Jinfang, *Dongtai yuyan yu wenhua*, 38–42.

31. SGZ 41: 1b. The name of the Ailao 哀牢 people, recorded in this area from the late second century BCE to the late first century CE, may have had an influence on the use of the term *Lao* for the people there at this time. The relationship between the two Lao is unclear, however. The characters were tonally distinct, *Lao* 獠 being a *shang* tone and 牢 a *ping* tone, and the prefix ai- (if it was indeed a prefix) is not recorded anywhere outside the confines of what is now Yunnan.

32. BWZ ch. 2: 24.

33. HHS 86: 19b–20a. This may in fact be the earlier record, but the book was not composed until the early fifth century, two centuries after the *Bowuzhi* and *Sanguo zhi*.

34. SJZ ch. 36: 1128–29.

35. JS 57: 5b.

36. TPYL 785: 8b. I infer this from the concentration of bronze drums in this area and their absence in other parts of the Two Rivers area.

37. SS 97: 4a.

38. SS 92: 4b–5a.

39. SS 61 14a–b.

40. NQS 15: 29a–b records five Lao commanderies (*Lao jun*) in Yizhou; LS 17: 7b–8a; JS 9: 1b; LS 53: 10a–b.

41. NQS 14: 26a; 41: 1b has "Lao bandits" (*Lao zei*).

42. CS 34: 24a.

43. CS 36: 2a.

44. Later renamed Shaozhou, in the vicinity of present-day Shaoguan.

45. SuS 80: 7a.

46. SuS 65: 12b.

47. Bai Yaotian has made a long but unconvincing argument for the derivation of the term *Li* from the Tai endonym *Yay* common in northern Guangxi and southern Guizhou. See Bai Yaotian 白耀天, "Li lun 俚論," *Guangxi minzu yanjiu* 廣西民族研究 no. 4 (1990): 28–38; "Li lun (xu)" 俚論 (續), *Guangxi minzu yanjiu* 廣西民族研究 no. 5 (1990): 52–64.

48. HHS 86: 9b records: "In the nineteenth year of Jianwu, Zhang You of the Man Li (里) outside the boundaries of the administration led his people to admire civilisation and become dependent [to the Han]. He was enfeoffed as the lord of the Li (里) who returned to the Han" (*gui han lijun*). To this the comment "Li (里) is another name for *Man*, nowadays these are called Li (俚) people" was added, either by Liang commentator Li Xian or Tang commentator Liu Zhao. My own reading is that in the original text this character *Li* referred to villages rather than to kinds of people, and that Zhang You was in fact enfeoffed as "lord of the Man *villages* who submitted to the Han." In other places, such as the 1793 edition of the *Taiping huanyuji*, 里 is used where other texts use 俚.

49. TPYL 785: 8a–b.

50. SS 92: 7b–8a.

51. SS 92: 8a.

52. SS 54: 10a.

53. SS 92: 5a.

54. CXJ 8: 40a.

55. TPYL 785: 8a. According to this text, these Li had the alternative name of *Shi* or *Zhi* 㹴, an obscure word that appears in no other text and was perhaps taken from their spoken language.

56. TPHYJ 161: 8a–b.

57. TPYL 820: 6b. This Gùizhou is present-day Liuzhou.

58. TPYL 347: 8a.

59. NQS 18: 20a.

60. LS 13: 7b. For the second record, see note 63.

61. NS 51: 4a.

62. This was in the districts of Chaozhou and Xunzhou, where Li commander Yang Shilue surrendered the two provinces to the Tang in 622 (ZZTJ 190: 5943).

63. The one exception to this is where they appear in a list of foreign/indigenous peoples under the control of Qianzhou (now Pengshui in northern Guizhou); TPHYJ 120: 12a–b. The list also contains other unusual names such as Gùizhou and Kunming, both of which were a considerable distance from Qianzhou.

64. NFCWZ, quoted in YWLC 82: 11a, says that the Li collect a certain type of ivy, but QMYS 10: 36a–b quotes the same text saying that it is the Wuhu who do so. TPHYJ 166: 10b notes that Wuhu are a kind of Li.

65. CS 9: 6b.

66. LS 32: 11b.

67. Taylor, *Birth of Vietnam*, 149.

68. SuS 47: 4a; 65: 10b; 67: 9a–b; 80: 6a, respectively.

69. SuS 2: 16b–17a; 53: 9a; 56: 5a, respectively. See Taylor, *Birth of Vietnam*, 152–55, 158–62, for an account of his political career.

70. ZZTJ ch. 204: 6445.

71. ZZTJ ch. 204: 6445; JTS 190a: 8b.

72. Dikötter noted that this concept related back to whether they consumed their food cooked or raw. Frank Dikötter, *The Discourse of Race in Modern China* (Stanford, CA: Stanford University Press, 1992), 9–10. Magnus Fiskesjø makes the interesting argument that the concept of "raw" barbarian (he says less about the "cooked" variety) was rooted more in classical conceptions of Chinese sovereignty and the benevolence of civilization than about the nature of the barbarians themselves; they were merely the permanent exceptions to civilized behavior—the peripheral people who had to exist in order for the civilization of the center to make sense. Unfortunately, his discussion of the terms is limited to the post-Tang period. Magnus Fiskesjø, "On the 'Raw' and the 'Cooked' Barbarians of Imperial China," *Inner Asia* no. 1 (1999): 139–36.

73. These two terms appear only twice before the seventh century. The term *raw Lao* first occurs in the *Wei shu* (WS 101: 32.b); *raw Man* was first used in the *Song shu* (SS: 24b).

74. "Cooked" Lao did exist, but not within the Two Rivers Region. SuS 46: 11a records them in what is now Yunnan. There are no records of "raw" Li.

75. NQS 58: 15a–16b.

76. Holmgren, *Chinese Colonisation*, 125–36.

Chapter 4

"Masters of Their Small Domains"

Local and Imported Traditions of Leadership

In the very earliest records of Li and Lao from the third and fourth centuries, the Li, Lao, and Wuhu political structures appear alien to the Chinese chroniclers and their customs are presented as impenetrable and barbaric. At this time it is easy to distinguish the "native" leadership structures of bronze drum–owning chieftains from the "foreign" administrative structures of imperially appointed bureaucrats of provincial and commandery centers. By the late sixth century, however, this had altered to the extent that the Li-Lao political structures between the Two Rivers closely resembled models of local government in other parts of the empire, and it became difficult for writers from outside the Two Rivers Region to distinguish Li-Lao chieftains from imperially appointed governors. On the one hand, there were chiefs with Chinese surnames who held imperial administrative titles, and on the other, there were representatives of families whose ancestors came from elsewhere, but who had lived in the Two Rivers Region for long periods of time whose members also held administrative titles. Sometimes these groups intermarried as well. Change in Chinese power structures was also a significant factor in the confusion between these two groups of people, as the meritocratic system of appointing local governors used by the Han had gradually shifted to a hereditary system in which official positions were inherited within great local families, which then formed a privileged ruling class in their own areas. So the growing resemblance of the Li-Lao chiefs to the heads of Chinese great families was not the result of a linear process of their acculturation to Chinese ideals of culture and government. It was also due to internal change in Chinese political structures and the influence of Li and Lao political structures on Chinese families who migrated to the area and developed into local elites. Political change in the Red River Plain occurred slightly differently from that of the lower Pearl River area or the Li-Lao heartland, and therefore requires separate treatment and explanation.

NATIVE POLITICAL STRUCTURES: *DONG* AND *DULAO*

As noted in the previous chapter, throughout the third and fourth centuries, tens of thousands of people inhabited the lands between Jiaozhou and Guangzhou who were outside imperial control. Unfortunately, in contrast to their detailed descriptions of imperial political structures, the Chinese texts offer only the merest tantalizing glimpses of the political structure of Li-Lao societies, and there is a need to glean evidence beyond and between the lines of the written sources.

No single large centralized Li-Lao polity existed between the Two Rivers before the sixth century; written records of the time provide names of individual leaders, but no large political structure such as a kingdom is ever mentioned between the rivers. The most common way of referring to Li-Lao political structures was by the term *dong*, which probably began as a Tai word for a mountain valley or level ground between cliffs beside a stream.[1] The floors of such valleys could sustain agriculture, while the forested, uncultivated upland areas between them would have made natural divisions between one group of people and another, so it was only natural that the local name for such valleys as a geographical feature eventually acquired the extended meaning of a political unit or chiefdom. This extended meaning was the sense that was borrowed into Chinese.[2] The territorial reach of the various Li and Lao *dong* between the Two Rivers is difficult to plot, but can be ascertained more or less from a combination of evidence from different sources. Wan Zhen describes the geographical location and political organization of the Li people as a patchwork of small independent villages:

> South of Guangzhou there are bandits known as Li, they live in the five commanderies south of Guangzhou: Cangwu, Yulin, Hepu, Ningpu and Gaoliang, the centre of their territory stretches for several thousand *li*. They usually live in separate villages and have no commanders or lords, taking refuge in places difficult of access in the mountains, they have no use for kings.[3]

The area described in this text lies at the boundaries of the five commanderies, and no commandery centers, provinces, or counties were founded in this locality until the last decades of the fifth century. The area also corresponds more or less to the locations where the majority of finds of Heger II bronze drums are concentrated, and it also contains many physical examples of *dong* in the geographical sense; the peaks of the various mountain ranges rise to heights of over a thousand meters, and from their slopes flow many small rivers and streams that create isolated valleys perfect for the maintenance of independent Li and Lao chiefdoms. The extent and location of some individual *dong* is hinted at in a few instances. There was an undated military campaign against a Gudang *Dong* a few miles northwest of present-day Yulin,[4] and in 622, Nanfuzhou was founded on the territory of the Luo and Dou *Dong* centered on the locality between the present-day cities of Xinyi and Zhanjiang in western Guangdong.[5] Shuangzhou (south of present-day Luoding in Guangdong) was founded by the Liang on the territory of the interestingly named "Twin-Head Dong" (Shuangtou *Dong*) during the Dàtóng period (535–546),[6] a Dalian *Dong* existed somewhere in the vicinity of Hepu,[7] as well as a Long *Dong* on the Zuojiang to the southwest of Nanning.[8] These *dong* eventually ended up as the provinces of Dangzhou, Douzhou, Shuangzhou, Lianzhou, and Longzhou under the Tang, and each of them is said to have taken its name from that of the preexisting *dong*. The small territorial extent of these provinces suggests that they may well have reflected the geographical extent of the former *dong*.

In his *Guangzhou ji* (Records of Guangzhou), written somewhere between 317 and 420, Pei Yuan describes the nature of the leadership of a *dong* in a description of a Li-Lao ceremony to celebrate the casting of a new bronze drum:

> The Li and Lao value bronze drums highly, and consider only those which are more than a *zhang* [about 2.5 meters] across as especially unusual. When first completed they are hung up in the courtyards, and on an appointed morning they set out wines and invite those of the same tribe. The guests crowd the gates, and the sons and daughters of the rich and prestigious people among the guests take gold and silver made into large forks, and after beating on the drums with it they then leave it for the owner of the drum. These they call the "bronze drum forks." It is their custom to be fond of battle and they often make deadly enemies. When they wish to go to war against one another, they beat these drums to assemble their forces, who arrive like the gathering of clouds. Those in possession of these drums are extremely powerful.[9]

The tradition of casting bronze drums did not spread to the mountains to the north of the Yu River until at least two or three hundred years after this text was written,[10] so this description almost certainly points to the lands between the Two Rivers. An almost identical text describing the Li and Lao bronze drums is included in the geographical treatise contained in the *Sui shu*, but ends with the addition of the following:

> Those in possession of the drums have the title of *dulao* and are selected by popular sentiment. Investigating the origin of this Commissioner Tuo [that is,

Zhao Tuo, the King of Nan Yue] called himself "great and venerable chief of the Man and Yi" when speaking to the Han, that is why the Li people still call those they respect *daolao*; because this has become corrupted in speech they also say *dulao*.[11]

It is more than likely that the *Sui shu* is actually quoting Pei Yuan for this passage and has merely retained more of the original text than the later quotations preserved in Song encyclopedias. The term *dulao* has been interpreted as a transliteration of a Tai term meaning "great man,"[12] but it is much more likely to be a translation of "great noble," which would have sounded something like *taaw-laau*, which corresponds more closely to the form *daolao* that the text considers to be the original uncorrupted form of the word. This *taaw* is still commonly used to refer to members of the nobility in many Tai languages.[13]

These two records paint a nice vignette of what must have been a common occurrence in the Li-Lao country throughout the Jin and Six Dynasties periods, and contain much secondary information about the nature of the Li-Lao leadership, for instance that the owners of drums had control over the assembly of war parties, held large banquets as a show of status, and received offerings of tribute in gold and silver from the children of other powerful members of the community. How the *dulao* received their positions is unclear; however, "selection by popular sentiment" probably referred to the selection from a pool of smaller chieftains who inherited their positions within smaller communities, as it is hard to believe that just anyone would have been permitted to contend for the position. "It is their custom to be fond of battle" indicates the importance of military competition among the chiefdoms, sometimes against one another or sometimes united in a show of military strength against Chinese imperial forces. Just how large an assembled war party of Li and Lao could be can be estimated from scattered records. In the lands between Hepu and the Red River Plain, the Li and Lao chieftains of Shiqi[14] provided five to six thousand troops to help the rebel Lu Xun attack Governor Du Huidu in Jiaozhou in 411, and by the seventh century, *dong* that were farthest from imperial administrative centers were capable of raising armies of thousands. In 631, Feng Ang led twenty thousand troops against an uprising by the Luo and Dou *Dong* in which the opposing force was said to have been in the tens of thousands, and during which his troops took a thousand heads.[15] Over seven thousand men and women were said to have been captured during a battle with the same *dong* in 640.[16] War parties numbering in the thousands probably involved alliances of many *dong*.

Comparing the records of the *dulao* in the fourth century CE back to those of the indigenous leaders in the Red River Plain under the Han five centuries previously, there are many similarities between them and the local ruling class in the Red River Plain, who were also in possession of bronze drums. Selection by popular sentiment as leader for a particular period of time was common throughout the Two Rivers Region under the Han, and such rulers seem to have been able to raise large forces from disparate areas in very short periods of time. In 40 CE, the Trưng Sisters of the Red River Plain were supported in their uprising by the people of Hepu, Jiuzhen, and Rinan. In 178 CE, the Wuhu Man of Jiaozhi and Hepu rebelled, sparking an uprising against the Han that involved tens of thousands of people in all the commanderies to their south and west and lasted four years,[17] during which time they called upon several tens of thousands of people of Jiuzhen and Rinan to attack and destroy commanderies and counties.[18] It is extremely unlikely that the Wuhu of Hepu and the people of Jiuzhen and the Red River Plain belonged to the same ethnic or linguistic group, and the widespread support for these uprisings across wide stretches of territory may be evidence of what O. W. Wolters believed to be characteristic of premodern Southeast Asian societies' selection of leaders, which was based on indifference toward lineage descent, and instead on identification of personal achievement in each generation.[19] General Ma Yuan's conquest of the Trưng Sisters in 43 CE resulted in the destruction of this style of leadership in the Red River Plain, and for the two centuries immediately following, the rulers of the region were titled officials appointed by the imperial court. By the time Pei Yuan wrote his description of bronze drum–owning chieftains, almost four centuries had passed since the extinction of this type of leader in the Red River Plain, and the only leadership within living memory in Jiaozhou held Chinese titles such as inspector and governor. It is unlikely that anything was remembered about the former rulers there except in the remotest of legends. Because no such destruction occurred in the Li-Lao country, the bronze drum–owning *dulao* were able to outlive the native rulers of the Red River Plain by more than half a millennium. They were to meet their end in a different manner that did not involve any great upheaval or large-scale military action on the part of their conquerors, but rather in a slow, localized manner, whereby they could demand many concessions from the side of the imperial administrations.

HAN TO JIN: PROTO-COMMANDERIES AND LEFT-HAND COMMANDERIES

How the Chinese empires initially gained the cooperation of local rulers of the Li and Lao was through various forms of mutual alliance involving ritual incorporation as part of imperial administration systems. Although this was portrayed as a process of administrative incorporation in which local leaders recognized the superiority of the empire, the outcome of these alliances was usually that the local leaders retained direct control over their own people while supplying tribute products desired by the Chinese in the guise of taxation. Leaders who agreed to such an alliance were given seals, ribbons, and ceremonial clothing as emblems of their investiture in the imperial system, and in later periods were referred to by the Chinese with certain administrative titles.[20] These alliances had a long history in the Two Rivers Region: Yoshikai Masato has concluded from his study of Nanyue-period seals found throughout the Two Rivers area that the Nanyue kingdom made alliances like this in its outlying territories, in which case later empires were merely continuing a practice that Nanyue had found successful.[21] The Chinese referred to the chiefdoms and polities that agreed to such alliances as if they were special administrative units within their empires, using a few different names for these in different periods. In the pre-Tang period, the units thus formed were named either *proto-commandery* (*chujun*), *dependent state* (*shuguo*), or *left-hand commandery* (*zuojun*).[22] In the seventh century under the Tang, the term *halter-and-bridle* (*jimi*) became the standard term for the practice, and *halter and bridle provinces* (*jimizhou*) were the units formed from it. These were the result of alliances in lands to the far west of the Li-Lao country; no *jimizhou* existed between the Two Rivers. From the Chinese side, these units were always portrayed as a functioning part of imperial administrative systems as forms of devolved control of native peoples, but in reality these remained the territory of native rulers. For the Chinese empires, such alliances provided revenue and security without the need for costly military invasion. For the native rulers, the Chinese empires provided a powerful ally and potential trading partner.

Details are scarce about the Two Rivers Region during the Western Han (206 BCE–9 CE), but in most areas throughout the region local rulers seem to have continued to rule their own people under what the Han referred to as "proto-commanderies." Sima Qian recorded that following the Han conquest of the Two Rivers Region and the Yi of the southwest (*Xinan yi*) in 111 BCE, the Han Empire founded seventeen proto-commanderies in their territories, covering an area from the west of Panyu (Canton) to the south of Shu (Sichuan). Sima Qian also noted that these proto-commanderies were "governed in accordance with their old customs and were not subject to tax or corvée."[23] Three commanderies that are now in Vietnamese territory (Jiaozhi, Jiuzhen, and Rinan) were also given this status, but they were not exceptional. Within the Han imperial system, no special status was bestowed on the areas of the Two Rivers Region that were to eventually become Vietnamese that was not given to the rest of the region. Although the proto-commanderies were said to be exempt from taxation and corvée labor, this did not mean that they were exempt from the payment of tribute, nor were native rulers left completely to rule their own people by themselves. Local leaders were responsible for collection of revenue for the empire in their own districts through local tribute products, and in the heavily populated regions of the Red River Plain and to its south, the Han was already sending officials to rule in parallel to local leaders.

There is no record of when the system of proto-commanderies was finally abandoned, but in the Red River Plain it almost certainly disappeared with Ma Yuan's destruction of the native leadership, as subsequent administration of this area was solely the responsibility of appointed officials. Regular records of named Han administrators in the plain begin near the end of the Western Han before Ma Yuan's time, which suggests that rule of the commandery centers was already beginning to pass out of the hands of locals at around this time,[24] and the power struggle between the appointees from the north and the local ruling class was one of the possible contributing factors to the Trưng Sisters' uprising. Han administrative units in the Red River Plain were clustered together in great numbers on the large plain, whereas those in the rest of the region were isolated from one another and strung out along major river courses or the coast. Further away from these rivers were a few outlying county outposts, but between these were whole regions containing neither county nor commandery centers in which most of the actual population still lived outside the imperial administrative system.

Attempts at alliance making in areas between the Two Rivers that were peripheral to the main Han administrative centers do not seem to have started until the second half of the second century CE. Initially, it involved a practice similar to the foundation of proto-commanderies, which involved the creation of administrative units (counties) within the territory of "barbarian" groups controlled by their own rulers. The first recorded example of this in the Li-Lao country concerns the area upriver to the southwest of the seat of Yulin commandery (present-day Guiping) on the Yu River. The *Hou Han shu* records that in 170 CE, Gu Yong, the governor of Yulin, gained the submission of over 100,000 Wuhu people through his "kindness and trustworthiness" and proceeded to found seven counties on their territory, giving them hats and sashes.[25] No records exist of the names of these seven counties or where they were founded, but a Tang commentator notes that they were in Yulin County belonging to Guizhou (present-day Gui County).[26] In contrast to these records, only six counties are recorded for Yulin Commandery under the Wu, a reduction from the Han total of twelve.[27] Despite the creation of the seven counties in Yulin, the territory covered by the Han commandery shows a decrease in registered population between the Western Han census of 2 CE and the Western Jin census of 280 (unfortunately, no figures are available from the Eastern Han census of 140 CE),[28] and because they were unnamed and uncounted, it is likely that these counties were not actually a proper functioning part of the imperial administrative system. As in the proto-commanderies, political power probably remained in the hands of their local leaders, the only difference being that this was no longer part of a region-wide policy for entire commanderies and was practiced on a small-scale, localized level.

The foundation by the Wu Empire of Jiude Commandery in the lands to the south of the Red River Plain a century later seems to have involved a similar process. According to the *Shuijing zhu*, this area was once ruled by a Man chieftain named Lu Yu. He was succeeded by his son Bao Gang, whose clan was then said to have "followed Wu to be transformed," leading to the foundation of the new commandery.[29] Although no date is attached to this record, a comparison with other texts makes it clear that Bao Gang's eagerness to follow Wu was connected to the military campaigns carried out by Tao Huang, governor of Jiaozhou, against neighboring groups of people. Wuping Commandery was founded after Tao's military conquest on the territory of the Yi people of Fuyan in 271 CE.[30] Its establishment is noted in the *Jin shu* as connected to the foundation of Jiude and Xinchang Commanderies. It was noted that before Tao Huang made war on these areas, "the lands that are now Wuping, Jiude and Xichang were steep and inaccessible, the Yi and Lao were stubborn and intractable and had not submitted for successive generations."[31] Like the foundation of the six Wuhu counties to the north, the foundation of Jiude does not appear to have transformed Bao Gang's homeland into an ordinary functioning part of the Wu Empire. Ten years later, in the Jin census of 280, no registered households were recorded in Jiude, suggesting that it existed initially as a commandery in name only and that the Jin administration did not or could not collect taxes there.[32]

Tao Huang's military campaigns leading to the establishment of the three new commanderies in 271 also resulted in the foundation of the "dependent state" of Jiuzhen and over thirty counties within it.[33] This is significant as the first record for the Two Rivers Region of a new type of administrative practice for dealing with non-Sinitic peoples. The term *dependent state* (*shuguo*) was said to refer to non-Chinese polities or peoples that accepted imperial overlordship and submitted to the Chinese ruler.[34] Two "dependent states" were recorded in the Two Rivers Region and both were attached to commanderies, one to Jiuzhen and the other to Hepu. The location of the dependent state of Jiuzhen is unknown, and like Gu Yong's seven Han counties, the more than thirty counties mentioned as having been founded in the state do not seem to have been part of the functioning administrative system of the Jin. The *Jin shu* geography records only seven counties for Jiuzhen Commandery, suggesting again that these new counties were led by their own rulers and were different from the tax-paying counties in the Red River Plain. The dependent state of Hepu has a similarly obscure history. It was a small area along the Yu River at the northern end of the Ningpu Pass (present-day Heng County), and three early texts give details about its foundation first as a county in 217 CE, the appointment of a head of military forces known as a defender (*duwei*), in 260, and its conversion to the commandery of Ningpu in 286.[35] Defenders were appointed to dependent states as well as to ordinary commanderies, and the post of defender of Northern Hepu was probably filled by imperial appointees to ensure that the Ningpu Pass to Jiaozhou remained unobstructed. The conversion from dependent state into Ningpu Commandery at this time is part of a larger trend of expansion of imperial rule during the first decades of Jin rule in the Taikang period (280–289) upstream along the Yu River, finally reversing the decline of imperial influence and interest in the area that had been a trend since the Western Han. Jinxing Commandery was founded in the area of what is now Nanning,[36] and this was the first time since the Han that any administrative unit had been founded to the west of Lingfang County (present-day Binyang in Guangxi). Another example of an alliance made around the same time was with the "bandit leader" Gaoliang, Qian Bo, who in 291 surrendered to Lü Dai, inspector of Jiaozhou, and was subsequently awarded the title of protector of the western region of Gaoliang Commandery.[37] A little farther to the north, Dingliu County was established somewhere in Cangwu Commandery in 318, reportedly as a result of the submission of the Man and Yi people there.[38]

Although couched in terms of submission and the foundation of new administrative units, the system of alliance practiced from the Han to the Jin often seems to have involved little more than renaming areas controlled by well-disposed local leaders as proto-commanderies, counties, or dependent states. This practice gave local leaders the legitimacy and prestige that came with the link to powerful outsiders without giving them the same administrative responsibilities as the appointed magistrates of true counties or commanderies. In the six centuries after the first conquest of the Li-Lao country south of the Yu River until the end of the fifth century, this practice was carried out only within the areas close to imperial administrative centers. Judging by the lack of records of named proto-commanderies and the large empty spaces on a map of Jin administrative units, Li and Lao farther away from the main river courses and cities still functioned according to their own rules under their own leaders without any close connections to the Chinese empires, and judging by their spread and numbers, bronze drums remained a more important status symbol in these areas during this period than the seals, ribbons, or titles handed out to the Li and Lao who lived closer to the large rivers.

SONG TO SUI—FROM SPECIAL UNITS
TO GRADES OF PROVINCE

The Liu-Song continued the Jin expansion of administrative units up smaller watercourses further into the Li-Lao country. The new province of Yuezhou was founded in 471 from the eastern reaches of Jiaozhou and ruled from the Hepu area. The foundation of the province is more connected to military campaigns against the Li-Lao than strategic alliance making with them, so it will be discussed in the following chapter. Under the Liu-Song, new names were adopted for allied areas, namely "left-hand commanderies" (*zuojun*) and "left-hand counties" (*zuoxian*). Like the proto-commanderies and dependent states of earlier eras, these were named in the manner of auxiliary administrative units adjacent to ordinary commanderies and counties, but were in fact controlled by local rulers.[39] The *Nan Qi shu* records five special commanderies for Lao, the *Lao jun* in the valleys of the upper Yangtze River,[40] but there is only one named case of a special unit in the Two Rivers Region, somewhere in Yuezhou, a special "Li commandery" (*Li jun*) named Wuchun, founded in 488.[41] It did not contain any subordinate counties, suggesting that it was of a similar status to the dependent states of the Wu and Jin Empires, that is, untaxed and ruled by local leaders.

The Southern Dynasties marked the end of specially named administrative units for Li and Lao self-rule between the Two Rivers. From this time onward, the distinction is made only between ordinary units of imperial administration such as provinces (*zhou*) and commanderies (*jun*) and the independent *dong* chiefdoms that were clearly autonomous Li-Lao polities. When the term *dong* is mentioned, it is safe to assume that we are dealing with a text relating to an area ruled by Li and Lao, but the status of local administrative units such as provinces and commanderies and their rulers is less clear-cut. In many cases, these terms could refer to Li-Lao areas as well as to ordinary functioning imperial administrative units. The ambiguity is the result of confusion between the administrative titles held by Li-Lao rulers through strategic alliances and those held by members of localized great families. The *Sui shu* treatise on food and goods offers a retrospective description of the usual policy for Li-Lao chieftains under the Southern Dynasties:

> The customs south of the Yangtze are fire-ploughing and water-weeding, the earth is poor and wet and there are no assets of farm-animals. All the *Man* hide in *Li* grottoes (*Li dong*). From those who have become civilized, tribute is collected according to their level to provide for the state. Then there are the chieftains from beyond the passes who, on account of the abundance of slaves, pearls, rhinoceros and elephants, are the masters of their small domains. Because of this the imperial courts gave many of them temporary appointments to obtain

benefits from them. Throughout the Song, Qi, Liang and Chen this was the case and no reforms were made to it.[42]

"Chieftains from beyond the passes" is a reference to the Li-Lao rulers of the Two Rivers Region.[43] Their economic strength as the proprietors of luxury goods enabled them both to remain "masters of their small domains" and to gain temporary titles from the Southern Dynasties in exchange for the supply of such goods.

Although Chinese descriptions of the system of alliances couch it in terms of a civilizing process and bestowal of legitimacy on local rulers, this system did not deprive Li-Lao chieftains of legitimacy among their own people or assimilate them to Sinitic models of behavior. It was a symbiotic arrangement that cemented the Li-Lao chieftains in power over their own people, allowing them to become richer and more influential in their own districts at a time when Chinese dynastic government and its imperial military machine were too weak to pursue any other policy toward them. By the beginning of the seventh century, Li-Lao rulers had become local dynasties ruling over territories similar in size to some imperial provinces. Unlike the unnamed Wuhu chiefs of old, by the beginning of the seventh century members of these dynasties were the powerful heads of well-known local clans and it was essential for the imperial court to gain their cooperation in order to have passage through their territory, obtain sought-after luxury items, and avoid armed conflict with them. The ephemeral nature of the alliances thus formed is confirmed by later descriptions of Sui and Tang dealings with the Li and Lao south of the Yu River. Up until the middle of the seventh century, there were regular insurrections in this area, even though it was no longer classified as a newly conquered territory. The last great administrative expansion into the heart of the Li-Lao country south of the Yu River had occurred one hundred years before this period of insurrection in the third decade of the sixth century. Map 4, showing the commanderies founded during this time, seems to leave few gaps for the Li-Lao *dong* even in the mountainous areas between present-day Beiliu and Xinyi. Nevertheless, forty years after the end of Emperor Wu's reign, the Sui Empire, although strong enough to conquer the last southern dynasty, the Chen, was still reliant on alliances with local leaders between the Two Rivers to achieve peace in the area, and even sixty years on the Tang still had problems gaining control over the Li and Lao who dwelled there.

As far as the number and spread of administrative units in the Li-Lao country is concerned, the reign of Emperor Wu of the Liang (502–549) was a time of great expansion. The number of provinces in the empire as a whole increased from twenty-three provinces (*zhou*) in 511 to 107 by the end of the Dàtóng period (535–546).[44] However, in the Li-Lao country the increase and spread of administrative units did not improve the efficacy of the imperial administration, a seeming contradiction that can be explained by the manner of the increase of units and the nature of the administrators who controlled them. Liao Youhua believed that administrative expansion under the Liang was merely a cosmetic measure rather than a necessity because the number of administrative units at the subcommandery level (particularly counties) showed no substantial increase during this time.[45] This belief was echoed in the wry comment of Li Bole (565–648), author of the *Bei Qi shu* (Book of Northern Qi), that "provinces were founded for towns of one hundred houses and commanderies founded for three households to inflate their number."[46] A reorganization of provinces carried out in 539 at the request of Zhu Yi, senior recorder for the Liang, supports these opinions. In that year, Zhu Yi submitted a memorial to the throne requesting the division of provinces into five different grades. It is clear from this memorial that by the sixth century the term *province* no longer referred to units of uniform size, and that Zhu Yi merely wished to recognize this formally in administrative regulations. The specifications for the upper four grades of province are not given in the record of the memorial, but the following text gives details about the lowest grade of province, of which there were to be twenty-one:

> At that time they [the Liang Empire] had just been concerned with military campaigns to enlarge the borders, crossing the Huai and Ju in the north, defending Pengcheng in the east, opening up Zangke in the west and pacifying the Li *dong* in the south. There was an abundance of disorder, so Zhu Yi asked that they should be divided up. The provinces of the lowest grade were all occupied by foreigners (*yiguo zhi ren*). Where provinces existed in name only and had no territory, or at villages where the people of the wild borderlands dwell, provinces, commanderies and counties were founded in which their own people were employed as governors, prefects, and magistrates.[47]

So the lowest grade of province was to be found around the "wild borderlands" or where "foreigners" lived. The mention of the opening up of Zangke and the pacification of the Li *dong* confirms that it was in these areas that most of the lowest-grade provinces were concentrated, as the northern and eastern campaigns were carried out against the armies of the northern dynasties, either as a defensive measure or in the hope of regaining control of the old Chinese cultural heartland, not against the "people of the wild borderlands." Most significantly, it is clear that these provinces were not to be controlled by officials sent from Jiankang, but by the local leaders themselves. This is the key to understanding the continuation of independent Li-Lao power structures over the following century and a half.

In the Two Rivers Region, during the reign of Emperor Wu of the Liang, there was an increase in the number of provinces from four to thirteen. South of the Yu River, six new provinces (Luozhou, Shuangzhou, Jianzhou, Xinzhou,

Nanhezhou, and Gaozhou) were founded, and the seats of these were closer to the heart of the bronze drum country than any previous provincial centers. Aside from provinces, the Liang founded many new commanderies south of the Yu River, perhaps as many as eighteen.[48] The two significant commanderies were Liangde Commandery[49] and Jianling Commandery.[50] The centers of these commanderies sit well within the area where excavations of Heger type II drums are concentrated. Taking the numbers of new administrative units at face value would seem to represent a consolidation of Liang power upstream along smaller rivers toward the last Li-Lao chiefdoms, but the details of Zhu Yi's administrative reform show the actual workings of the Liang administrative system toward the Li and Lao were no more than a continuation of the system of alliances carried out by previous empires in which the native rulers maintained their rule over their own people while receiving an official title. Characteristic of these new commanderies founded by the Liang between the Two Rivers was their small size compared to those founded under previous dynasties, the fact that many contained only a single subordinate county,[51] and that they were founded in territory where there had previously been no administrative units. Despite sharing the names *province* and *commandery* with the imperial administrative units close to the Liang capital and governed by Chinese, these were close in function to the dependent states and counties founded by earlier empires. Many of the new commanderies founded by the Liang south of the Yu River were abandoned or downgraded to counties after the Sui conquest as the Sui made the commandery the new basic unit of local administration to replace the province. It is worth noting that although some of these old commanderies were reinstated as counties under the Tang, in the heart of the Li-Lao country some Sui commanderies were abandoned altogether.[52] The short-term nature of these abandoned commanderies, the fact that they contained only single counties, and the later history of their territories as centers of Li-Lao resistance against the Tang, make it all the more likely that these areas were part of the system of alliances described as "temporary appointments" in the *Sui shu* as the usual policy of the Southern Dynasties toward local chieftains.

RESULTS OF ALLIANCE BUILDING

A result over the long term of the policies of alliances with the Chinese empires for the Li and Lao was a shift in the way they governed themselves. From the third century onward, the leadership of Li-Lao societies south of the Yu River gradually transformed from a cluster of independent chiefdoms beyond imperial control to a system based increasingly on hereditary rule over defined territories that reached its peak under the Sui and early Tang.

Looking back from the twelfth century, Fan Chengda described the change in the following manner: "Over time some Lao gradually picked up names that indicated superior and inferior rank, and these were then taken up by the *Man* barbarians."[53] As Li-Lao leaders were granted an increasing number of official titles and their territories either corresponded in size to imperial administrative units or were nominally subordinate to them, those who described them found it increasingly difficult to distinguish them from the local ruling class of ordinary provinces whose ancestors were of northern Sinitic extraction. This growing similarity of the Li-Lao leadership to the local Chinese ruling classes did not mean that Li-Lao rulers were cooperative with the wishes of the imperial courts; on the contrary, in chaotic years of the later Six Dynasties period, official title did not necessarily entail official-like behavior, and at that time they appear to have been no more fond of resisting the commands from the imperial capital than were their Chinese counterparts.

CHANGE IN IMPERIAL ADMINISTRATIVE PRACTICES

The increasing similarity of Li and Lao modes of leadership to those practiced within imperial administrative units can be read as a step on the road toward eventual assimilation to Chinese norms of government, as can the confusions between those who were named Li or Lao and those who were merely "people" or "subjects" discussed in the previous chapter. To view this transformation solely as a result of Li and Lao acculturation to Chinese political and behavioral norms neglects the changes in Chinese administrative practices that were happening over the same period. The boundaries between "people" and Li-Lao and those between "governors" and "chiefs" became increasingly indistinct during the Southern Dynasties, not only because the Li and Lao leaders looked ever more like Chinese administrators, but also because of the increasing resemblance of Chinese administrators to Li and Lao leaders. As Li and Lao political structures were growing in size, the territories of Chinese commanderies and provinces were shrinking; as more families of Li and Lao chieftains were given imperial titles and were recognized as hereditary rulers over certain districts, inspectorates and governorships were no longer held by appointees from the capital and positions came to be inherited within localized families. This was especially common in the Red River Plain and areas away from the main urban centers, and the imperial courts of the Southern Dynasties were forced to rely on the cooperation of local elites for economic and military control of most regions outside the immediate vicinity of Jiankang, just as they were forced to rely on the political acquiescence of the Li and Lao chieftains for the supply of certain products and access to transport routes. The combination of these changes over time not only made Li-Lao chieftains resemble provincial governors, but also made provincial governors look increasingly like Li-Lao chieftains.

In regard to the size of Chinese administrative units, after the proliferation in the number of new provinces in the first half of the sixth century, the term *province* (*zhou*) referred to an administrative unit only a fraction of the size of its namesake under the Han, and the subordinate grade of unit known as the commandery had been reduced to approach the size and population of some of the larger *dong*. A province in the Han administrative system had no similarly sized equivalent under the Liang system, but the use of the name *zhou* as the primary unit of local government remained unchanged until it was abolished under the Sui in 583. The single Han province of Jiaozhou in the first century CE had encompassed the entire Two Rivers Region, and by the mid-sixth century there were nineteen provinces covering the same area. South of the Yu River, there were more provinces in the area covered by Hepu Commandery in Han times than there had been counties subordinate to the commandery under the Han.[54] What this meant was that sixth-century inspectors of provinces (*cishi*) and especially commandery governors (*taishou*) had authority over much smaller areas than those who had held the same titles in the first centuries CE under the Han, Wu, and Jin Empires. In Han times, commanderies would have dwarfed the tiny *dong* chiefdoms, but by the sixth century some of them had become comparable in size. As previously mentioned, by the sixth century names for administrative units no longer indicated an equal administrative status. Some provinces were large, populous, and contained many subordinate commanderies and counties. Within the provinces, commanderies were similarly varied in their sizes and functions. Some contained over ten subordinate counties, and others only single counties.[55] The basic pattern of distribution was that the commanderies in provinces near to older established administrative centers in the Two Rivers Region (Guangzhou, Gaoliang, Hepu, and Jiaozhou) had many subordinate counties and resembled more closely the administrative pattern of the areas around the imperial capital Jiankang. Those remote from such centers, and especially those that were distant from the main river courses and contained only one or two counties, came to resemble the *dong* in size, location, and function.

From the late second century CE onward, the way leaders for Chinese administrative units were selected shifted from a system of centralized appointments from the court to one in which positions were the hereditary property of local great families. In the Two Rivers Region under the Han, the high-level positions of inspector and governor were mostly held by outsiders, and at this time there was a clear-cut distinction between the bearers of imperial authority and local Man chieftains. However, after Han times it became increasingly common for administrative positions to be inherited within established powerful families native to the area with the agreement of the imperial court, and this was the common practice throughout the Jin Empire and the early Liu-Song. Looking at the situation in the Red River Plain, Jennifer Holmgren has referred to the holders of administrative titles as members of "a semi-independent Vietnamised bureaucracy with hereditary privileges" and noted that the process of their creation began with the Shi family in the third century.[56] The development of such localized hereditary bureaucracies was not confined to the Red River Plain, but was part of a larger trend in imperial politics from the fall of the Western Han onward, which began to favor hereditary privilege and local power over merit for the selection of official posts. The development of local gubernatorial dynasties was a typical feature of imperial rule throughout the entire Two Rivers Region from the third century up until the end of the fifth century, and many of the families Holmgren and Taylor mention as "Vietnamized" actually held positions throughout the whole of the Two Rivers Region, and not just in the area that was to become Vietnam. In addition to the Red River Plain, they held positions in future Chinese areas such as Cangwu, Hepu, and Nanhai, so referring to this phenomenon of localization as "Vietnamization" is therefore not only anachronistic but also geographically inaccurate.

Shi Xie (173–226), who is sometimes known by the Vietnamese transliteration of his name Sĩ Nhiếp, ruled the Red River Plain during the chaotic period from the downfall of the Han to the rise of the Three Kingdoms state of Wu and was written into Vietnamese national histories of later periods as a specifically Vietnamese character. However, the Shi family did not come from the Red River Plain, nor was their influence limited to within the boundaries of present-day Vietnam. In the early third century, members of the Shi clan also controlled areas of what is now China. Even though his father had served as governor of Rinan Commandery in the far south, Shi Xie himself did not begin his life in the Red River Plain, but in Guangxin, the commandery seat of Cangwu. His brother Shi Yi had control over Hepu, and his next eldest brother, Shi Wei, was originally county magistrate of Xuwen before Shi Xie appointed him governor of Jiuzhen. Shi Xie also appointed his youngest brother, Shi Wu, to the governorship of Nanhai Commandery at Canton.[57] Later examples of similar localized families claimed for the Red River Plain, and consequently for the Vietnamese national history, were the Tao, the Du, and the Teng, but like the Shi family, members of these families were also involved in local politics of Guangzhou and their activities were never restricted just to the Red River Plain.

The Tao family was the most politically influential family in the Red River Plain in the second half of the third century, and four generations of the family served as inspectors of Jiaozhou. Tao Ji had been inspector of Jiaozhou under the Wu, his son Tao Huang, Tao Huang's son Tao Wei, younger son Tao Shu, and Tao Wei's son Tao Sui all served as inspectors of Jiaozhou.

Members of the family also held posts outside the Red River Plain in Guangzhou: both Tao Huang and his son Tao Wei served as governors of Cangwu Commandery.[58] So although the later members of the family became settled in the Red River Plain, the two middle generations were also connected to Cangwu.

The Du family held the post of inspectorate of Jiaozhou for three generations over twenty-eight years from 399 to 427. This family was much more connected to the Red River Plain than the aforementioned two families. Du Yuan was officially inspector of Jiaozhou for ten years from 399, but had probably held de facto power since around 380.[59] His ancestor Du Yuán was said to have served as governor of Ningpu. Du Yuan's son Du Huidu was born in the Red River Plain and served as inspector of Jiaozhou there for over a decade until his death, and his son Du Hongwen also served in the post. Sometime during his father's tenure as inspector, Du Hongwen led an army of three thousand soldiers to Canton with the intention of aiding in a campaign against the Northern Wei in Luoyang, and later in 427, despite ill health, he set off to court when summoned and died during the journey at Canton.[60] These two events show that even after generations in the Red River Plain, members of the Du family did not necessarily think of themselves as outsiders in regard to the imperial administrative system.

The Teng family was a localized family of Guangzhou. Teng Xiu was twice inspector of Guangzhou under the Wu. His grandson Teng Kan was inspector of Guangzhou and Kan's nephew Teng Dunzhi was sent to serve as inspector of Jiaozhou in 380, but was supposedly prevented from taking up office there by a local named Lý Tốn.[61] There were many more families such as these in the Two Rivers Region in the fourth century.[62] Hereditary dynasties of governors began to develop in the Guangzhou area over the same period as in Jiaozhou, but none of these families managed to inherit positions to the fourth generation in the manner of the Tao in Jiaozhou. There were also periods in that province in which governors and inspectors were appointed who do not seem to have come from localized families. From 269 to 322, the position of inspector of Jiaozhou lay mostly in the hands of localized families, the Tao and the Gu,[63] and the Du family controlled the post from 399 to 427, but in the gap between 322 and 399, the post was held by a succession of ten court appointees who did not follow the pattern.[64] Holmgren has suggested that these were mainly sent to deal with the Chams and that the real control of the area still lay with the great families rather than the appointees from the north.[65]

It was only in the late fifth century that the politics of leadership in the Red River Plain began to diverge from those of Guangzhou. At this time, appointees to the inspectorate of Guangzhou were posted from Jiankang rather than from the ranks of local families, but this was followed by a gradual shift toward employing members of the imperial household of each dynasty for such roles, whereas the Jiaozhou area remained under the control of powerful local families. Despite the security of their power base in Jiaozhou, these local leaders, with the exception of Lý Bôn, do not seem to have been interested in leading the people of the Red River Plain as the kings or emperors of an autonomous state. Even those celebrated as national heroes in later Vietnamese histories, such as Lý Trương Nhân and his cousin Lý Thúc Hiến, were only interested in imperial recognition as self-appointed inspectors of Jiaozhou, and Lý Thúc Hiến was even eventually granted the post by the Southern Qi in 479.[66] Even so, because of the relative isolation of Jiaozhou, the trend toward autonomy continued, and by the sixth century the Liang and Chen Empires were never able to gain firm control over the Red River Plain, and the area enjoyed de facto independence for most of the first half of the sixth century, with a twenty-five-year period (516–541) in which no inspectors were even appointed to the region.[67] Even though local families of the Red River Plain did enjoy a kind of dynastic status, and during the sixth century exceptionally long periods of autonomy, these should also be seen in the context of the general weakness and instability of the short-lived Qi, Liang, and Chen Empires, rather than as an indication of the Vietnamese recovering their long-lost independence under new leaders.

In the eastern Two Rivers Region, the Liang Empire took a different approach by appointing members of the royal house as administrators in the main provincial seats. Eight members of the imperial family were appointed to Guangzhou as inspectors and governors during the Liang,[68] but it was difficult to do this in the Red River Plain, where local families had developed their own power base in isolation from the rest of the empire. The imposition of a member of the imperial household in the Red River Plain was met with opposition from the local ruling families. After a twenty-five-year period of not appointing inspectors, Xiao Zi, a nephew of Emperor Wu, was appointed as inspector of Jiaozhou, but is said to have lost the hearts of the people through his cruelty and violence, a situation that the famous Lý Bôn was able to work to his own advantage by grouping together the local powerful families of several provinces to lead them in revolt. Lý Bôn eventually declared himself Emperor of Yue in 544, but his initial frustrations with the Liang Empire seem to have been due to resentment at his inability to advance in the administrative system.[69] It is important to note that Lý Bôn was not considered a foreigner or a barbarian in Chinese texts; in the eyes of those who wrote of his deeds in the *Nan Qi shu* and *Chen shu*, he appears simply as another rebellious upstart from a regional governing elite who had wished to found his own dynasty. This was the usual view chroniclers held of localized families in the Red River Plain; whether rebellious or obedient to the orders of the court in Jiankang, they were still considered as part of the civilized world by those who wrote about them. With few exceptions, they were usually not referred to as anything other than "people" (*ren*), only sometimes as Li, and never as Lao, and their leaders were usually known by administrative titles denoting legitimacy in the eyes of the empires, such as governor and inspector, never as chieftains or commanders. What made the Red River Plains people really different from those of the lands closer to the imperial capital at Jiankang was that they were cut off from the danger of competing with other powerful factions for centuries by the Li and Lao chiefdoms. In other parts of the empire, families who supported regional upstarts risked attack and punishment by rivals who might act out of their own interests with the excuse that they were in fact doing it out of loyalty to the emperor. The Red River Plain was fairly rich, self-sufficient in agriculture, and isolated from strong rivals to leadership positions, and the result of this isolation was that local dynasties became more ingrained in society and tended to last through more generations than the areas around Guangzhou.

Chinese sources from the later Southern Dynasties usually record only more important appointments in the larger urban centers; in smaller administrative units, the picture is less clear. Records survive of the names of Liang inspectors of Gùizhou, Dingzhou (upgraded to a province from Yulin Commandery), Xinzhou, Gaozhou, and Guangzhou, but not those of the other smaller provinces. A record from the *Chen shu* notes that local government in the south of the empire had the following characteristics: "At the time in the provinces of the south, most of the administrators were village chiefs (*xiangli qiuhao*) who did not obey official decrees, so Emperor Wen sent [Hua] Jiao to control them with the law."[70] This suggests that under the Chen, in areas away from the provincial capitals the administration had remained in the hands of local families and that it was felt necessary to try to assert the centralized power of the empire. The "provinces of the south" here is almost certainly a reference to the Two Rivers Region because this area made up most of the southern region of the Chen Empire. Whether these village chiefs were descended from migrants from the north or were Li-Lao chieftains who had been appointed as administrators is unclear, as the practice of using members of localized families as officials and giving chieftains official appointments had by this time blurred any distinction between the two.

From the third to the eighth century, there were also Lao between the Two Rivers who remained beyond the reach of Chinese administrative systems, but closer to the rivers, changes in administration practices and the trend toward hereditary dynasties of governors in the smaller provinces of the region, combined with the alliances between Southern Dynasties, caused the Li-Lao leadership to become indistinguishable from the local Chinese leadership. The willingness of local rulers to ally themselves with larger empires has traditionally been interpreted in Chinese scholarship as a result of the prestige of the superior civilization, and granting of administrative titles and use of "halter-and-bridle"–style practices as evidence of the beneficence of imperial power that could use persuasion rather than brute force to gain its ends. However, what the long-term continued use of such strategies by the Chinese empires in their interactions with the Li and Lao actually shows is that the empires after the Han were too weak to take control of the Li-Lao country by force. The need for compromise with the local leadership in order to collect tribute products gave the ultimate advantage not to the imperial court, but to the Li-Lao chieftains themselves, and ended up having the opposite effects from what was perhaps hoped from the Chinese side. From an imperial perspective, an appointment and regalia were methods of taming and civilizing the Li and Lao, giving imperial legitimacy to people they were unable to control in exchange for goods it was difficult to procure by force. For the Li-Lao chieftains, on the other hand, an alliance with the Chinese empires offered the chance for prestige, self-enrichment, and consolidation of their rule over their own people.

NOTES

1. Pulleyblank, "Chinese and Their Neighbours," 430. *Dong* is written with the same character as a Chinese word for "cave" and Schafer and others therefore translate it with its Chinese meaning as "grotto." Vietnamese has the word đồng for a dry field, and Nguyễn Ngọc San (*Tiếng Việt Lịch Sử*, 140) says the Vietnamese term derives from an original Tai *tổng* with the same meaning. Li's reconstruction (*Comparative Tai*, 105) would give a proto-Tai **djoŋ* with the meaning "plain" or "open field." Li (*Dongtai yuyan*, 290) discusses the relationship of the two terms *long* and *dong*, which he believes to be alternative pronunciations of a word meaning "flat field." David Holm's *Recalling Lost Souls—The Baeu Rodo Scriptures: Tai Cosmogonic Texts from Guangxi in Southern China* (Bangkok: White Lotus, 2004), 6, compares the archaic forms of the terms *Dong* and *Zhuang*, and suggests that the origin of the term *Zhuang* also referred back to a term for a flat fertile river valley, and was synonymous with *dong*.

2. There is evidence that the meaning of the word in the geographical sense was also known to Chinese authors. A tenth-century description of the customs in the district around modern Enping and Yangjiang records that "agriculture is mainly carried out in the *dong*" (TPHYJ 158: 6a). The context suggests a geographical feature rather than a political unit.

3. TPYL 785: 8a.

4. TPYL 172: 8a; TPHYJ 165: 4b. The TPYL records this as coming from the *Nanyue zhi* but because Dangzhou was not founded until the Tang it is more likely that this was actually a quotation from another work, perhaps that named *Xu Nanyue Zhi* 續南越志 (The Continued Annals of Nanyue) of the late Tang, which is also quoted in the TPYL and TPHYJ.

5. TPYL 172: 5a records that the province was later renamed Douzhou in 634 after the name of the *dong*.

6. TPHYJ 164: 4b, 5a; TPYL 172: 4a–b. The second source quotes the *Nanyue zhi* again. Both sources mention these two versions of the name. Both characters are and were historically homophones. The province of Shuangzhou covered the districts around present-day Luoding.

7. XTS 43a: 9a.

8. TPYL 172: 13a.

9. GZJ, quoted in TPYL 785: 8b.

10. Yoshikai, *Dōko saihen no jidai*, 211–13, dates the move north of the river to the ninth or tenth century.

11. SuS 31: 15a.

12. Wade, *Lady Sinn*, 133, and Li, *Dongtai yuyan*, 159, both offer explanations for the **tue* (now a classifier for animals and people only in a pejorative sense but once applied to gods). The modern distribution of **lau*, meaning "great" or "big," is now restricted to northwestern varieties of Tai spoken in Yunnan and northwest Guangxi, whereas those in other regions use *lung* or *hung* (Zhang, *Zhuangyu fangyan yanjiu*, 756), but its continued use in Kam and other related Kadai languages shows that the term was once widely used in the Li-Lao country, and that this interpretation of the name is more likely. See Wang Jun 王均, ed., *Zhuangdong yuzu yuyan jianzhi* 壯侗語族語言簡志 (Beijing: Minzu chubanshe, 1984), 858–59.

13. Condaminas, *From Lawa to Mon*, 113, defines *tao* as "a noble, a man belonging to the aristocratic class." The change from *dao* to *du* is not an isolated event; it is also attested in the old Chinese name for the mangosteen, *dunianzi* 都念子, noted in LBLY ch. 2: 10 as a corruption of the name *daonianzi* 倒捻子. A fanciful explanation is given for the origin of the name, "to pinch upside down" (*daonian* 倒捻), referring to the way the fruit is eaten holding on to the peduncle.

14. SS 92: 5a.

15. XTS 110: 2a.

16. XTS 222c: 19a.

17. HHS 86: 14a.

18. HHS 8: 10a.

19. Wolters, *History, Culture and Region*, 151.

20. HHS 86: 2b–36b records seven incidences of the Han Empire bestowing seals and ribbons (*yinshou*) on local leaders in this manner, including those on the borders of Rinan and those to the north of the Two Rivers Region like Yelang and Changsha.

21. Yoshikai Masato 吉開將人, "Shirushi kara miru nanetsu sekai (zenpen; chūhen; kōhen)—ryōnan kodai sekiin kō" 印からみた南越世界 (前篇; 中篇; 後篇)—嶺南古璽印考, *Tōyō bunka kenkyūjo kiyō* 東洋文化研究所紀要 no. 136 (1998): 89–135; no. 137 (1999): 1–45; no. 139 (2000): 1–38.

22. For a good overview of these systems throughout this period up to Song times and their fundamental similarities, see Okada Kōji 岡田宏二, *Zhongguo Huanan minzu shehui shi yanjiu* 中國華南民族社會史研究, translated by Zhao Lingzhi 趙令志 and Li Delong 李德龍 (Beijing: Minzu chubanshe, 2002), 1–18.

23. SC 30: 18a–b. For a detailed study on the "first time commanderies," see Hu Shaohua 胡紹華, *Zhongguo nanfang minzu shi yanjiu* 中國南方民族史研究 (Beijing: Minzu chubanshe, 2004), 34–46.

24. The first recorded administrator in the Red River Plain, for example, was Xi Guang, who served as inspector during the reign of Emperor Ping (1–5 CE). HHS 76: 6b.

25. HHS 86: 14a. Obviously not all of the Wuhu were happy with such arrangements, as the great rebellion of Wuhu of 178 occurred only eight years after the foundation of these counties.

26. TPHYJ 166: 11a. Although no record exists of these counties, comparison of the geographical treatises in the HHS 23: 21b and JS 15: 9b shows that in the area that was the Han Commandery of Yulin, four counties were lost and eleven were gained. The location of only one of these new counties is known, at Yuping (present-day Gui County). A comparison of locations and names of counties that appear in the *Hou Han shu* geography based on the census of 140 CE with those of the new counties in the *Jin shu* geography dating from 280 CE seems to point toward the location of the counties in the area around the confluence of the Yu and Tan Rivers close to the seat of Yulin Commandery.

27. Liao, *Lishi dilixue*, 115–16; 122–23.

28. The territory of Yulin Commandery in the Western Han census corresponds to that of Yulin and Guilin Commanderies under the Jin. The figure for the households in the Western Han census of 2 CE (HS 28b: 10a–11b) gives a household count of 12,415 compared to 8,000 for Yulin and Guilin Commanderies combined in 280 (JS 15: 9b).

29. SJZ ch. 36: 1136.

30. SS 38: 40b. The commandery founded in this area was given the name Wuping, meaning "militarily pacified."

31. JS 57: 5b.

32. JS 16: 9a.

33. JS 57: 5b. Taylor construes this passage as meaning that the thirty counties were established in the three new prefectures, but neglects to mention that they were within a dependent state.

34. Definition from Hucker, *Dictionary of Official Titles*, 435: "a reference to non-Chinese states or peoples that accepted China's overlordship and submitted tribute to the Chinese ruler."

35. SS 38: 38a quotes three sources: a Jin geography (*Taikang dizhi* 太康地志, usually known as *Taikang diji* 太康地記) from the Taikang period (280–290), which noted that there was a dependent state of Hepu there that survived until 286 when it was changed into Ningpu Commandery; Zhang Bo's *Wulu dilizhi* noted that a defender or commander of military forces had been posted to the area, named as "defender of Northern Hepu" since 260; and an anonymous *Guangzhou ji*, which states that a county was created there in 217 CE.

36. SS 38: 32b says it was founded in 318, but Bai Yaotian makes a convincing argument for the earlier date. Bai Yaotian 白輝天, "Jin zhi jinxing jun kao" 晉置晉興郡時間考, *Guangxi difangzhi* no. 1 (1997): 46–49.

37. SGZ 60: 8a–b.

38. SS 38: 25b.

39. Kawahara Masahiro 河原正博, *Kan minzoku Kanan hattenshi kenkyū* 漢民族華南發展史研究 (Tokyo: Yoshikawa Kōbunkan, 1984), 65–81. Kawahara explains the system in great detail, but his conclusion that the *zuo* of *zujun* derived from the name of the ancient kingdom of Chu seems a little far-fetched.

40. NQS 15: 29a/b.

41. NQS 14: 28a.

42. SuS 24: 3b.

43. Because this referred to the land "beyond the passes," both Katakura, "Chūgoku shihaika no betonamu," 31, and Lü, *Beishu shidai de Yuenan*, 99, believed that this system was relevant to the discussion of the situation in the Red River Plain. However, *chieftain* was a term confined to those who did not have political legitimacy in the eyes of the court and was not applied to the rulers of the Red River Plain.

44. SuS 29: 2a–b.

45. Liao, *Lishi dilixue*, 71. In the Red River Plain, the number of commanderies remained unchanged, but the number of counties decreased from thirty to twenty-seven (see table in Holmgren, *Chinese Colonisation*, 169). Note that Holmgren prefers to translate the term *xian* as prefecture rather than county.

46. BQS 4: 25b.

47. ZZTJ 158: 4903–4. The commentary adds: "this means they employed local people from the area."

48. Because no geographical treatise survives from Liang times, this figure is an approximation based on BLJYZ 4893–905.

49. YDGJ 37: 3b.

50. SuS 31: 11a.

51. Liao, *Lishi dilixue*, 67–71. Single-county commanderies were especially common in the land between the Leizhou Peninsula and the south bank of the Yu River. Gaozhou had six out of a total of eleven. To its north, all three commanderies subordinate to Shuangzhou were single-county commanderies. The entire province of Luozhou to its west consisted of a single commandery containing one county. In contrast, the reduced province of Guangzhou, which by the end of the Liang only controlled the area around Canton, contained five subordinate commanderies with a combined total of twenty-eight subordinate counties.

52. Some examples: Liang founded Nanba Commandery to the west of the present-day city of Gaozhou, which was downgraded to a county under the Sui (DMYTZ 81: 23b). Kaiyang Commandery, south of present-day Luoding, was abandoned completely by the Sui (DMYTZ 81: 13b). Another abandoned commandery was Haichang (SuS 31: 9b), which lay very close to the heartland of the bronze drum–producing area, inland from the present-day city of Maoming.

53. GHYHZ 43.

54. HS 28b: 11a. In 2 CE, Hepu Commandery had only five subordinate counties, but by 550 the same area contained seven provinces—Yuezhou, Luozhou, Hézhou, Anzhou, Huangzhou, Shuangzhou, and Gaozhou.

55. Yan Gengwang 嚴耕望, *Zhongguo difang xingzheng zhidu shi* 中國地方行政制度史 (Taipei: Zhongyang yanjiuyuan lishi yuyan yanjiusuo, 1963), 3: 19–22.

56. Holmgren, *Chinese Colonisation*, 115–21; Taylor, *Birth of Vietnam*, 70–80; Stephen O'Harrow, "Men of Hu, Men of Han, Men of the Hundred Man: The Biography of Si Nhiep and the Conceptualization of Early Vietnamese Society," *Bulletin de l'École Française d'Extreme-Orient* 75 (1986): 249–66.

57. SGZ 49: 9a–b.

58. JS 57: 4b–6b.

59. Holmgren, *Chinese Colonisation*, 123.

60. SS 92: 4a–8b.

61. Taylor, *Birth of Vietnam*, 110.

62. Hu, *Lingnan gushi*, 130–49, lists a Xiu family, a Wang family, and two Liu families, the members of which inherited positions in the Pearl River drainage area in the fourth century.

63. This was Gu Bi, whose two sons also held the post after him.

64. Holmgren, *Chinese Colonisation*, 116. The ten listed in Holmgren's table are Wang Liang, Liang Shuo (Holmgren romanizes this as Liang Shi), Tao Kan, Ruan Fang, Zhang Lian, Jiang Zhuang, Zhu Fan, Yang Ping, Ruan Fu, and Wen Fangzhi.

65. Ibid., 121–22.

66. For Lý Trương Nhân, see SS 8: 16b, and for Lý Thúc Hiến, see NQS 2: 6a.

67. See Holmgren, *Chinese Colonisation*, 134.

68. Hu, *Lingnan gushi*, 177–82.

69. ZZTJ ch. 158: 4909.

70. CS 20: 6a–b.

Chapter 5

"To Overawe the Li and Lao"

Attempts at Military Conquest

Interactions between the Southern Dynasties and the Li and Lao were by no means limited to peaceful alliance and cooperation. In the Southern Dynasties period in particular, the Chinese written record documents many instances of warfare, albeit mostly on a small scale and ultimately unsuccessful when it came to gaining a permanent foothold for imperial power in the Li-Lao country between the rivers. In the centuries preceding the Southern Dynasties, native political structures of the Two Rivers had been no match for the military might of the empires in the north. After the conquest of Nanyue in 111 BCE, the Han Empire spread southward over a greater territory than any its successor states would ever be able to maintain, and its armies had the capacity to defeat and quell resistance over the entire Two Rivers Region for around three centuries before its power began to wane. The foundations of the future geopolitical shape of the Two Rivers Region were laid down at this time as the Han focused its military and administrative energies on securing important population centers like the Red River Plain and the regions farther south as the gateways to the trade with Southeast Asia and the Indian Ocean. It was during this era of northern military supremacy that the Han neglected to secure the country that offered them overland access to these areas, even though these regions continually caused them trouble. The failure to make a conclusive conquest of the lands between the Two Rivers and leaving the people there in control of their own affairs were strategic mistakes that in the long term would cause problems for imperial rule in the Red River Plain: after the disintegration of the Han Empire in the third century CE, none of the empires that succeeded it had sufficient military power to impose their will on the areas that had been bypassed in this initial expansion southward. Not only were the post-Han empires smaller and militarily weaker, from the mid-fourth century onward they also had the added distractions

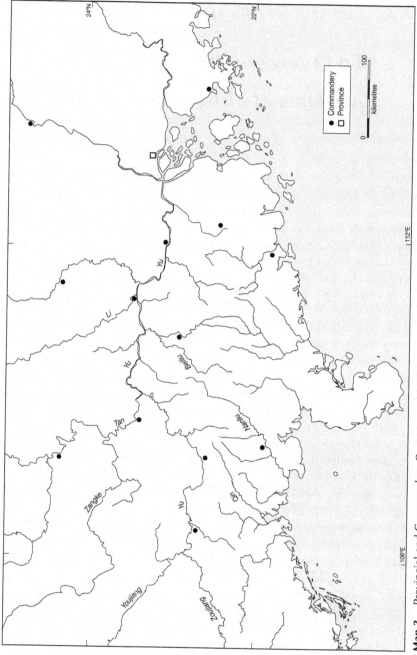

Map 3. Provincial and Commandery Centers, ca. 300 CE

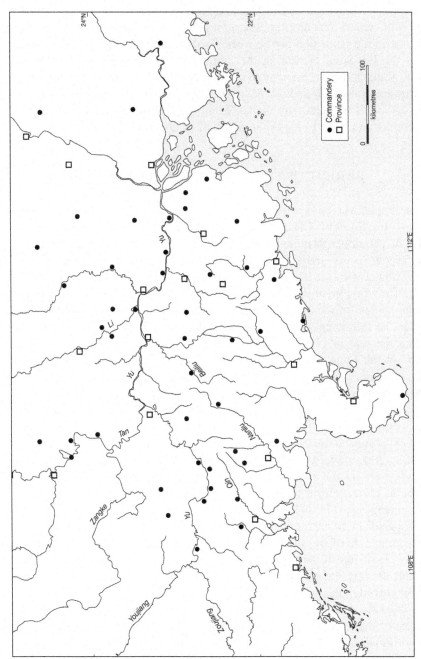

Map 4. Provincial and Commandery Centers, ca. 550 CE

of needing to defend their borders from competitor empires in the north and to suppress internal political chaos and military uprisings. Even so, from the late fifth century onward, the Southern Dynasties began to take more of an interest in the lands that lay between Jiaozhou and Guangzhou. This began with the Liu-Song increasing the number of counties and commanderies along water routes in the area to encircle the Li-Lao chiefdoms and secure the trade routes to Jiaozhou. Military action was then used against the Li and Lao with frequency by the Qi, Liang, and Chen Empires, and reached its climax under the Liang in the first half of the sixth century.

EARLY CONFLICT WITH THE LI AND LAO

Even though Ma Yuan's troops passed through the Li-Lao country on their way to Jiaozhi in 40 CE, there is no evidence that they engaged in conflict with its people, even though some of these people had lent their support to the Trưng Sisters' uprising. Left to their own devices at this time, the Li and Lao between the Two Rivers eventually began to make trouble for the Han. Their first great uprising occurred in 115, over seventy years after Ma Yuan's defeat of the Trưng Sisters, in which the Wuhu of Cangwu rose up and in the following year led a force of thousands from Yulin and Hepu to attack the seat of Cangwu Commandery. Instead of sending a general to defeat them, Empress Dowager Deng decided to avoid conflict and instead sent attendant censor Ren Chuo with a proclamation to grant them amnesty.[1] The next uprising occurred in 178 and was started by the Wuhu of Jiaozhi and Hepu,[2] who managed to assemble a force of tens of thousands from these areas as from regions further south, such as Jiuzhen and Rinan, to attack and occupy commanderies and counties. This time the inspector of Jiaozhi, Zhu Juan, took troops to attack and defeat them.[3] It is likely that these Wuhu of Jiaozhi were inhabitants of the hill country to the northeast of the Red River Plain, as almost all other references to the Wuhu show them as inhabiting that general area. In 248, a man named Lu Yin was appointed by the Wu as inspector of Jiaozhou, as well as to the military post of commandant for the pacification of the south; he was then sent to deal with uprisings of the Yi people of Jiaozhi and Jiuzhen, who had attacked and occupied cities and commanderies.[4] Other sources note that a certain Triệu Âu or Lady Triệu was involved in this uprising at Jiuzhen.[5] The uprisings of the Trưng Sisters and Triệu Âu are often depicted as connected in Vietnamese national history as part of the long struggle to end foreign domination, but the uprisings of 248 originated in a different region and are unlikely to have had any continuity or connection with that of the Trưng Sisters. Like those that occurred in the second century CE, the 248 uprisings were initiated by the peoples of the hill country rather than those of the plains and were linked more to imperial encroachment into this country than to a continuation of resistance to an already centuries' long occupation of the Red River Plain. Nor was the discontent in the hill country in this year confined to the lands that were to form the core of a future Vietnam; Lu Yin's first task upon entering the south was to deal with Huang Wu, a "great commander" (*jushuai*) of Gaoliang to the southwest of Canton who had also risen up against the Wu. He was said to have to obtain Huang Wu's surrender with favors and trust, and let him lead out over three thousand of the families under his leadership to surrender as well. The term *commander* was not an imperial administrative post; it referred to autonomous local leaders outside the imperial system. Judging by his title and where he lived, Huang Wu is probably an early example of a named leader of Li and Lao. After dealing with the situation in the Red River Plain, Lu Yin returned north to attack the "bandits" of Jianling in Cangwu.[6] Another uprising occurred in 291, when the "Yi bandits" (*yizei*) of Yulin attacked and surrounded its commandery and county seats, but were defeated by Lü Dai, inspector of Jiaozhou.[7] Around the end of the third century, conflict occurred between the people between the Two Rivers and Chinese imperial forces: Teng Xiu, the inspector of Guangzhou, informed Tao Huang, his counterpart in Jiaozhou, that he had attacked the "southern bandits" (*nanzei*) many times but had been unable to control them. Tao Huang suggested the following solution:

"Those on the South Bank look to us for salt and iron. If we cut off our trade with them they will melt down [their iron] to make farming tools, if we do that for two years we can then wipe them out in one battle." It is recorded that Xiu was able to successfully defeat them by following this plan.[8]

The "south bank" was a reference to the lands south of the Yu River.[9] "Bandits" was a pejorative term often applied to those outside the imperial administrative system and was often prefixed with an ethnic term, such as the "Yi bandits" of Yulin mentioned earlier. That the term *bandit* was a reference to the Chinese perceptions of these people's political behavior as uncivilized rather than to their mode of existence can be deduced from the fact that the "southern bandits" required iron for farming tools and were able to trade goods for it (even though what they traded is left unmentioned). This indicates that they were leading a settled existence based on farming and trading rather than bandit incursions into Chinese-populated areas. After Teng Xiu's battles, no further resistance requiring outside military assistance is recorded between the Two Rivers for another two centuries, and the Li and Lao seem not to have been involved in military conflicts with the Wu's successor empire, the Jin. This period of peace corresponds to a halt and slow retreat of what little imperial presence there was between the rivers from the end of the third century until the middle of the fifth, and it was at this time that the Li and Lao chiefdoms were able to flourish without the threat of Chinese military incursions. There is also evidence that this period coincided with a change in Li and Lao military technology between the rivers, a shift from dependence on a supply of imported iron to self-sufficiency in the production of iron, which enabled them to produce their own iron weaponry.

CHANGES IN LI-LAO MILITARY TECHNOLOGY

The record of Teng Xiu's plan for defeating the "southern bandits" to the south of the Yu River is particularly significant for our knowledge of early Li-Lao weapon-making technology, as it shows that the Li and Lao of the time were heavily dependent on trade with the Chinese for a supply of iron. However, there is evidence of the use of iron in the Two Rivers Region long before Teng Xiu's time. In his study of the spread of metallurgy in Southeast Asia, Charles Higham noted that iron was known in the Lingnan region as early as the fourth century BCE, the evidence for this being a large collection of iron artifacts found in a pre-Qin tomb excavated on Yinshan near Pingle on the Li River, the main route to the north through the "Magic Trench" canal.[10] Nevertheless, textual and archaeological evidence suggests that knowledge of iron weapon–making technology in the Two Rivers Region in the last centuries BCE was a rarity even among those who had migrated there from the north. In the first years of the first century BCE, during a period of hostility between the Han Empire and the Kingdom of Nanyue, Empress Gao of the Han (240–180 BCE) was persuaded to prohibit the importation of iron weapons into the kingdom in the belief that this would have an adverse influence on its military strength.[11] The lack of a developed iron weapon–making industry is further supported by the fact that after the Han conquest of Nanyue in 111 BCE, no officials were appointed to the Two Rivers Region to oversee the state monopoly in iron in the new province of Jiaozhi, even though many officials were appointed to do this in other provinces. Those iron tools that have been excavated in the region dating from the Nanyue period, such as those from Luobowan tomb in Gui County, were inscribed with place names from the north and are therefore unlikely to have been of local production. In other tombs, however, there were iron implements such as *ding* tripods that, although modeled on ritual implements from the north, betrayed their local origins in their design.[12]

Iron tools seem to have been more common than iron weapons, but their use was restricted mainly to people who lived close to the main river courses; Han tombs in which iron implements were found are situated in areas close to these rivers and the concentrations of Han administrative units. Sites of iron foundries dating from the Han era have been found in Pingnan County, only thirty kilometers away from a bronze foundry at Beiliu where many bronze drums were cast,[13] but knowledge of casting iron does not seem to have spread much further from these areas. As far as weaponry is concerned, the many swords, spears, and daggers that have been excavated from native tombs that predate the presence of the Han in the Two Rivers Region are usually made of bronze rather than iron. The most common weapons to be found in archaeological investigations are short double-edged swords and crossbows,[14] and many depictions of these can be observed in addition to long swords and spears in the ochre cliff paintings along the Zuojiang at Huashan close to the Sino-Vietnamese border, suggesting that these were the preferred weapons among the Li and Lao at the time.[15] Early written records of the Wuhu do not describe them using such swords, but mention instead their use of more exotic weapons such as bronze-tipped poisoned arrows and bamboo crossbows known as "fox crossbows" (*hunu*).[16] It may however be the case that more commonplace weapons such as swords were left unmentioned because they were not sufficiently exotic in the eyes of the Chinese to warrant a mention. It is also noteworthy that no common term for iron exists in the Tai languages of the Two Rivers Region—central and southwestern varieties have the three different terms *lek*, *va*, and *thit*, the first and last of which are Sinitic loans from different periods.[17] It is therefore unlikely that knowledge of the use of iron was spread universally throughout the Tai-speaking peoples of the Two Rivers Region before close contact with speakers of Sinitic languages.

Aside from Tao Huang's comment on the reliance of the "bandits" of the south bank on salt and iron, another piece of written evidence from the third century CE suggests that the Li and Lao between the Two Rivers probably did not have widespread knowledge of iron metallurgy before this time, and that knowledge of this skill became widespread only in the first half of the fourth century. The *Jin shu* records that before Emperor Kang's accession to the throne in 343,

> There had been many taxes and corvée in the East [referring to the eastern coast of central China] and the result of this was an out-migration of common people over the sea to Guangzhou. The inspector Deng Yue opened many foundries, and because of this all the Yi found out how to make weapons. [General] Yu Yi sent a memorial to the throne saying that the East was an asset to the state, and that with the unending disturbances absconders [from it] had gradually increased in number, and also that the Yi were always spying, and that once they had found out the benefits of casting iron it would become impossible to prevent them from doing it.[18]

Trade interactions and the close proximity of the Li and Lao chiefdoms to Chinese centers along the rivers were probably just as responsible for the transfer of knowledge of military technology as any activities of industrial espionage.

THE PROTECTOR OF THE WESTERN RIVERS
AND THE FOUNDATION OF YUEZHOU

If the two-century-long peace between the Two Rivers was indeed the transitional period from importation of iron to self-sufficiency in the casting of weapons among the Li and Lao, it probably contributed to their increased ability to defend themselves against the military incursions of the two centuries of conflict that were to follow. The new upsurge of military activity against the Li and Lao between the Two Rivers in the last two decades of the Liu-Song marked a change in the policy of the Southern Dynasties toward the Li and Lao, and records of military attacks against them become ever more frequent.

The foundation of new commanderies and counties between the Two Rivers began again under the Liu-Song. This was the beginning of a process of gradual encirclement of the heartland of the Li-Lao bronze drum culture, as new administrative units were founded farther up the major waterways in increasing proximity to its center, a process depicted on maps 3 and 4 of the commandery seats in the Two Rivers Region under the Western Jin (300 CE) and the last years of the Liang (550 CE). Some of these new commanderies and their subordinate counties probably existed in name only and were still autonomous entities, but records of the military maneuvers of the Liu-Song show that the empire had become interested in acquiring direct control over some territories where the imperial presence had formerly been thinly spread. The foundations of many of these units bear the hallmarks of military conquest (albeit small scale) rather than alliances with local rulers.

Studying the policy of the Southern Dynasties toward the Li and Lao, Peng Fengwen noted several characteristics of imperial military action against the people between the Two Rivers: that only a few actions were ordered directly by the court, that most were organized by local administrators, and that they were mostly localized and never concentrated over a large area.[19] Military attacks against the Li and Lao are usually referred to with the euphemism *ping*, which translates nicely into English as "pacification." The first record of such "pacification" activity relates to a campaign carried out by the Liu-Song general Tan Daoji, which was connected to the building of a stone fortress in 426 at the mouth of the Lingluo River.[20] As well as securing a port, control of the river mouth would have helped in making inroads to much of the country between what are now the towns of Luchuan and Suixi.

This action was followed soon after by the foundation of the new post of "Protector of the Western Rivers" (*Xi jiang duhu*). According to the *Nan Qi shu*, this position was established especially for the purposes of attacking recalcitrant Li and Lao.[21] The first recorded appointee to the position was Liu Mian in 459, then governor of Yulin, who went to fight against the forces of the "great leader" (*dashuai*) Chen Tan of Hepu.[22] Another record relates that a previous administrator, named Fei Shen, had previously attacked Chen Tan, but had been unable to defeat him, and that after Liu Mian took over the task he was able to force Tan into surrender.[23] The twist to Chen Tan's story is that after submitting to imperial authority, he was given the post of Dragon Galloping General, then only a year later in 460 he sent a request for an army to go and attack "those who had not yet submitted" and was rewarded for his loyalty to the Liu-Song with an official post as governor of Gaoxing alongside his post of general.[24] The method of dealing with Chen Tan is an example of both military action and cooptation into the administrative system through alliance, showing that both methods could be used concurrently. The advantage of this for local leaders such as Chen Tan was that an alliance could (and, in his particular case, did) provide the opportunity for their own imperially backed self-aggrandizement.

Further inroads were made into the territory of the Li-Lao north of Hepu following the foundation of Yue Province in 471 by Chen Boshao, another holder of the post of Protector of the Western Rivers.[25] The *Nan Qi Shu* notes:

> Yue province is governed from Linzhang Commandery. Originally it formed the northern frontier area of Hepu. Mobs of Yi and Lao live there, lurking in the crags and blocked-off places. They commit banditry and for the most part are not entered in the population registers as citizens. In the Taishi (465–472) period, Chen Boshao, protector of the Western Rivers, was hunting in the north when he saw two black buffalo run startled into the bushes. He sent people to pursue them but they couldn't catch them. He then marked the place, saying that it had a strange, auspicious omen and founded Yuezhou there. In the seventh year he founded the six commanderies of Boliang, Longsu, Yongning, Anchang, Fuchang, and Nanliu. In the second year of Yuanhui (474) Boshao was made inspector and for the first time a provincial centre was established to control it [the province]. He cut through the mountains to make a gate for the city, to overawe the Li and Lao.[26]

Yuezhou was founded to secure the routes up the Nanliu River to the Yu River tributaries, and it was a true frontier province, governed from an inland citadel as a military outpost built to control the surrounding countryside. That the province was more of an outpost than an ordinary functioning administrative unit is attested to by reports that its governor spent much of his time in battle on horseback.[27] Chen Boshao himself seems to have had a high degree of autonomy over affairs in the new province; according to a later source, he declared himself a prince.[28] Liao Youhua states that the administrative structure of Yuezhou was founded purely for military purposes, noting the lack of registered population figures for any of the commanderies in the treatise on geography in the *Song shu* and the suspicious lack of subordinate counties for certain commanderies, which suggests that many of the new administrative areas existed in name only at the time the list was made.[29] An alternative explanation for the absence of counties in the new Yuezhou commanderies is that the Liu-Song geographical treatise was based on the census from 464 that predated the foundation of the province, and that only the names of administrative units could be added into the treatise, as no counts had yet been made of their populations. During Chen Boshao's rule as protector, military pressure on the Li was also applied from the north, when Li Sidao, governor of Jinkang on the south bank of the Yu River, led an army to attack the Li but lost the advantage by disobeying orders and was later punished for this by Chen Boshao.[30]

The foundation of Yuezhou in 471 makes an interesting comparison to the situation in the Red River Plain: over four hundred years had passed since Ma Yuan's campaign against the Trung Sisters and yet the people of these "crags and blocked-off places," who were geographically closer than the Red River Plain to Canton and the imperial capital in Jiankang, were still largely autonomous at this time. Taylor has referred to Yue Province as the "new frontier of the Chinese Empire,"[31] but in the sense of a borderland between China and a future Vietnamese state. Yuezhou was indeed a frontier province, but the frontier country lay in the opposite direction from the Red River Plain in the expanse of hilly country to the north and east of Hepu. It was the people of this area that the fortification at Yuezhou was to guard against, not those of the Red River Plain. The building of forts and battles with locals to bring territory under direct imperial control had not been a feature of life on the Red River Plain since the time of Ma Yuan.

THE LI WARS UNDER THE LIANG EMPIRE

The short-lived Southern Qi Dynasty (479–502) did very little to expand administration south of the Yu River, aside from founding a new commandery at the strategic position Guangxi, south of present-day Luoding. The Qi court retained the position of protector of the Western Rivers and although one of the protectors, Zhou Shixiong, is known by name, no details survive of military campaigns against the Li-Lao in this period. These were to begin in earnest again under the Liang. As related in chapter 4, at the commencement of the reign of Emperor Wu of the Liang in 502, the entire Two Rivers Region contained only four provinces, but by the end of his reign in 550, the number of provinces in the region had more than tripled to a total of fifteen. Most of this administrative growth took place between 523 and 545, and around the same time there are frequent records of open warfare against the Li, usually referred to as "pacification of the Li *dong*" (*ping li dong*). Although the foundation of provinces and the need for "pacification" are almost certainly connected, a lack of precise dates and information means it is difficult to establish any pattern of cause and effect. The first recorded Liang military campaign against the Li was somewhere in Yulin Commandery, in which governor Xun Fei went to fight "Li bandits" but was hit by a stray arrow and died in battle. This occurred around 503.[32]

In 507, parts of Xiangzhou and Guangzhou were split off to create the new province of Hengzhou (in the vicinity of present-day Shaoguan),[33] and Gùizhou was split off from Guangzhou.[34] Gùizhou was originally Guilin Commandery on the Tan River and was upgraded to an independent province for the government of the northern tributaries of the Yu River. In 523, three new provinces were formed from Guangzhou by upgrading the former commanderies to provincial status. These were Jianzhou, centered on Guangxi Commandery, Chengzhou, centered on Cangwu, and Nandingzhou, made up from what had been left of Yulin Commandery after the detachment of Gùizhou in the northeast.[35] Yuezhou was then renamed Nanhezhou and was governed from Hepu. The foundation dates of other provinces are obscure, but most can be pinned down to the Dàtōng or Dàtóng eras of Emperor Wu (527–529 and 535–546, respectively).[36] The next new administrative unit to be founded was Gaozhou, which was said to have been "founded by the Liang after pacifying Li *dong*."[37] It was founded either during the Dàtōng period or in 535.[38] The Gaoliang area in which Gaozhou was founded had never been a stable part of the empire before this time; the Liu-Song had once founded a Gaoxing Commandery in the area, but soon abandoned it, whereupon it was "occupied by Yi and Lao,"[39] meaning that it had fallen back under local control. The upgrade of Gaoliang Commandery to a province was the suggestion of a former inspector of Guangzhou named Xiao Mai. He had recommended this to the throne as a necessary strengthening of defenses on the South River, where he considered the situation to be dangerous. His recommendation and former post obviously gained him a good reputation for being able to deal with the people of the Two Rivers Region, as he was later appointed to the post of Protector of the Western Rivers.[40] South of the Yu River were the new provinces of Anzhou, Luozhou, and Xinzhou. The first two were founded before 542[41] and the last some time during or before the Dàtōng period.[42] Another province was founded on the territory of a *dong* during the Dàtōng period, when the "Twin-Head *Dong*" (*Shuangtou Dong*) was split off from Xinzhou to form Shuangzhou.[43]

The foundation of the five provinces of Gaozhou, Xinzhou, Jianzhou, Luozhou, and Shuangzhou represents a further consolidation of Liang power upstream along smaller watercourses toward the heart of the Li-Lao country. Significantly, only the foundation of Gaozhou is explicitly mentioned in connection with military offensives against the Li and Lao, suggesting that some of these provinces may actually have been the domain of Li and Lao rulers. The number of records of warfare against the Li and Lao dating from the period of the foundation of the new provinces indicates considerable resistance to the rule of the Liang Empire among the Li and Lao. The *Sui shu* recorded the phrase "pacifying the Li *dong*" in a list of military campaigns under Emperor Wu, which saw the huge increase in the number of provinces between the Tianjian (502–520) and the Dàtóng (535–546) periods.[44] The foundation of new provinces was recorded elsewhere as having followed (among other campaigns) the recent "opening up" of the Zangke river country in the west and the "pacification of Li *dong*" in the south.[45] Aside from these references, there are several more records of warfare with the Li and Lao that point to the general area around Canton, and two that refer expressly to the Li and Lao on the south bank of the Yu River.

The *Chen Shu* records that during the Dàtóng period three men, Du Ceng-ming, his brother Du Tianhe, and Zhou Wenyu, had been very successful in expeditions against the Li and Lao for Lu Anxing, who held the post of Pro-tector of the South River at Canton, so they were appointed as the assistant defenders of Xinzhou.[46] The same book records a deputy official (*shilang*) of Wuling (now in southern Hunan) as having gone out from Panyu to attack the Li *dong*.[47] This was before 545, when he accompanied Protector of the Western Rivers (and later emperor) Chen Baxian to battle with Lý Bốn in the Red River Plain. Records such as these that refer only to raids on "Li *dong*" without specifying location are difficult to place, but the lack of references to Li dwelling to the east of Canton prior to the Sui (589–618), and the fact that the area directly to the north of the provincial seat at Canton was under the jurisdiction of a different province throughout the Six Dynasties Period, make it extremely likely that these raids were also against people who lived to the south and west of Canton.

There are specific mentions of a Li commander (*Li shuai*) named Chen Wenche who fought against Liang forces some time during the Dàtóng period.[48] Three versions of his story are found in three different sources, and each source supplies details missing from the other versions. Xiao Mai's biography records that Chen Wenche, Li commander from west of the river (*Jiang xi*),[49] came out to plunder Gaoyao (present-day Zhaoqing), at which time Xiao Mai was ordered to increase the length of his office as inspec-tor (presumably with the intent of defeating Chen Wenche), resulting in Wenche's surrender not long after.[50] Lan Qin was a military official who had held various positions in the Two Rivers Region, including overseer of mili-tary affairs in Hengzhou (Southern Jiangxi) and Gùizhou. His biography tells that he passed through Guangzhou and defeated Chen Wenche and his brothers in battle, taking them alive, and that upon his arrival at Hengzhou he was promoted to "general who pacifies the South."[51] The biography of Ouyang Wei, a friend of Lan Qin from a young age, records that Lan Qin went south from Hengzhou to attack the "Yi and Lao," capturing Chen Wenche alive and acquiring at the same time an "uncountable number of things," among which was a huge bronze drum "the like of which had not been seen for generations," which he then presented to the emperor as tribute.[52] The comment on the size of the bronze drum indicates that it was most likely a Heger II drum, and his connection with such a drum suggests that Chen Wenche came from somewhere to the south of the Yu River, as no Heger II drums have been excavated from anywhere north of the Yu River to the east of its confluence with the Zangke.

These records provide a little additional information about the type of society that existed outside the Liang imperial administration. Li leaders like Chen Wenche were rich, organized enough to make raids on Liang commanderies, and commanded armies of thousands. The motives for the "pacification" of the Li *dong* or Chen Wenche's raid on Gaoyao are not mentioned in the Chinese texts, but they are implied as justified action through the use of words such as "pacify," whereas the Li themselves are depicted as mere raiders and troublemakers lurking around the edges of civilized districts. However, through comparison of the time scale of the records of warfare with those of the Liang attempts at administrative expansion, it becomes clear that these two trends were closely connected. Initially the Liang encroachment into the Li-Lao country was a continuation of what had started under the Liu-Song, a slowly tightening noose of military and administrative control around the Li and Lao chiefdoms, but the rapid upsurge of Liang military incursions into the country between the Two Rivers in the 520s and 530s was unprecedented.

Any further consolidation of Liang power in the Two Rivers area ended as imperial attention was diverted to quelling the rebellion of General Hou Jing in 549. After his sacking of the Liang capital that year, local officials in the west of the Two Rivers Region began to fight among themselves with the aim of extending their own power bases in the region, and the Liang wars against the Li came to an end.[53] Chen Baxian, the first emperor of the Chen Empire in 557, had himself once held the post of Protector of the Western Rivers, but the empire he founded was not to make any significant territorial advances into the Li-Lao country south of the Yu River. The Chen was unstable and too weak even to concentrate its efforts on bringing larger populated areas such as the Red River Plain under its control, so it was unlikely to have been able to carry out large-scale military or administrative expansion into new districts in the Li-Lao country. This initial weakness of the Chen corresponds to an absence of records of attacks on the Li *dong* for two or three decades. During this quiet period in 576, Shen Jungao was appointed as inspector of Guangzhou; according to his biography, Shen was a literary official with no military ability who chose to deal with the Li-Lao in a peaceful manner. Apparently, prior to this the Li and Lao had been fighting and attacking each other for generations, and through determined effort he was able to achieve peace among them.[54] Unfortunately, Shen's manner of dealing with the Li-Lao seems to have been atypical, and he died in office after only two years. Military action against the Li and Lao resumed under an inspector of Guangzhou named Ma Jing, who served around the end of the reign of Emperor Xuan (reigned 569–583). It was recorded that he would make expeditions deep into the Li *dong* every year with a group of well-trained soldiers and that these were repeatedly victorious.[55] This record refers only to raids on "Li *dong*" without specifying location, but by Ma Jing's time the province of Guangzhou was much reduced in size. The Liang had split the old province so many times that its territory no longer stretched far to the west up the Yu River as it had previously. It is therefore probable that these raids were carried out closer to the seat of Guangzhou in Canton or even to the east of that city, rather than in the lands to the south of the Yu River.

In combination with the administrative incorporation of their leaders, these concentrated attacks on the Li and Lao south of the Yu River had the result of replacing the empty spaces on the Chinese map with a patchwork of provinces and commanderies. Significantly, as Peng points out, the military attacks occurred in the same area that was under the jurisdiction of the Protector of the Western Rivers.[56] However, the persistence of a strong Li and Lao leadership in the area after this time shows that neither the military campaigns nor the administrative expansion of the Southern Dynasties was effective in gaining completely centralized control over the Li and Lao. The description of the Li and Lao as having frequently fought among themselves shows their own lack of centralized government and explains why military activity against them was also localized and tended to involve armed sorties for raiding rather than the conquest of large new territories. Not only did the Southern Dynasties lack the military power for anything other than small conflicts, there was also no united Li or Lao political structure for them to conquer and control.

As noted in the previous chapter, without a wholesale eradication and replacement of local ruling elites in the style of Ma Yuan, the Li and Lao *dulao* of old slowly transformed into nominal inspectors and governors whose positions were inherited within their own clans. As these became more involved politically with the Southern Dynasties, local rulers slowly began to look similar to the lineages imported from the north.[57] Although the Li and Lao were never united under a single powerful ruler, during the second half of the sixth century a few of their leaders began to control much larger areas than small *dong* and their rulers had the ability to assemble and control ever larger armed forces, thus making the region even more difficult for the increasingly enfeebled Southern Dynasties to bring under direct control by force of arms.

Despite these periods of military conflict throughout the post-Han period, Chinese empires were simply not capable of or strategically poised for outright military conquest of the Li and Lao, and eventually had to resort to negotiation and alliances to secure their agreement. The necessity for negotiation stemmed not only from the Li and Lao chieftains' inconvenient occupation of strategic territories, or from their potential to cause trouble for the Chinese if left to their own devices; it was also because their lands contained an abundance of resources that were highly sought after in Chinese cities. If an empire could not simply go and occupy the country that produced these resources, it was necessary to go and engage its leaders in a trade relationship in order to acquire them. The nature of the trade relationship and its effects on Li-Lao society are the subject of the following chapter.

NOTES

1. HHS 86: 10b.
2. HHS 8: 10b.
3. HHS 8: 13a.
4. SKC 61: 13a–13b.
5. Taylor, *Birth of Vietnam*, 90, says that the Lady Triệu is not mentioned in Chinese sources, but he is mistaken. The first and most detailed record of her, upon which all subsequent records are based, is from Liu Xinqi's *Jiaozhou ji*, quoted at length in TPYL 371: 3b and 499: 10a–b.
6. SGZ 61: 13a/b. Jianling lay to the east of present-day Liuzhou in Guangxi.
7. SGZ 60: 8a/b.
8. JS 57: 5a. This probably took place in the last years of the Wu Dynasty (220–280). Teng Xiu served under the Wu as the regional inspector of Guangzhou in 277 and died in 288; Tao Huang was the prefect of Cangwu around that time.
9. Taylor, *Birth of Vietnam*, 96, has used the same quote as if the "southern bandits" referred to Linyi. However, Teng Xiu's post was in Guangzhou, not Jiaozhou, and elsewhere in Tao Huang's biography (JS 57: 6a) the "south bank" is a definite reference to the lands south of Guangzhou.
10. Higham, *The Bronze Age of Southeast Asia*, 135.
11. SC 113: 2a/b.
12. Zheng Chaoxiong 鄭超雄, "Guanyu lingnan yetie qiyuan de ruogan wenti" 關於嶺南冶鐵業起源的若干問題, *Guangxi minzu yanjiu* 廣西民族研究 45, no. 3 (1996): 50–56.
13. Ibid., 51–52.
14. Jeffrey G. Barlow, "Culture, Ethnic Identity, and Early Weapons Systems: The Sino-Vietnamese Frontier," in *East Asian Cultural and Historical Perspectives* and

Society/Culture and Literatures, ed. Steven Tötösy de Zepetnek and Jennifer W. Jay (Edmonton: University of Alberta, Research Institute for Comparative Literature and Cross-Cultural Studies, 1997), 1–15.

15. Wang Kerong 王克榮, Qiu Zhonglun 邱鍾侖, and Chen Yuanzhang 陳遠璋, *Guangxi zuo jiang yanhua* 廣西左江巖畫 (Beijing: Wenwu chubanshe, 1988), 193–95.

16. NZYWZ in TPYL 786: 3a. The word *fox* in the name of this type of crossbow is probably an attempt at transcribing a Tai word rather than a reference to foxes: Li Fang-kuei gives the proto-Tai as **hna*, remarkably close to Pulleyblank's Early Middle Chinese reconstructions of the pronunciations of the two characters 狐弩 **yɔ-nɔ*. Another word in which the same character occurs with a similar function is the name *Hu-Lao*, mentioned in chapter 3.

17. According to Thai historical linguist Pittayawat Pittayaporn, the word *lek* (or *luk* as it is pronounced in some districts) is descended from a Sinitic loan word that predates the first millennium CE; see Pittayawat Pittayaporn, "Layers of Chinese Loanwords in Proto-Southwestern Tai as Evidence for the Dating of the Spread of Southwestern Thai," *MANUSYA: Journal of Humanities*, Special Issue no. 20 (2014): 52–53. The geographical distribution of the words is also significant. In the varieties of Tai spoken in the hill country to the south and west of the Youjiang, variants of *lek* are the common term. In the areas close to the Youjiang, the Zangke, and the Yu River, the word is *thit*, which descends either from Early Middle Chinese or a more recent borrowing from Ping dialect or Cantonese. Where this term is used would have been the area of the most intense contact with Sinitic speakers. The etymologically unrelated term *va* is used only in the mountains to the north of the Zangke River; see Zhang, *Zhuangyu fangyan yanjiu*, 322.

18. JS 73: 10b. Yet even as late as the twelfth century, iron does not seem to have been universally available. Twelfth-century writer Zhou Qufei (LWDD ch. 6: 218) noted that people who along the coast southwest from Canton could not easily procure the iron nails used for making larger boats had to make do with rafts made from planks lashed together with vines.

19. Peng, "Nanchao lingnan minzu zhengce," 95.

20. TPHYJ 167: 9a. The present name of this river is the Jiuzhou Jiang.

21. NQS 14: 20a–b. Peng, "Xijiang duhu," 63–64, argues that the term had a broader meaning than the West River (Xijiang) of the present day, and therefore I translate the title with a plural as "Protector of the Western Rivers."

22. SS 97: 4a.

23. SS 86: 4a–b.

24. SS 97: 4a.

25. SS 38: 43b.

26. NQS 14: 25b–26a.

27. NQS 14: 26a.

28. TPHYJ 167: 9a.

29. Liao, *Lishi dilixue*, 133, notes three other commanderies in Yuezhou without subordinate counties.

30. SS 54: 10b.

31. Taylor, *Birth of Vietnam*, 122: "In 471 Yue Province was organised from portions of Guang[-zhou] and Jiao[-zhou]. The immediate reason for this was to recognise those portions of Jiao that were still under imperial authority, most important being the prefecture of Hepu, which became the headquarters of the new province. Yue Province in effect became the new frontier of the empire." (Romanization altered to Pinyin.)

32. LS 47: 4b. The approximate time is calculated from the time of his father Xun Fazhao's death in office as magistrate of Anfu at the end of the Xingzhong era of Qi (501–502). His brother Xun Jiang had not yet finished his three years of ritual mourning before he was killed, but Xun Jiang was eventually appointed as senior attendant-in-ordinary (*zuo changshi*) to Emperor Gao's second son, the prince of Yuzhang, who had this title from 504 onward. Xun Jiang died at age twenty-one.

33. LS 2: 15a.

34. LS 2: 15b.

35. LS 3: 4b.

36. During Emperor Wu's long reign, there were two reign periods called *Datong*; the first was Dàtōng 大通 (527–529) and the second Dàtóng 大同 (535–546). To avoid confusion, the tonal spelling has been retained for each transcription.

37. Fragment of a lost chapter of YHJXTZ, quoted in YDJS 117: 1b.

38. SuS 31: 12a. There is some confusion over the foundation date of Gaozhou. SuS says it was perhaps split off from Panzhou, but this is an anachronism, as Panzhou was not founded until the Sui, so this is likely to be a mistake for Guangzhou. NS 51: 4a–b says that it was upgraded after the defeat of the Li commander Chen Wenche, which must have been after 535 (see note 48).

39. YHJXTZ, quoted in YDJS 117: 1b.

40. NS 51: 4a–b.

41. Anzhou was upgraded from Songshou Commandery. YHJXTZ ch. 38: 952 says that Anzhou was founded by Emperor Wu of the Liang and centered on Qinjiang County on the Qin River. As for Luozhou, although the name ending in -*zhou* makes it appear to be a province, Luozhou existed already as a county during Liu-Song and Qi times at the northern end of Leizhou Peninsula. According to LS 3: 26b, these two provinces already had governors by 542.

42. CS 8: 1a–b. Xinzhou was upgraded from the former Xinning Commandery.

43. TPHYJ 164: 4b, 5a.

44. SuS 29: 2a–b.

45. ZZTJ ch. 158: 4903–4.

46. CS 8: 1a–b.

47. CS 12: 1a.

48. If Lan Qin's biography in LS 32: 10a–12a was arranged in chronological order, the battle with Chen Wenche can be dated to after 535, as the passage immediately preceding the description records a gift of horses from Western Wei general Yuwen-heitai, and the Western Wei was not founded until 535.

49. Near to Gaoyao the Yu River actually does flow in a north-south direction rather than from west to east, so the description "west of the river" probably refers to the south bank, rather than the lands to the west of Gaoyao.

50. NS 51: 4a.
51. LS 32: 11b.
52. CS 9: 6b.
53. CS 9: 7a.
54. CS 23: 3b.
55. CS 21: 17a.
56. Peng, "Xijiang duhu," 64.
57. This was not true everywhere, however, and even in areas that are now undoubtedly "Chinese," a more traditional Li-Lao structure of small-scale leadership survived well into the seventh century in small *dong* south of the Yu River, from which "wild" Li and Lao chieftains led resistance to the Tang from the 630s to the 650s. These were in what later became the three districts of Yuzhou, Yizhou, and Douzhou, at the heart of the bronze drum country and distant from the main river routes, in the districts of present-day Luchuan, Beiliu, and Xinyi. The first resistance war occurred in 631 (ZZTJ ch. 193: 6092), another occurred in 640 (XTS 222c: 19a), and the last in 651–652 (ZZTJ ch. 199: 6276).

Chapter 6

Gold, Silver, Snakes, and Slaves
Highland-Lowland Trade Relations

The desire of the Li and Lao between the rivers to possess their own drums is illustrated by a proclamation from the third year of the Taiyuan period of Emperor Xiaowu of the Jin (378 CE), which stated:

> Money is the precious treasure of the realm, so when mean folk desirous of profit continually melt it down and destroy it, officials ought to do something about this. The Yi people of Guangzhou esteem bronze drums highly as a great treasure, but Guangzhou produces no copper. I have heard that under these circumstances officials and private merchants are greedy and weigh coins incorrectly in order to take them to Guangzhou and sell them off to the Yi people, who then melt them down to make drums. This is to be strictly prohibited and those who receive them will be punished.[1]

Although this text refers to the drum owners only by the generalized term *Yi*, the fact that they are referred to as living in Guangzhou, coupled with the distribution of drum finds and the administrative boundaries of the fourth century, make it almost certain that the Yi people referred to in this text were those referred to elsewhere as Li and Lao who lived south of the Yu River. What were these people trading in order to obtain large quantities of copper cash, and why was it that copper held so little value for them in the form of coins that they acquired these only for the raw materials with which to cast drums?

We have already seen that some Li and Lao chieftains had special relationships through alliances with the Jin and the Southern Dynasties that enabled them to retain the rule of their own people beyond the direct authority of the Chinese empires, and that these were relationships primarily based on trade in sought-after products from the Two Rivers Region. The Chinese obsession with the exotica of the Two Rivers Region had a long history. The earliest Chinese records of the lands around Two Rivers Region make mention of it as an area rich in luxury goods. The book *Huainanzi*, compiled during the Western Han (206 BCE–9 CE), noted that it was first emperor of Qin's desire for the luxury goods from the region Yue, such as rhinoceros horn, ivory, kingfisher feathers, and pearls, that made him wish to conquer it.[2] Referring more specifically to the lands between the rivers, the *Han shu* noted that the commandery of Hepu, which nominally administered the country north of the Gulf of Tongking to the south of the Yu River, "abounded in rhinoceros and elephants, tortoiseshell, pearls, silver, copper, fruit and cloth."[3]

Although the Han had military strength sufficient to conquer the interior hill country of the Two Rivers Region, this area seems to have held little attraction for them. It was easier to concentrate effort on controlling and taxing the local population in highly fertile plains at river mouths and points along the larger rivers and the coast, such as Hepu, Cangwu, and Jiaozhi, than on the many small *dong* that were more difficult for them to unite and tax under a centralized control. So the Han presence between the rivers was mainly limited to these places of strategic and economic importance, and the long-term result of such a policy was that after the fall of the Han the country away from the commandery seats consisting of hills, plains, and large stretches of coast still remained in the hands of the Li and Lao. Control of these lands gave the Li and Lao three key advantages in their relationships with the Chinese in the coming centuries: control over sought-after resources, self-sufficiency in food production, and proximity to markets.

The regions that the Li and Lao controlled were not only rich in the aforementioned luxury items so sought after by the Chinese, but also held an abundance of mineral resources such as gold, silver, and copper, of which the Han seemed to be unaware. By the time of the Southern Dynasties, when gold and silver were employed as the main trading currency of the neighboring imperial provincial capitals, the Li and Lao chieftains happened to be sitting on some of the richest gold and silver resources on the East Asian Mainland, and their dominion over the hill country and the sea coasts adjacent to their *dong* would have allowed them to easily organize the collection of local products that remained in perennial demand in the Chinese cities. There is much evidence to show that trade in the luxury products from the hill country and coast was reliant on the cooperation of local people who were familiar with the areas where particular flora and fauna could be collected. Some of this evidence is by direct citation, some is indicated by geographical reference, and then some only by clues in the names of products traded, which seem to indicate that the Chinese gained knowledge of them through peoples who spoke Tai-Kadai languages. The environment inhabited by the Li and Lao was also highly advantageous for the development of their political autonomy, as it allowed their populations to be agriculturally self-sufficient. The *dong* south of the Yu River were situated in a fertile climate warm enough for two harvests of rice per year; the double harvest was a well-known feature of the Red River Plain during the Southern Dynasties,[4] whereas double cropping at Xuwen on the Leizhou Peninsula led to the saying, "If you wish to lift yourself out of poverty, go to Xuwen."[5] In the present day, a double harvest of rice is possible in all the lands south of the Yu River and most parts of the provinces of Guangdong and Guangxi.[6] Aside from salt in some of the *dong* that lay distant from the ocean, the Li and Lao would not have needed to rely on supplies of imported foodstuffs. A final strategic advantage for the Li and Lao of the *dong* was that, although they remained politically autonomous, they lived relatively close to the two urban centers of the region to which they could easily trade their goods.

The Southern Dynasties were often barely capable of imposing their will on some provinces of their own empire, let alone the unconquered areas, but the products of the Two Rivers Region remained in demand in the cities. Therefore, in order to obtain the products they desired from the Li and Lao–controlled regions, it was necessary for the people of the Southern Dynasties to engage Li and Lao leaders in trade relationships; however, they seem to have had very little to trade in return, as only the three products, salt, iron, and copper, have been recorded as having been traded into the lands of the Li and Lao. This trade relationship with the imperially controlled lowlands resembles those typical of Southeast Asian lowland-highland trade patterns in later periods: mutually beneficial forms of exchange in which highland peoples would gather forest products in exchange for salt and other trade products of the coast.

Certain groups of Li and Lao were undoubtedly self-sufficient in copper, and as we have seen in chapter 5, by the fifth century some were also self-sufficient with regard to iron production, whereas those who lived on the coast would also have had access to the means of producing their own salt. What the empires could offer were trade alliances with the Li-Lao chieftains as leaders in their own right through the policy of what they referred to as temporary appointments. Studying the history of this policy during the fourth and fifth centuries, Peng Fengwen concluded that it was little more than a burdensome forced taxation and that the local leaders received no benefit from it.[7] Although it is true that there is no textual evidence for direct material gain for the Li and Lao directly related to the policy, this does not mean that alliances with the Southern Dynasties were not beneficial to their rulers. Over the three centuries that the policy of alliances was made, several changes occurred in the society between the rivers that indicate the rising power of the Li and Lao chieftains. These were the growth of chiefdoms from small *dong* into large alliances of many *dong* under powerful Li commanders, the enrichment of many Li commanders and their families, and the continued retention of Li-Lao political autonomy between the Two Rivers well into the seventh century. I argue that these changes were directly related to the system of alliances in exchange for the supply of luxury goods. Imperial inability to conquer the interior of the Li-Lao country, appoint administrators, and tax the Li-Lao as registered citizens led to a situation highly beneficial to the chieftains of the *dong*; they enjoyed a trade imbalance in their favor, which resulted in agreements guaranteeing the safety of specific chieftains and their people from the depredations of venal imperial officials. The Li and Lao were lucky enough to dwell in proximity to regions where their trade products were desired and at the same time remain beyond their direct control.

Francis Allard has described a similar process of enrichment through trade relations with a large state in another part of the Two Rivers Region during the Warring States period in the north of China (475–221 BCE), a time when local leaders prospered through their control of the sources in the trade in luxury goods with the neighboring state of Chu, resulting in an abundance of rich burials stocked with bronze artifacts in the archaeological record. The grave sites that indicated the most prosperous of these leaders were mainly concentrated along the river routes connecting the Pearl River drainage area to the lands of Chu, namely the Nankang, Shian, and Linhe passes detailed in chapter 2.[8] The proliferation of bronze drums dating from the period from the third through the seventh century suggests that the Li-Lao chieftains were indeed enriched, both materially and politically through their contact with the Chinese empires over this time as the existence of large numbers of drum finds indicates many stratified societies able to support teams of artisans and laborers for their creation. Like the Lingnan bronze cultures described by Allard, the bronze drum cultures of the Li and Lao lay outside the direct political control of centralized states (Chu and the Southern Dynasties, respectively). There is, however, a significant difference between the distribution of Allard's rich burials and the bronze drums of the Li and Lao; finds of drums are mainly concentrated away from the main river routes that pass through the area to connect Jiaozhou and Guangzhou. This suggests that it was not the interprovincial trade between the two territories under imperial control of Jiaozhou and Guangzhou that enriched the Li-Lao chieftains, but rather the trade between forested uplands under their own control with these two heavily populated centers on the two river plains.

I digress for a moment to note that around the same time as the system of trade alliances was initiated, the Jin Empire made an effort to tax foreign people on the peripheries of their empire, and that this may have included some of the Li-Lao who lived adjacent to commanderies and counties in the Two Rivers Region. In 280, the Jin introduced a household taxation system (*hudiaoshi*) with grades based on age and physical distance from the capital.

Yi people were also included in this system but were taxed differently from ordinary citizens. Their distance from the capital or from the commandery seat also had an effect on the amount of tax they were required to pay. The *Jin shu* described the tax as follows:

> After conquering Wu, the Jin made a system of household taxation, a household led by a man of full age had to provide three bolts of cloth, and three catties of floss silk, households led by women or men not of full age would have to provide half this amount. Those who lived in the border commanderies were to provide two-thirds of this amount and those who lived far away only a third. Yi would pay a "Yi cloth tax," each household had to provide a bolt of cloth, the distant Yi would only have to give a *chang* [about 2.5 meters]. . . . The distant Yi who paid no tax on their fields had to give three bushels of public rice, five pecks for those living further away. For those who lived furthest away the tax was paid in cash, at twenty-eight pieces per person.[9]

This probably did not affect the Li and Lao who lived to the south of Cangwu. Governor Tao Huang's letter to Emperor Wen quoted in chapter 2 dates from around the same time as the application of this new taxation system, but contains a description of the fifty thousand households who would not submit to authority on the south bank of the Yu River. This makes it seem highly unlikely that the Li and Lao of the interior were included in this system, even under the category of "distant Yi." As the power of centralized empires began to wane in the Two Rivers Region, so did their organization of taxation structures and ability to collect revenue. For the most part, the average members of a Li or Lao chiefdom between the Two Rivers would have had no direct relationship with the imperial administration, as its influence was probably confined to the indirect order through a chieftain for the collection or supply of particular products. The nature of these products and the effects that their collection had on the Li and Lao chiefdoms is outlined below.

GOLD AND SILVER

The Li-Lao country between the Two Rivers produced metals that were much sought after in the cities of the empire, particularly gold and silver, but there seems to have been little awareness of the fact in Han times. Although the earliest surviving record of the products of the Two Rivers Region from that period does mention silver and copper resources,[10] the people of the Han Empire and perhaps even the Li and Lao themselves do not seem at that time to have been aware of the mineral riches that were hidden away between the

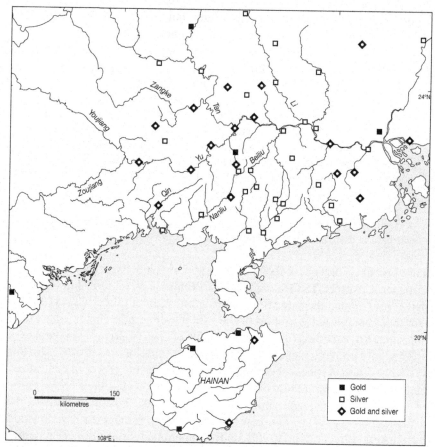

Map 5. Districts Recorded as Giving Tribute in Gold or Silver from the Sixth to the Tenth Centuries CE (from records in JTS, TD, TPHYJ)

Two Rivers. As such, in the early period of imperial rule in the region, the Han Empire and its smaller successor state in the south, the Wu, were mainly interested in the exotica of the region such as aromatics, pearls, rhinoceros horn, and ivory, and by the time that Chinese empires became aware of the full extent of gold and silver resources of the interior of the Li-Lao country, they no longer had sufficient military power to bring them under their own jurisdiction.

The edict from 378 describing what the "Yi of Guangzhou" did with the smuggled copper coins they had procured from the north showed that these people had no interest in copper in the form of coins and wished only to transform them into drums, the status symbols that made sense in the context of their own societies. The spread of excavated bronze drum finds, coupled with the historical extent of the province of Guangzhou, clearly indicates that the people referred to in the edict must have been living south of the Yu River to the west of Canton, inhabiting as far to the west as the Yunkai Mountains, as this was the only area said to be under the authority of the province of Guangzhou during the period of drum production. Use of Chinese coinage between the Two Rivers is not attested in the archaeological record; Han *wushu* coinage has been found in the Han Dynasty tombs close to the coast and the great river courses, but not in the heart of the Li-Lao country, and finds of other coins from the pre-Tang period in the area are also rare.[11] This absence of early Chinese coins probably corresponds to the high level of interest in their raw materials to the prospective Li-Lao drum caster.

However, this lack of interest in copper coinage was not restricted to the Li and Lao; even the people of Jiaozhou and Guangzhou were not properly incorporated into the cash economy of the Southern Dynasties, and preferred instead to trade either in gold or silver or in kind. The importance of gold and silver as currency in the centers of Jiaozhou and Guangzhou is well documented; a geographical work dating from the Jin notes that in the markets of Guangzhou, officials exchanged silver for grain.[12] The *Sui shu* notes that around the time of the foundation of the Liang Empire at the beginning of the sixth century, the provinces of Jiaozhou and Guangzhou were using gold and silver as currency rather than coinage.[13] The same work noted that by the commencement of Chen rule in the second half of the sixth century, the people of the provinces of Lingnan were mostly bartering with salt, rice, and cloth rather than using cash, perhaps an indication of an economic downturn and devaluation of currency in a time of political chaos.[14] In discussion of the records of the use of gold and silver coinage in Guangzhou during this period, it has been suggested that these are evidence for the importance of Guangzhou as the major end point of the maritime silk route and its connection to interregional trade networks, and that the gold and silver arrived there as a result of maritime trade.[15] The immense gold and silver wealth held by Linyi, which offered tribute of tens of thousands of catties of both metals,[16] and the finds of Persian silver coins at Yingde, Qujiang, and Suixi in southwestern Guangdong certainly seem to confirm that this was often the case.[17] There is, however, still an abundance of evidence pointing generally to the lands occupied by the Li-Lao chieftains as the origin of at least some of the gold and silver that was circulated as currency in Guangzhou and Jiaozhou, and even more specifically to the Li-Lao country between the Two Rivers. Gold and silver resources between the Two Rivers were certainly there for the taking; records from the Sui and Tang show a distribution of gold and silver given as tribute that corresponds with many of the areas where concentrations of bronze drums have been excavated. Even in the present day in the same area, gold dust can be found in rivers and gold nuggets are still extracted from the ground.[18] The paucity of early records directly related to the Li and Lao ownership and exploitation of these resources is most likely due to Chinese ignorance of the interior of the Li-Lao country, the extent of which during this period is reflected in the fantastic descriptions of the area and its menacing inhabitants mentioned in chapter 2. It should therefore come as no surprise that the edict of 378 was also incorrect in its assertion that "Guangzhou produces no copper." Although this seems to have been true for the eastern half of the province of Guangzhou around Canton, the western region of the province was in fact extremely rich in copper resources.

Such a statement was probably made out of ignorance, as much of the territory supposedly under the control of Guangzhou was not actually part of the administrative system and was therefore largely beyond the limits of Jin knowledge. South of the Yu River, the component metals for bronze smelting were very easy to find, and the area around modern Beiliu and Yulin where finds of Heger II drums are most concentrated had abundant natural resources of copper. Three drum production sites dating from the Southern Dynasties period have also been found near Beiliu, lying right at the heart of the concentration of Heger II drum excavations and conveniently close to natural resources of copper.[19] Although they are mentioned in the *Han shu*, the copper resources of this area seem to have passed out of the knowledge of the centers of imperial power until they were rediscovered in Tang times.[20] In light of this, similar levels of ignorance regarding the extent of gold and silver resources of the area are not surprising.

Before the sixth century, most of the records of gold and silver in the region come from Shen Huaiyuan's *Nanyue zhi* (Annals of Nanyue) and relate to areas on the edge of the Li-Lao country with which the Chinese were most familiar, namely those close to Canton and the main river courses. Shen Huaiyuan noted that Ningpu was known as the "Golden City" during the Jin because of its abundance of gold,[21] and also that there was a "silver cave" near Suicheng County on the south bank of the Yu River near Cangwu.[22] Sihui County had a Gold Mountain where one could find gold dust, and people who passed by the mountain often saw gold by its side.[23] Another Gold Mountain near Canton produced gold dust and was said to emanate a spirit in the golden figure of a man who was often seen wandering its peak.[24] Gold dust could also be collected from the Kettle Pond (Futang) in Rongcheng County near Cangwu.[25] Gangzhou, a Li-Lao–controlled territory just southwest of Canton, was named after the Gold Hill (*Jin gang*) there.[26]

A fuller picture of the extent of potential gold resources available to the Li and Lao chieftains can be constructed from the various lists of tribute products contained in Tang and Song geographies.[27] The Tang records of tribute in the *Xin Tang shu* (New Book of the Tang) treatise on geography shows tribute of gold from twenty-eight provinces, eleven of which lay completely or partly south of the Yu River in Li-Lao territory before the sixth century.[28] According to the records of tribute in the first years of the Tang contained in Du You's institutional encyclopedia *Tongdian*, almost all of the commanderies south of the Yu River gave a tribute of twenty taels of gold, and Xinxing (present-day Xinxing County in Guangdong) gave fifty. Records of silver tribute from the Li-Lao country are even more common; of the forty-six provinces recorded as giving tribute in silver in the *Tongdian*, twenty-five are in Li-Lao areas south of the Yu River.[29] Although it is possible that some of the gold and silver given as tribute may have been traded into the area from elsewhere, the tenth-century geography *Taiping huanyu ji* records silver as a local product of the provinces of Yulinzhou, Guizhou, Enzhou, and Xinzhou, and silver as a local product of the same provinces with the addition of Hengzhou.[30] The same book provides some extra details from older texts, noting three gold mines near Wuzhou,[31] and that the rebel Lu Xun had collected silver in Xinzhou in the fifth century.[32]

The occupation of lands rich in gold and silver resources is one thing, and the exploitation of such resources is yet another, but the Jin records of the ceremonies given by *dulao* in honor of a new drum suggest very strongly that the Li and Lao had gold and silver to spare, were well aware of their value, and were quite capable of extracting and working them themselves. Shen Huaiyuan recorded that Furen Mountain in Suicheng County south of the Yu River by Cangwu was a Silver Cave (*Yinxue*) where the Li would collect silver dust and smelt it into silver.[33] Feng Ziyou, a seventh-century chieftain of Panzhou (present-day Maoming) who will be discussed in more detail in chapter 7, was also known to be liberal with his gifts of gold and silver and was said to have taken an entire barge full of gold with him to present to the Tang court. With the access to these kinds of resources, we can conjecture that at least from the fifth century onward the Li and Lao chieftains were at a great advantage when trading with the people of the nearby urban areas that relied on gold and silver as their main currency. The extraction of metals would have required a large labor force, and not only would have encouraged competition between the Li-Lao chieftains over territory in which precious metals and copper were to be obtained, but also over the control of populations that could be employed in their extraction of such metals, through either mining or panning.

HUMAN TRAFFICKING AND SLAVERY

The trade in slaves is also attested as an economic activity of the Li and Lao chieftains. Human trafficking out of the Li-Lao country must also have become commonplace in the sixth century, as slaves were noted as one of the benefits that the Southern Dynasties gained through cooperation with the Li-Lao chieftains.[34] Nanhai Commandery was said to have imported slaves from Gaoliang around the beginning of the Tianjian period (502–520).[35] These were probably either people captured in conflicts between different Li and Lao groups and subsequently sold into slavery or those captured in Chinese raids against the Li and Lao. Many imperial administrators of the time treated Li-Lao people as the legitimate plunder of conquest. Such attitudes are apparent from the description of the activities of Xiao Mai, Liang inspector to Guangzhou during the Tianjian period (502–520):

> When he attacked recalcitrant Li, he would take slaves and treasures and keep only what was required for the upkeep of the military, and offer the rest to the throne, unlike other inspectors who would keep hold of such things in order to enrich themselves. Because of this he was considered to be an upright official.[36]

Similarly, Ouyang Wei and his brothers, who oversaw the military affairs of the three provinces of Guangzhou, Hengzhou, and Jiaozhou under the early Chen dynasty (Wei died in 563), is recorded as having supplied slaves, bronze drums, and other rarities to the Chen court during his period of duty.[37] Such activities seem to have been a common pastime of Chen officials; before Emperor Wen of the Sui launched his conquering attack on the Chen in 588, he made an enumeration of their many crimes as justification for the deed, in which he criticized them for their treatment of people of the southwest of their empire, mentioning such activities as annual military attacks and the enslavement of the population.[38] The Chen had no control over Yunnan and little effective control over the Red River Plain at the time, so "southwest" in this context is almost certain to have been a reference to the lands between the rivers.

As far as trade in human beings among Li-Lao chieftains is concerned, it is unlikely that the Li-Lao chieftains would have happily sold members of their own *dong* into slavery, as this would have reduced the potential labor and military force under their own control. It is more likely that they acquired captives through the oft-mentioned warfare with other *dong* and that those surplus to requirements were sold for profit down the rivers to the people of the Chinese-controlled provinces and commanderies. With regard to slave ownership among the leaders of the Li and Lao themselves, seventh-century leader Feng Ang was said to have owned over ten thousand slaves,[39] and it is doubtful that he was the sole slave owner among the powerful class of chieftains.

On an individual level, there were also those among the Li and Lao who would choose to sell members of their own families. Wan Zhen's *Nanzhou yiwu zhi* of the third century CE noted that the Li were not interested in their own flesh and blood, but were greedy for treasures, and that if they saw a merchant with riches or livestock, they would swap their own sons for these.[40] There was also the notorious "pointing at belly sale," whereby a pregnant woman would arrange in advance for the sale of her unborn child to be handed over when the child had reached a certain height.[41] Records of such practices may well have been attempts to dehumanize the Li and Lao by giving examples of their behavior running counter to the strict familial relations that were norms of the civilized behavior for the Chinese, but they do have parallels in later records of similar customs in certain societies of Southeast Asia, where people had become aware that even they themselves had a tradable value as assets.[42]

The exchange of human beings as property among the Li and Lao had various benefits for the chieftains who acquired them. Slaves taken in warfare not only reduced the manpower of one's potential enemies, but were also a useful asset in gaining or maintaining an alliance with the Chinese if transferred on to them, whereas slaves retained as workers would increase the capacity of a *dong* for food production, increase military manpower, and aid the labor-intensive extraction of gold, silver, and ores used in the manufacture of weaponry and status symbols such as the bronze drums.

KINGFISHER FEATHERS

Kingfisher feathers were used to make a blue pigment for jewelry and costume[43] and had been part of the tribute of luxury items from the Two Rivers Region even in Han times, when Zhao Tuo, the king of Nanyue, had presented a tribute of forty pairs of live kingfishers and a thousand dead to the Han court.[44] Kingfisher feathers were frequently mentioned as a special product of the south and probably came from either the white-throated kingfisher *Halcyon smyrnensis perpulchra* or the black-capped kingfisher *Halcyon pileata*. Both of these species have iridescent blue feathers and at present both are still found in the Two Rivers Region. The white-throated kingfisher is more widely distributed than the black-capped variety, which is found year-round only in the coastal regions east of the Leizhou Peninsula.[45] One Southern Dynasties record notes the birds as native to the lands to the south and west of the Li-Lao country in Jiuzhen, Jiaozhi, and Xinggu, but that the people who caught them ate their meat without knowing the value of the feathers.[46] Other locals certainly considered the feathers as treasures; an early text, dating from either Han or Wu times, notes that Wuhu people lived in the mountains and shot kingfishers in order to collect their feathers,[47] and Guo Yigong's fifth-century work *Guang zhi* (Annals of Guang) noted that the people of Jiaozhi and Cangwu had the habit of using kingfisher feathers in turbans, conical caps, or headdresses.[48] Perhaps this was a continuation of the construction of large elaborate headdresses depicted on Heger type I bronze drums and the red ochre cliff paintings at Huashan, in which peacock feathers also seem to have been employed. The kingfisher is an extremely territorial bird; a study of the density of the white-throated kingfisher in the marsh-lands of Bangladesh noted an average of only 4.58 individuals per square kilometer,[49] and although the more sparsely populated lands between the Two Rivers could probably support more highly concentrated populations, orga-nized collection of birds for large amounts of feathers for any purpose would have required a leader to control a wide territory. The trade in feathers with the Chinese would therefore have been another impetus for the expansion of the territory of one's *dong*.

IVORY AND RHINOCEROS HORN

Ivory and rhinoceros horn were two more commonly mentioned luxury prod-ucts from the Two Rivers Region and were two of the products mentioned as sought after by the Chinese empires in exchange for a "temporary appoint-ment." By the fourth century, elephants were still common in the Two Rivers area, and they continued to inhabit isolated areas of the region right up until the eleventh century.[50] Unfortunately, there are few records from the Six Dynasties that deal directly with Li-Lao involvement in the collection and trade of ivory and rhinoceros horn, only those that noted where elephants and rhinoceros were to be found.

From Han times onward, there are records of live elephants being sent to the court in the north, but many of these seem to have come from areas to the south of the Li and Lao, such as Jiuzhen and Rinan. Elephants were known in the Li-Lao country, however, and at one time the use of elephants for riding or warfare was common as far to the east as Fujian, as is attested in the Liang work *Jian'an ji* (Records of Jian'an), which recorded that in ancient times the king of Yue had ridden an elephant to go hunting.[51] In the Taikang period (280–290) after the conquest of Wu, Nanyue sent tribute of tame elephants to the Jin court, and the emperor asked for a huge cart to be built for the elephants to push and for Yue people to ride the elephants,[52] and during the second month of 531, a tame elephant sent as tribute to the Liang court from Nanyue went mad and trampled people.[53] Writers of the Southern Dynasties tend to use Yue and Nanyue to refer to the Yu River drainage area rather than to the Red River Plain, so it is possible that these records refer to elephants from the lands that are now Guangdong and Guangxi. There was also a myth related to the Two Rivers Region recounted over the centuries that elephants shed their tusks annually and buried them in a certain place.

Those who discovered this cache of ivory and wished to keep the supply going would have to make imitation tusks to replace those they had taken, otherwise the elephants would realize this and find a new place in which to hide them.[54] Elephants do not actually shed their tusks more than once in a lifetime and the story of them burying their tusks seems to be a local variation on the well-known tale of the elephants' graveyard, where piles of precious ivory await discovery by adventurous explorers.

As for rhinoceros horn, Wan Zhen noted that huge rhinoceros lived on the sea coast in Ping County in Gaozhou, probably a reference to the area around Enping County in Guangdong.[55] Shen Huaiyuan noted that the Li and Lao of Xinning County (now Xinxing in Guangdong) were skilled at making armor from rhinoceros skin, which they plated with tin,[56] but it seems that by Tang times the wild rhinoceros was already scarce in the Li-Lao country. The *Taiping huanyu ji* notes the presence of rhinoceros only in Yulinzhou,[57] and the Tang tribute in rhinoceros horn is mainly from other areas of the empire such as the present-day provinces of Yunnan, Hunan, and Guizhou. By the Song, rhinoceros horn was being traded by "Jiao people" (that is, people from the former Jiaozhou) at Yongzhou (Nanning) and Qinzhou,[58] so presumably by this time there were few rhinoceros left in the country closer to Canton. As with other products obtained from hunting, a chieftain would have needed control over large tracts of land to be able to collect and send regular supplies of ivory or rhinoceros horn as tribute products.

CASSIA BARK AND OTHER PLANTS

Another product that is likely to have been traded by the Li-Lao was the bark of the cassia or cinnamon tree (*gui*). This tree was native to the Two Rivers area, and its bark was used both as medicine as well as a condiment for food[59] and may have been exported from the region to as far away as India.[60] The fourth-century botanical work *Nanfang caomu zhuang* described its habitat as follows: "The cassia is found in Hepu growing on the top of high mountains. It is always green in summer and winter. The tree forms a pure forest of its own without mixing with other kinds of trees. In Jiaozhi there are established gardens of cassia."[61] The high mountains of the Hepu Commandery of the fourth century lay distant from the flat country on the coast where Chinese settlement was concentrated, so many of these natural stands of cassia undoubtedly lay within the territories of Li-Lao chieftains.

Even the people whom the Chinese texts describe as the most primitive, those said to nest in the trees and eat their food raw, made their living from collecting aromatics for trade with the lowlands,[62] and there are also records of Li and Lao collecting and even cultivating other kinds of plants that grew within their territories. The sixth-century agricultural manual *Qimin yaoshu* recorded that the Wuhu of Jinfeng Mountain[63] were involved in the collection and selling of *jiao* vine (*jiaoteng*), from which a red dye could be produced. This vine was said to come from Xinggu, to the far west of the Li Lao country. There are also two records from the third century CE of people growing tropical fruits highly prized by the Chinese; it was known that lychees were grown in the mountains of Gaoyao County in Cangwu,[64] and that longans were produced in the mountains of Cangwu, Jiaozhi, Hepu, and Nanhai.[65] The early date of these records, coupled with the fact that Chinese settlement was restricted mainly to the riversides and plains, again suggests that these plants were being grown by Li and Lao people.

There was presumably a trade in timber from the mountains downriver as well, but there are few records of this in pre-Tang texts.

TRADE PRODUCTS OF THE SEA

The Li and Lao were not limited to commerce involving sought-after items from mountainous regions; there is also ample evidence that they took part in the collection and trade of products from the sea. There are several early records that refer to trade in products from the sea from Yulin Commandery. Ren Fang's *Shu yi ji* (Records of the Relation of Oddities), a collection of curious anecdotes compiled in the first decade of the sixth century, records:

> In the second year of Yuanfeng [111 CE] Yulin Commandery gave a coral woman as tribute, and the emperor commanded that it be placed in front of the palace and called it "woman coral." Suddenly one morning it burst into branch and leaf, but by the time of Emperor Ling the branches had died, and all thought of it as an omen that the house of the Han would soon perish.[66]

Another quote from the same work relates:

> In Yulin Commandery there is a coral market, a place where sailors can sell coral. Coral is emerald green in colour and grows at the bottom of the ocean, one tree has ten branches, but there are no leaves among the branches, big trees can be five or six *zhi* (feet) tall and even especially small ones are more than one *zhi* (foot) long. Mermaids it is said, have a palace of coral on the sea.[67]

An early-fifth-century work named *Gujin zhu* (Commentaries on the Ancient and Modern) contains two records of pearls coming from Yulin in Han times. In 89 CE, a large pearl from Yulin Commandery was found that was three inches around, and in 103 CE, the surrendered peoples of Yulin had found a large pearl five inches around that they presented as tribute.[68] Liu Mian, the governor of Shian, reported that in 463 auspicious intertwined coral grew in Yulin.[69] All of these records contradict later opinions about imperial administrative geography in the Two Rivers Region in a manner that is highly significant for considering the true extent of the Chinese presence in the lands along the coast of the Gulf of Tongking. Administrative histories state that the territory of the Han commandery of Yulin was never supposed to have reached the sea coast of the Gulf of Tongking, as during Han times jurisdiction of most of this coast, as well as the entire coast southwestward from the mouth of the Yu River, was said to have been the responsibility of Hepu Commandery. The point at which the territory of Yulin Commandery is thought to have come closest to the gulf coast is near the mouth of the Qin River, but the idea that the area around the mouth of the Qin River was once subordinate to Hepu Commandery under the Han traces its origins only as far back as a ninth-century Tang geography.[70] The first administrative unit in the area, the commandery of Songshou founded in the second half of the fifth century, was created as subordinate to Jiaozhou, not to Yuezhou or Guangzhou, suggesting that the area in fact had more to do with the Red River Plain than it did to Hepu. Whether subordinate to Hepu or to Jiaozhi, the consensus of these geographies was that it did not belong to Yulin, which remained a landlocked commandery throughout its six centuries of existence, but the foregoing four records relating to coral and pearls indicate that there was some confusion about its exact boundaries. A probable explanation for this is that there were no fixed boundaries for Yulin, and that long stretches of the Gulf of Tongking lay beyond imperial administration altogether; therefore it was entirely natural that any trade carried out inland from the Gulf of Tongking into the lands drained by the Yu River would be classed as having taken place at Yulin. It is also noteworthy that after the Yunkai Mountains, the second concentrated cluster of Heger II drums is found around the upper waters of the Qin River by the Ningpu Pass, suggesting that any trade that passed into Yulin from the coast would need to have passed through the territory of many rich and powerful *dulao* chieftains. This trade may also have been one of the reasons for their enrichment.

There was no imperial administrative center on the coast between Hepu and the mouth of the Red River until the county of Haiping (in the vicinity of present-day Hạ Long), situated on the coast to the east of Jiaozhi, was founded in the fifth century,[71] and nothing along the coast stretching southwest of Canton down to Zhuyai Commandery on the southern tip of the Leizhou Peninsula. There were only three commanderies at Xinhui (present-day Jiangmen), Gaoliang, and Gaoxing (both close to present-day Yangjiang), up until the late fifth century when a new commandery, also by the name of Gaoxing, was founded by the Qi in the vicinity of present-day Huazhou.[72]

This meant that up until the second half of the fifth century, the imperial presence in most of this coastal region was thinly spread, and that most of the land remained the hands of the Li and Lao. This southern coast produced an abundance of sought-after luxury goods from the sea such as pearls, coral, and cowrie shells,[73] and there is also evidence that there were Li and Lao dwelling along the coast were involved in the collection and trade of these. The most famous product of the sea coast was undoubtedly its pearls. These were a famous trade product even in Qin times, and the rulers of the Nanyue kingdom seem to have had access to vast quantities of them. It was recorded that the tomb of the third ruler of the Nanyue kingdom, Zhao Yingqi (reigned 122–113 BCE), was ransacked by assistant inspector of Jiaozhou Lü Yu by imperial order in 226 CE and contained several barrels of golden silkworms and white pearls.[74] Schafer has already made an exhaustive study of the pearl trade in the Gulf of Tongking,[75] and it remains necessary here only to conjecture how the Li and Lao were involved in this trade. The South Sea coast and Gulf of Tongking certainly had the most abundant pearl fisheries known to the Chinese of the Southern Dynasties, particularly the area around Hepu. Hepu seems to have been able to survive economically from this trade in pearls and relied on the Red River Plain for supplies of rice in exchange for the pearls. Once it was recorded that the pearl supply ran out through overfishing, and that as a consequence the people of Hepu died of starvation on the roads.[76] In the late third century, Tao Huang's report to the throne contained a similar description of the economy of Hepu, noting that the commandery had a rocky soil unsuited for farming, and so the local people did not farm, but only collected pearls, which they traded with merchants for rice. The Wu Empire had forbidden the locals from collecting pearls privately out of fear that they would take the best specimens. This also resulted in starvation, as the local people had nothing to trade for food.[77] Although the imperial authorities could make rulings on pearl collection, these were not always strictly obeyed; the local people were skilled at diving down to collect pearls for themselves, and when officials forbade them from such activity, they would simply dive down and cut the pearl oysters open underwater, secreting the pearls in their mouths before resurfacing.[78] As for those who lived outside the control of the imperial administrations, they were obviously free to do as they pleased, and there is evidence of a pearl trade that was carried on among the people between the Two Rivers, in records of the Wuhu as collectors of pearls and of areas that were said to be rich in pearls but lay far from any imperial administrative seat. Aside from mentioning the Wuhu as keen collectors of kingfisher feathers, the *Jiaozhou yiwu zhi* noted that they also cut open oysters for pearls.[79] Presumably, this record referred to mountainous areas close to the sea coast, perhaps again the area around Qinzhou. The Lao were also said to have used pearls for their own decorative purposes. The book *Guang zhi* (Annals of

Guang) records how the Lao of Zangke, Xinggu, Yulin, Jiaozhi, and Cangwu would stick pearls onto hides to make helmets.[80] The fact that pearls reached these mountainous inland regions suggests an internal trade carried out by the Li and Lao in items like pearls from the coast inland through channels other than the main sea trade and river routes to and from Jiaozhou and Guangzhou. A Tang text records that in Baizhou, east of Hepu, there was a stream known as "Green Pearl Well" (*Lüzhu jing*), where an official in Liang times had gathered three barrels of pearls.[81] In the tenth century, the provinces of Huazhou and Baizhou were still famed for their pearls.[82] Prior to the foundation of Yuezhou in 474, there were no counties or commanderies in these districts, but there must certainly have been Li and Lao living along the coast before this time. The *Nan Qi shu* tells of a Li of Gaoliang to the south of Yuezhou (presumably somewhere along the Leizhou Peninsula) who dredged up a bronze statue of an animal while he was out fishing in 485,[83] and another record from the Tang relates that in Leizhou, along the corners of the coast, the people were still a mixture of Yi and Lao who lived in houses called *lan* (in fact, this is the Tai word for "house" transcribed here into Chinese in the sense of "stilt house")[84] to avoid the frequent pestilences.[85] These texts make it clear that not only were there populations of Li and Lao along the coast, but also that some must have been making their living from fishing. Surely such people would also have been aware of the value those who dwelled inland attached to pearls, coral, and cowries. Another economic activity connected to the sea coast was the collection of shell aromatic (*jiaxiang*). This was a medicinal substance made by the burning of sea snail opurcula and good for preventing stomach aches and diarrhea.[86] The *Taiping huanyu ji* recorded at Hepu that there were Yi people by the name of Yueyi who made their living from the collection of shell aromatic.[87] Much further along the coast, closer to Canton, the people of Enzhou were also said to make their livelihood through its collection.[88]

CULTURAL EXCHANGES THROUGH TRADE INTERACTIONS

There are a few indications that the material culture of the Li and Lao had some influence on the material culture of the Chinese over the long term. These cultural transmissions are mainly related to the use of specific plants and animals, and were probably the result of the trade in such produce into Chinese cities. An additional route for the transmission of cultural knowledge may have been the slave trade, which would have brought populations of Li and Lao into contact with the inhabitants of Chinese cities.[89]

One of the most interesting examples of cultural borrowing is that of the medicinal and culinary use of the python. Two species of python are found in the

Two Rivers Region at present; these are the Burmese or Indian python *Python molurus bivittatus* (Thai *nguu laam*) and the reticulated python *Python reticulatus* (Thai *ngu leuam*). While the latter species does not seem to be present in southern China, it is still found in northern Vietnam.[90] The name, geographical location, and records of use of this python in Chinese texts and spoken language all point to the snake as a probable trade product from the Li-Lao country and the name as a borrowing from their language. The character used to write the name of the python found in old Chinese texts relating to the south is now pronounced *ran*, but according to Pulleyblank's reconstruction, the Early Middle Chinese pronunciation was closer to **ɲiam*. This word first appeared written with the character for "beard" 髯, which led some writers to assume it was a snake that grew whiskers.[91] In the Sinitic languages spoken in the region at present, the python is known by names sounding similar to *naam*, which are usually associated with the written character 蚺.[92] Li Fang-kuei's reconstruction of proto-Tai would give the ancestral form of the word in the three varieties of Tai as **lhiam* or **nhiam*, which is very close to the Early Middle Chinese pronunciation. The first pharmacopeia to note the medicinal use of the snake was the mid-seventh-century manual *Xinxiu bencao* (Newly Amended Materica Medica), which mentioned the medicinal properties of its gall and fat.[93] Modern Chinese pharmacopeia state that the *ran* snake is used for its meat, fat, and gall,[94] and that the gall in particular is used to clear the lungs, stop coughing, stop vomiting, calm the stomach, melt phlegm, and calm someone who has suffered shock.[95] The reticulated python or *ngu leuam* was the one usually used in Thai traditional medicine.[96]

The earliest Chinese record, in the *Huainanzi*, records: "When the Yue people catch a *ran* snake they regard it as the greatest delicacy, but when the people of the central lands (*zhongguo*) catch one they throw it away as useless."[97] The *Shuowen jiezi* of the second century defines it succinctly as "a large snake which can be eaten,"[98] but makes no mention of eating it as a specifically southern custom. An early description from an Eastern Han work notes: "The *ran* is a large snake, not only large but also very long. It is variegated in colour like the pattern of a tapestry; it eats pigs and swallows deer."[99] The *Shuijing zhu* notes how the people of Wuping killed snakes that had recently devoured a meal, with a view to making a meal of it themselves: "When the Yi of the mountains see that the snake is not moving they take large bamboo skewers and skewer the snake through from its head to its tail. Having killed it they then eat it, considering it to be a rare treat."[100] The *Taiping huanyuji* quotes *Jiaozhi ji* (Record of Jiaozhi) as an authority for the following quote about the *ran* snake under the entry on Dragon Cave Mountain (Longxue Shan) in the vicinity of Wuping: "The *ran* snake comes from the south. It is several metres (*zhang*) long. It swallows deer right up to their antlers, waiting for them to digest and rot inside after gulping them down. The

Lao people eat its fat and gall in order to cure all kinds of illnesses."[101] This record of the medicinal use of snake fat and gall by the Lao as medicine suggests, along with the quote from the *Huainanzi*, that the use of the snake for medicine and food was a piece of Li-Lao medical knowledge adopted by the Chinese. The earliest record of its medicinal use by the Chinese dates from the fourth century and recounts the story of a certain Yan Han who wished to cure the sickness of his sister-in-law, who had lost consciousness. A doctor told him to use python gall as a remedy, but he couldn't get it anywhere. Eventually it was delivered to him by a fairy boy wearing green clothes, who gave him a green bag containing some gall, upon which he changed into a bird and flew away.[102] Although this actually predates the piece from the *Jiaozhi ji*, the natural distribution of the python in the south and its borrowed name *ran* both point to the transmission of medical knowledge from the Li-Lao to the Chinese during the early Six Dynasties period.

Descriptions of the snake in Early Medieval texts locate its habitat in the Red River Valley and the three commanderies of Wuping, Jinxing, and Jin'an.[103] Records from the Tang and early Song show a similar distribution. The Tang work *Beihu lu* (Records from the North-Facing Window) records that the four provinces of Guizhou, Hezhou, Quanzhou, and Guangzhou had to alternate in giving a tribute of python gall.[104] In a list of tribute from different Sui commanderies, the Tang administrative encyclopedia *Tongdian* records python gall as tribute from the commanderies of Chaoyang (Chaozhou), Nanhai (Canton), Annan (Hanoi), Gaoliang (Yangjiang), and Haifeng.[105] The *Taiping huanyuji* notes eight provinces as producers of python gall, all but one of them in the Two Rivers Region,[106] and elsewhere in the same book the python is mentioned in connection with Yulinzhou (Yulin).[107] So overall, the records of this snake are limited to the provinces along the southeast coast of China and from the Red River Delta northeastward. The provenance of python gall as a tribute product, the fact that the Burmese python was common in Li-Lao areas, and that the name and earliest records of the snake are all connected to the Li-Lao in some way, indicates that pythons were an important trade product for mountain and forest dwellers who would have known their habitat best.

Clues to a trade in plants, or at the very least the acquisition of botanical knowledge from the Li-Lao, may be seen in the names of forest products found in the oldest botanical treatise on the Two Rivers Region. Some of the plants noted as native to Guangzhou and Jiaozhou in the sixth-century agricultural manual *Qimin yaoshu* are prefixed with the character *gu* (古, Early Middle Chinese pronunciation *kɔ*), which is very close to the proto-Tai numerical classifier for trees and plants, as well as to that used in the Tai languages spoken throughout Guangxi and Yunnan.[108] The *gudu* 古度 tree was mentioned first in the Rhapsody on the Wu Capital,[109] and refers to one of four species of fig tree.[110] This is actually very close to the name of the fig tree in modern Thai *ma deuua*, in which the *ma* is the classifier for trees in place of the *ko* prefix.[111] The earliest word for the cotton tree *Bombax malabaricum* in Chinese is *gubei* 古貝, which was pronounced something like **kɔ-pajʰ* in Early Middle Chinese.[112] Related names such as *faai*, *phaai*, and *waai* survive in most Tai languages.[113] The *gubei* was first recorded in the *Nanshi* (History of the South) as the name of a tree from Linyi,[114] although it had been described earlier in Zhang Bo's third-century work *Wulu dilizhi* (Geographical Gazetteer from the Records of Wu) as *mumian* or "tree thread," a product of Jiaozhou and Yongchang (present-day Yunnan). The phonetic form of the prefix and the word in modern Tai languages suggest that this word was actually borrowed first into a proto-Tai language, and then subsequently into Chinese as a disyllabic word with the Tai prefix for plants added. The cotton plant *Gossypium herbaceum* was first named the *guzhong* vine (*guzhongteng*), recorded in Shen Huaiyuan's *Nanyue zhi* as a product of Fengshui County in Gùizhou, which the Li people would weave into cloth.[115] Other plants with a similar prefix are the citron, known as *gouyuanzi*,[116] and the poisonous gelsemium vine *Gelsemium elegans*. The latter had the Chinese name *yege*, but also had a native name explicitly referenced by Wan Zhen in connection with Li people as *gouwan* or *gouwen*. It was said that the "Li bandits" would eat this vine to commit suicide on the doorstep of someone who had an unpaid debt to their family with a view to getting it paid back.[117]

A further cultural borrowing accompanied by a loan word was the practice of growing living fences of bamboo around settlements as defensive walls. The earliest written reference is from a letter by Liu An (179–122 BCE), prince of Huainan and author of the *Huainanzi*, written to dissuade Emperor Wu from sending troops to attack the kingdom of Min Yue (Fujian). The letter describes, "I have heard that the Yue have no cities, towns or villages, and live in small river valleys in bamboo thickets."[118] Later descriptions of life in the Two Rivers Region make it clear that the people there were not simply living in bamboo thickets; they had cultivated these as protective walls around their settlements. The type of bamboo used for such walls was thorny bamboo (perhaps the species *Bambusa stenostachya*), which went by the Chinese name of *cizhu*, literally "thorny bamboo." This type of bamboo grows in clumps and can reach heights of twenty meters, many branches sprout out from each section, and the lower branches of the plant are hard and thorny. Although *cizhu* is the common term used in modern Mandarin for thorny bamboos, another word exists for these that is peculiar to the Two Rivers Region and is widely used in Cantonese and other southern Chinese languages. This is *lezhu* or *lakjuk* in Cantonese, a name in which the *lak* refers both to the species of plant and alternatively to its thorns.[119] Like the python, the fig, and the gelsemium vine, the word used for thorny bamboo betrays its foreign origin; the Tang writer Liu Xun noted in the ninth century that the southern word for thorns was *le* 勒; this was very likely the ancestral form of the word as it now appears in Cantonese because the character *le* was pronounced **lək* in Early Middle Chinese.[120] The common words for "thorn" in the Tai speech of present-day Guangxi are unrelated: *nam* in the southwest and *wan* in the north, but the ordinary word for "bamboo" is in fact *dok*,[121] a word that Yongxian Luo has reconstructed as proto-Tai **drok*.[122] It is probable that the word was a Tai borrowing, but that the sense of the word was narrowed in Chinese to refer to the distinctive feature of the plant, rather than to the plant itself. The use of this plant had been known for centuries; Tai Kaizhi's manual of bamboo species, the *Zhu pu*, records that it was found in all commanderies of Jiaozhou and that the people there grew it for walls, so that soldiers could not attack them.[123] The habit of growing bamboo in this manner is thus first attested for small settlements of locals who wished to keep imperial troops at bay, but it was soon adopted by the Chinese for the defense of their larger administrative centers. Tang sources record that it was grown as protective walls around the provincial seats of Nan'enzhou,[124] Xinzhou,[125] and Yongzhou,[126] and as a twelve-*li*-long (approximately 4.5 kilometers) city wall of Jiaozhi, then seat of the protectorate of Annam. Here the bamboo was planted at the behest of Protector-General Wang Shi as a defense against the attacks of Man warriors,[127] an interesting twist as technology adopted from the Man was now being used to guard against them.

THE EFFECTS OF TRADE ON LI-LAO SOCIETY

The Li and Lao were fortunate enough to occupy areas of the Two Rivers Region that were rich in the products desired by the people of the Chinese empires. Their leaders were also fortunate that for several centuries the Chinese empires were not capable of an outright conquest of these lands to acquire their products by force. During this period, the Li and Lao traded these products to the people of the Chinese empires and in return they received copper, salt, iron, and alliance agreements that gave them the nominal status of imperial administrators. Alliances for a Li-Lao chieftain presumably had the dual advantage of raising their status among their own people as a great ruler and gaining recognition by the empire as the legitimate ruler of a defined area. The latter would have significantly reduced the possibility of incursions from imperial troops in their own regions. This close trade contact with the Chinese empires throughout the Six Dynasties period seems not to have tamed the Li-Lao leadership, nor were they entirely assimilated through it to Chinese models of behavior. Drums were a symbol of barbarism for imperial administrators, but a symbol of political legitimacy and power for the Li and Lao chieftains who acquired riches in the hope of being able to cast their own.

Even those who lived in the east of the Li-Lao country closer to Canton and further from natural sources of copper in the ground gravitated toward the behavior patterns of the drum-owning Li and Lao chieftains, rather than to the world of the imperial administrators in Canton by choosing to melt copper coins into drums. Aside from the acquisition of copper for drums and iron for weapons, the chieftains of the *dong* would have desired the benefits of recognition as the autonomous and unchallenged leaders of their own people. This in turn would have encouraged competition among them to acquire more territory and manpower with a view to supplying Chinese demands for gold, silver, slaves, and other local products. Those who could supply more would become more valuable as allies to the Chinese empires and would be able to consolidate their own positions among their own people. Trade contacts with the Chinese empires and the political alliances the Li and Lao made with them triggered change in Li and Lao societies, as competition and internal conquests strengthened the Li-Lao leadership, transforming them from the politically fragmented societies composed of small individual *dong* in the third century into the larger conglomerations of many different *dong* under the control of powerful local dynasties that finally appeared in the seventh century.

NOTES

1. JS 26: 11a.
2. HNZ 18: 18a.
3. HS 28b: 36b.
4. QMYS 10: 1b.
5. TPHYJ 169: 6b.
6. Spencer, *Asia East by South*, 322.
7. Peng, "Nanchao lingnan minzu zhengce," 97.
8. Francis Allard, "Interaction and Social Complexity in Lingnan during the First Millennium BC," *Asian Perspectives* no. 33 (1994): 322–24.
9. JS 16: 7b–8a.
10. HS 28b: 36b.
11. See Li Xipeng 李錫鵬, "Xinhui chutu de gu qianbi" 新會出土的古錢幣, in *Zhongguo kaogu jicheng (huanan juan)* 中國考古集成 (華南卷) (Zhengzhou: Zhongzhou guji chubanshe, 2005), 3: 2234–39, and Chen Dayuan 陳大遠, "Guangdong luoding xian faxian jiaozang tongqian" 廣東羅定縣發現窖藏銅錢, *Kaogu* no. 3 (1992): 282–83.
12. GZJ, quoted in TPYL 812: 6a. CXJ 27: 4a has a slightly different version meaning "the officials use silver and grain to trade." This work could be either Pei Yuan's or Gu Wei's *Guangzhouji*; both date from the Jin but the author of this particular fragment is not specified in either source.

13. SuS 24: 20a. The text includes information about what was used for currency in other parts of the empire: use of copper cash was limited to the area around the capital at Jiankang, along the southeast coast, and the provinces along the Yangtze River as far west as Yunnan, whereas the remaining provinces traded using a mixture of grains and silks.

14. Ibid., 24: 21a.

15. Wang Guichen 王貴忱 and Wang Dawen 王大文, "Cong gudai zhongwai huobi jiaoliu kan Guangzhou haishang sizhou zhi lu" 從古代中外貨幣交流看海上絲綢之路, in *Zhongguo kaogu jicheng (huanan juan)* 中國考古集成 (華南卷) (Zhengzhou: Zhongzhou guji chubanshe, 2005), 2: 1067–73.

16. NQS 58: 4b.

17. Wang, "Guangzhou haishang sizhou zhi lu."

18. Zhu Xia 朱夏, *Zhongguo de jin* 中國的金 (Shanghai: Shangwu chubanshe, 1953), 72–73. These are the present districts of Teng County, Rong County, He County, Shaoping, Cangwu, Beiliu, Luchuan, Bobai, Yongning, Binyang, and Shanglin.

19. Yao Shun'an 姚舜安, "Beiliu xing tonggu zhuzao yizhi chutan" 北流型銅鼓鑄造遺址初探, *Kaogu* no. 6 (1988): 558–61.

20. Writing in the twelfth century, Zhou Qufei mentions the abundance of copper resources in the area that is now Guangxi, particularly around what is now Nanning (LWDD ch. 7: 276). TPHYJ 164: 13a records a copper mountain, copper lake, and cinnabar sand to the southwest of Rongcheng County on the south bank of the Yu River. The geography of the *Xin Tang shu* records copper resources between the Two Rivers at a place called "copper mound" (*Tongling*) Qìnzhou, just to the north of present-day Yangchun (XTS 43a: 3a), but mainly to the north of the Yu River at Hezhou and Lianzhou, the present He and Lian Counties (XTS 6b–7a).

21. TPHYJ 166: 14a.

22. TPYL 812: 6a; CXJ 27: 4a.

23. YWLC 6: 4b.

24. NYZ, quoted in TPHYJ 157: 6b.

25. NYZ, quoted in TPYL 74: 1b. The name *Rongcheng* is misprinted as Dancheng 丹城.

26. ZZTJ ch. 190: 969.

27. A study has been made of these: Zhongguo lianhe zhunbei yinhang diaocha shi 中國聯合準備銀行調查室, *Tangsong shidai jinyin zhi yanjiu* 唐宋時代金銀之研究 (Beijing: Zhongguo lianhe zhunbei yinhang diaocha shi, 1944).

28. XTS 43a: 2a–8b. These eleven provinces were Kangzhou, Xinzhou, Qìnzhou, Enzhou, Yongzhou, Héngzhou, Xúnzhou, Qinzhou, Baizhou, Xiuzhou, and Dangzhou. Four provinces from north of the Yu River also gave gold tribute, as did five of the provinces of Hainan, and five from Annam (northern Vietnam).

29. TD ch. 6: 34–38. These were the provinces of Kangzhou, Shuangzhou, Duanzhou, Xinzhou, Panzhou, Chunzhou, Luozhou, Bianzhou, Gaozhou, Yongzhou, Qìnzhou, Enzhou, Hengzhou, Xúnzhou, Luanzhou, Qinzhou, Gongzhou, Tengzhou, Rongzhou, Laozhou, Shunzhou, Dangzhou, Douzhou, Yuzhou, Lianzhou, Yizhou, and Luzhou.

30. TPHYJ 158: 4a–70: 11b. Gold-producing provinces: Enzhou, Xinzhou, Xúnzhou, Chéngzhou, Rongzhou, Yulinzhou, Héngzhou, Danzhou, Yaizhou, and Qiongzhou. Silver-producing provinces: Enzhou, Xinzhou, Guizhou, Liuzhou, Chengzhou, Yulinzhou, Yaizhou, and Fengzhou.

31. TPHYJ 164: 10b.

32. TPHYJ 163: 5a.

33. NYZ, quoted in TPHYJ 164: 12a.

34. The practice persisted well into Tang times. See Schafer, *Vermilion Bird*, 55–56, for a description of the continued Tang trade in slaves from the Two Rivers Region.

35. LS 32: 2b; James K. Chin, "Ports, Merchants, Chieftains and Eunuchs: Reading Maritime Commerce of Early Guangdong," in *Guangdong: Archaeology and Early Texts*, ed. Shing Muller, Thomas Hollmann, and Putao Gui (Wiesbaden: Harrassowitz Verlag, 2004), 228, and Geoff Wade, *The Lady Sinn*, 134, have both construed this passage to mean that the slaves were the goods sold for half price, but it is more likely that the slaves from Gaoliang and the foreign merchant ships are mentioned as two separate sources of wealth, not that the Gaoliang slaves were actually brought to Canton on such ships. Wang Gungwu, *Nan-hai Trade*, 91–92, agrees with my interpretation.

36. NS 51: 4a.

37. CS 9: 6b.

38. QSW 17: 5b.

39. JTS 109: 1b.

40. TPYL 492: 4b.

41. Schafer, *Vermilion Bird*, 56.

42. Concrete records are lacking, but Li-Lao involvement in the capture and trade of slaves from rival groups was perhaps similar to that encountered by Europeans in Southeast Asia a thousand years later, where control over manpower was seen as the important indicator of status and power. For a fuller discussion of slavery in premodern Southeast Asian societies, see Reid, *Southeast Asia in the Age of Commerce*, 129–36.

43. For the many uses to which the kingfisher feathers were put, see Beverly Jackson, *Kingfisher Blue, Treasures of an Ancient Chinese Art* (Berkeley, CA: Ten Speed Press, 2001).

44. HS 95: 12a. In addition to this, he sent ten rhinoceros horns, five hundred purple cowries, a jar of beetles that lived on cassia bark, and two pairs of peacocks.

45. John MacKinnon and Karen Phillips, *A Field Guide to the Birds of China* (Oxford: Oxford University Press, 2000), 95–96, plate 17.

46. NZBJYWZ (an anonymous work that predates the *Qimin yaoshu* of the sixth century), quoted in TPYL 941: 7b.

47. JZYWC, quoted in TPYL 941: 6a.

48. TPYL 687: 3b.

49. A. H. M. A. Reza, M. M. Feeroz, M. M. Islam, and M. M. Kabir, "Status and Density of Kingfishers (Family: Alcedinidae, Halcyonidae and Cerylidae) in the Sundarbans Mangrove Forest, Bangladesh," *Bangladesh Journal of Life Sciences* 15, no. 1 (2003): 55–60.

50. See also Mark Elvin, *The Retreat of the Elephants—An Environmental History of China* (New Haven, CT: Yale University Press, 2004), 9–17.

51. JAJ, quoted in TPHYJ 100: 13b.

52. JS 25: 4a.

53. LS 42: 2b.

54. NZYWZ, quoted in CXJ 29: 3b.

55. NZYWZ, quoted in TPYL 890: 3a. This is impossible unless the text has been altered in some way, as Gaozhou was not founded until the first half of the sixth century. The text is probably referring to Siping County in the vicinity of modern Enping (perhaps Siping is in fact a mistake for Enping, as the first character of the two names is graphically very similar), which dates from Han times. The name was probably redacted at some point from Gaoliang Commandery to Gaozhou.

56. TPHYJ 164: 9b. This Xinning is probably a mistake for Ningxin County, recorded as a subordinate county to Cangwu Commandery in the late fifth century; NQS 14: 21b.

57. TPHYJ 165: 6a.

58. LWDD ch. 5: 195–96.

59. Li, *Nan-fang ts'ao-mu chuang*, 83; Schafer, *Vermilion Bird*, 195–96.

60. Hall, "Economic History of Early Times," 186.

61. Translation from Li, *Nan-fang ts'ao-mu chuang*, 83.

62. LYJ, quoted in SJZ ch. 36: 1138.

63. QMYS 10: 36b. There was a Fengshan Commandery in the northwest of Yuezhou, which contained a county called Anjin. It is probable that this name was garbled from Anjin and Fengshan, as this area was closer to Xinggu and was part of the area where Wuhu lived.

64. WLDLZ, quoted in TPYL 971: 8a.

65. JYYNYWZ, quoted in the poem "Rhapsody on the Wu Capital" (*Wu du fu* 吳都賦), WX ch. 5: 100.

66. TPYL 807: 4b.

67. Ibid.

68. *Gujin zhu* (Commentaries on the Ancient and Modern), a fourth-century work quoted in TPYL 803: 5a. "The surrendered folk" probably refers to people who had submitted to the rule of the Han.

69. SS 29: 42a.

70. YHJXTZ ch. 38: 952. This work was then quoted as an authority in YDJS 119: 1a.

71. Until the foundation of Songshou Commandery under the Liu-Song Empire (in the vicinity of present-day Qinzhou), a trade could have been carried on here without imperial involvement, perhaps up the Qin River passing from the coast into the territory of Yulin before being transferred northward.

72. The name first appears in this context in NQS 14: 27b.

73. NZYWZ, quoted in YWLC 84: 6b with regard to large variegated purple cowries that were found in the South Sea "north of Jiaozhi." WLDLZ, quoted in TPHYJ 170: 5a notes that coral was also a prized product of the area around Jiaozhou and was collected from the bottom of the sea with iron nets.

74. Gu Wei's GZJ, quoted in TPYL 825: 5b. The character "white" (*bai* 白) in this text is corrupted to (*yue* 曰) "to say."

75. Edward Hetzel Schafer, "The Pearl Fisheries of Ho-p'u," *Journal of the American Oriental Society* 74, no. 4 (1952): 155–68.

76. HHS 76: 19a. See Schafer, "Pearl Fisheries," 156–57, for a translation and explanation of the full text.

77. JS 57: 6a–b.

78. NZYWZ, quoted in TPYL 803: 10b.

79. Quoted in TPYL 941: 6a.

80. TPYL 356: 7b.

81. LBLY ch. 1: 2. "Green Pearl" was the name of a woman, however, not of a type of pearl.

82. TPHYJ 167: 8a; 167: 11b.

83. NQS 18: 24a. Gaoliang was actually meant to be under the jurisdiction of Guangzhou, so this is perhaps a mistake for Gaoxing Commandery, which had been made subordinate to the province of Yuezhou.

84. See Li, *Dongtai yuyan*, 239–40.

85. TPHYJ 169: 6a.

86. XXBC ch. 16: 251. Edward Schafer and Benjamin E. Wallacker, "Local Tribute Products of the T'ang Dynasty," *Journal of Oriental Studies* no. 4 (1957): 232, translate it as "plate aromatic."

87. TPYL 167: 4a. This is from an obscure Tang work composed of ten chapters entitled *Junguozhi* 郡國志, the provenance of which I have been unable to trace.

88. TPHYJ 158: 6a.

89. Bryce Beemer has argued for the importance of captured Thai slaves in Burma in the transmission of culture in more recent times, as a case study of a wider, but neglected, field of study. Bryce Beemer, "Southeast Asian Slavery and Slave-Gathering Warfare as a Vector for Cultural Transmission: The Case of Burma and Thailand," *Historian* 71, no. 3 (2009): 481–506.

90. See John C. Murphy and Robert W. Henderson, *Tales of Giant Snakes: A Historical Natural History of Anacondas and Pythons* (Malabar, FL: Krieger, 1997), 10, 14. See also David G. Barker and Tracy M. Barker, "The Distribution of the Burmese Python, *Python molurus bivittatus*," *Bulletin of the Chicago Herpetological Society* no. 43 (2008): 33–38.

91. This explanation derives from the early transcription of the name using a character containing the "hair" radical *biao* 髟, originally reserved for writing a word for "whiskers": *ran* 髥 (HNZ 12: 14a). The form with the "insect" radical *hui* 虫, *ran* 蚺 also appears very early as the form recorded in the dictionary *Shuowen*. TPHYJ mainly uses the "insect" form, but uses the "beard" form once and notes that the snake was so called because of its profuse beard (TPHYJ 159: 3a).

92. From my own personal knowledge. The literary reading of this character in Cantonese is *im*, which would correspond to Early Middle Chinese *ηiam, as the initial *η- (corresponding to Mandarin *j*-) disappears in Cantonese. Bernard F. Meyer and Theodore F. Wempe, *The Student's Cantonese Dictionary* (Hong Kong: Catholic Truth Society, 1947), 151, use the reading *im* and define it as an "edible snake." It is a paradox why the usual pronunciation *naam* seems to be borrowed from the Tai word for a reticulated python, rather than the Burmese variety, when reticulated pythons are not known in China.

93. XXBC ch. 16: 244.

94. Jiangsu yixueyuan 江蘇醫學院, ed., *Zhongyao dacidian* 中藥大辭典 (Hong Kong: Shangwu yinshu guan, 1978–1979), 2109–10.

95. Su Delin 粟德林, *Zhongguo yaowu da cidian* 中國藥物大辭典 (Beijing: Zhongguo yiyao keji chubanshe, 1991), 869.

96. Jean Mulholland notes that in Thailand it is the reticulated python that is usually used for medicinal purposes. Jean Mulholland, *Herbal Medicine in Paediatrics: Translation of a Thai Book of Genesis* (Faculty of Asian Studies Monographs New Series: New Series No. 14; Canberra: Faculty of Asian Studies, Australian National University, 1989), 302.

97. HNZ 12: 14a.

98. SWJZ 13a: 16a.

99. JZYWC, quoted in SJZ ch. 37: 1156.

100. SJZ ch. 37: 1156.

101. TPHYJ 170: 9a. *Jiaozhi ji* is probably an alternative title to *Jiaozhou ji*.

102. This story is contained in JS: 88–8b. According to ZZTJ ch. 95: 3024–25, Yan Han was alive in 338.

103. The last three place names correspond to the hill country north of Hanoi (SJZ ch. 37: 1156), the area around Nanning (Pei Yuan's GZJ, quoted in TPYL 934: 1b–2a), and southern Fujian (NS 70: 15a–b), respectively.

104. PHL ch. 1: 8.

105. TD ch. 6: 34–38.

106. TPHYJ 161: 3a–107: 11a. These are Shaozhou in present-day northern Guangdong and Hezhou, Gùizhou in northern Guangxi, Gaozhou, Yungzhou (Nanning), and Fengzhou in the Red River Plain and the outlier Quanzhou (TPHYJ 102: 3a) in Fujian. Schafer and Wallacker, "Local Tribute Products," 226, note a similar distribution from Tang tribute lists, translating it into English as "whiskered snake bile."

107. TPHYJ 165: 5a.

108. Zhang Junru, *Zhuangyu fangyan*, 794.

109. The Rhapsody on the Wu Capital also contains a reference to a kind of cotton tree called the *julang* (Early Middle Chinese *ku-lang*) from Guangzhou, which possibly contains the same prefix (WX ch. 5: 98).

110. The modern equivalents of all the plant names in this paragraph come from Gao Mingqian 高明乾, *Zhiwu gu Hanming tukao* 植物古漢圖考 (Zhengzhou: Daxiang chubanshe, 2006), 86–87.

111. QMYS 10: 50a–b quotes GZJ and JZJ for the name.

112. The reconstruction is according to Pulleyblank, *Dictionary of Reconstructed Pronunciation*. In later texts, such as the *Ling wai tai ta*, the spelling is *ji-bei* 吉貝 (Early Middle Chinese *kjit-paj^h*), but this was probably a graphical error. Zhou Qufei (LWDD ch. 6: 228) states that it is actually the 古貝 spelling that is the corruption. Paul Pelliot believed it originated in a Prakrit word *karpāi*, descended from an earlier Sanskrit *karpāsa*. See Paul Pelliot, *Notes on Marco Polo: Ouvrage Posthume* (Paris: Imprimerie Nationale, 1957–1973), 1: 429–59. Another form of the word may have arrived through the southern maritime route, the Malay *kapas*, which was also a Sanskrit loan word. See Han Zhenhua 韓振華, *Zhufan zhi zhubu* 諸蕃志注補, Centre

of Asian Studies Occasional Papers and Monographs no. 134, vol. 2 (Hong Kong: Centre of Asian Studies, University of Hong Kong, 2000), 386–94, for a discussion of the many different names of this plant. I believe the loan directly from the Prakrit *karpāi* to be more likely as its phonetic form is a closer fit than *kapas* to the Early Middle Chinese **pajʰ*.

113. According to the principles outlined in Li, *Handbook of Comparative Tai,* the proto-Tai reconstruction would be **fai*. It would have been borrowed into Early Middle Chinese as **pai*. The labiodental fricative *f-* sound had not yet developed in the Sinitic languages in the period under discussion here. Edwin G. Pulleyblank, *Middle Chinese: A Study in Historical Phonology* (Vancouver: University of British Columbia Press, 1983), 68–69.

114. NS 68: 1b.

115. NYZ, quoted in TPYL 820: 6b. The attribution of this quote to the NYZ is suspicious, as Gùizhou was not founded until the sixth century, so perhaps it belongs to a later work (see chapter 4, note 4).

116. Early Middle Chinese **kəw-jwian*. The unrelated word *som* is the ordinary Tai for citrus fruits in the present day.

117. NZYWZ, quoted in TPYL 990: 4b–5a.

118. HS 64a: 3a. The word used for "thicket" here is *huang*.

119. It is also used in the compound *lak wai*, meaning "a hedge." Meyer and Wempe, *Student's Cantonese Dictionary*, 298–99.

120. LBLY ch. 2: 10. The meaning of the character is "bridle," but here it was obviously being used for its sound.

121. Zhang Junru, *Zhuangyu fangyan yanjiu*, 633.

122. Yongxian Luo, "Expanding the Proto-Tai Lexicon—A Supplement to Li (1977)," *Mon-Khmer Studies* 27 (1997): 293.

123. ZP 1: 4a.

124. YDJS 98: 3a. Present-day Enping.

125. LWDD ch. 8: 296–97. Present-day Xinxing.

126. LBLY ch. 2: 10. Present-day Nanning.

127. XTS 167: 9b.

Chapter 7

Last of the Bronze Drum Chiefs

The Rise and Fall of the Great Families

As the preceding chapters have shown, the rise of the bronze drum culture between the rivers was a combination of geography, patterns of trade, and the special relationships between the Li-Lao chieftains and the Chinese empires that enriched the Li and Lao while ensuring they retained autonomous rule over their own territories. The decline of the drum-casting tradition was connected to the end of independent political structures among the Li and Lao. The section on Southern Man people contained in the *Sui shu* describes their demise in the following manner:

> The Southern *Man* people live mixed together with the Hua people. They are called Dan, Rang, Li, Lao, and Yi. None of them have lords, they live in the mountain valleys, and of old they were known as the Hundred Yue. Their custom is to crop their hair and tattoo their bodies. They are fond of fighting with each other, and through this have gradually became diminished and weak and ended up subordinated to the Central States. They were all arranged into commanderies and counties and became the same as ordinary subjects, and no more details of them were recorded. During the Daye period (605–617) over ten countries from the southern wildernesses presented tribute, but these have since all dissipated like wisps of smoke and no more is heard of them. Now only four countries are still recorded.[1]

As the *Sui shu* was completed in 636, this text describes what had occurred over the first decades of the seventh century. Comparing the situation of the Li and Lao in these decades to what it had been in the early sixth century, it certainly would have appeared that they were less powerful than they once had been. The description of their disappearance in the *Sui shu* is typical of the way contact between non-Sinitic peoples and Chinese empires is portrayed in Chinese texts, whereby Chinese administrative control and increased contact

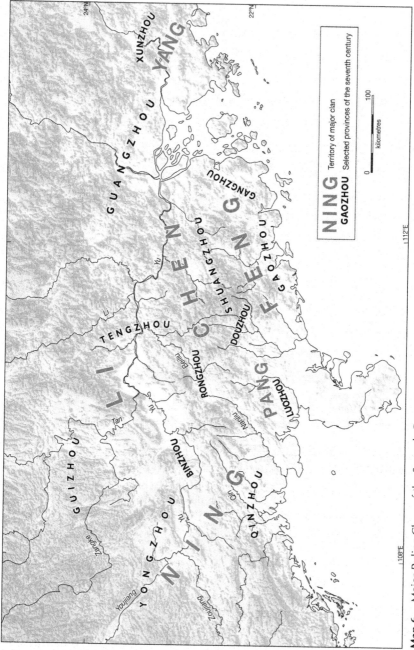

Map 6. Major Ruling Clans of the Seventh Century

with the empires inevitably leads to cultural assimilation, transforming them from named categories of foreigners into ordinary subjects. Although this was the long-term fate of the Li and Lao over the millennium of their contact with Chinese empires from the Han onward, what happened over the short term of three or four centuries between the third and eighth centuries CE shows the opposite process at work. The *Sui shu* declared the indigenous people of the Two Rivers Region to be a spent force, but it seems that this was a premature judgment, as native political structures reasserted themselves in the following century. Schafer's overview of the situation in that century was as follows:

> In the seventh century, native resistance [to the Tang] was concentrated in the western administrations of Jung and Yung, especially in the coastal counties between Canton and Hanoi. The Feng and Ning tribes were always prominent in this resistance, which always threatened the main line of communications through Nam Việt.[2]

The Li and Lao between the rivers were still a match for the Tang, and their political structures in this period differed greatly from those of the preceding centuries in the size of their territories. The small *dong* of previous centuries barely rated a mention as individual polities, and their names were mostly left unrecorded. By the Tang, Li and Lao political power was no longer scattered throughout a honeycomb of small *dong*, but was instead concentrated in the hands of a small number of great families such as the Feng and Ning. The leaders of these families constituted a new class of ruler between the rivers. They possessed Chinese surnames, controlled more or less fixed territories in which they inherited administrative posts, and although they ruled their own people in the manner of the chieftains of old, they also had close connections to the imperial courts and military. The growth of larger conglomerations of Li-Lao political power under these ruling families was the end result of the administrative and economic policies of the Southern Dynasties toward the Li-Lao chieftains, which encouraged them to forge relationships with the empire based on trade, which in turn encouraged them to control larger territories. Their resemblance on a superficial level to other great families, such as the fact that they held Chinese surnames and positions at court, seems at first to back up the narrative of the transformative power of Chinese civilization to assimilate foreigners. However, if one looks at the writings of those who recorded their activities, the members of the ruling class between the rivers were usually not depicted as ordinary civilized people, and were often referred to by ethnonyms such as Man, Li, or Lao that indicated barbarity and foreignness. Like other large and powerful families in other parts of the Sui and Tang Empires, they took part in imperial military campaigns, enjoyed imperial titles and rewards and the favor of the courts, but in the eyes of those who wrote about them, they were significantly less "Chinese" than the administrators in the Red River Plain or at Guangzhou, and this way of looking at them was not altogether without basis. Descriptions of their life in their home territories indicate that some of them owned bronze drums and commanded sizable private armies, and that they still commanded the loyalty of the Li-Lao people in their own home districts in the role of chieftains. Viewed from this angle, they appear to be a continuation of the old Li and Lao ruling class, and their posts as inspectors of provinces were the outcome of alliances with the Sui and Tang, not the result of court appointments. They were an ensconced ruling class who monopolized the politics of their own localities by a prestige derived from the people who lived there, and although their imperial titles and administrative positions afforded them legitimacy at court, it was their position as Li-Lao chieftains in a local context that gave them legitimacy in the eyes of the populace of their respective districts, making them useful allies for the Sui and Tang Empires.

As a consequence of their dual roles, sometimes they were referred to as Man chiefs and Li leaders, and at other times referred to by their official administrative titles, but they were different from the appointed administrators of other provinces and retained a political autonomy of their own. Although some chose arrangements with the empires, some resisted imperial rule and raided neighboring provinces, and some alternated between doing both within a matter of years. They deserve attention not only as the representatives of the last and most powerful generations of local rulers between the Two Rivers, but also because of their ambiguous status that challenges the erroneous idea of fixed distinctions between the Chinese and non-Chinese and of historical boundaries between different minority nationalities that have been written retrospectively into Chinese history.

This chapter gives an overview of the three major ruling families that flourished south of the Yu River throughout the sixth and seventh centuries, concentrating on the rise and fall of those that Schafer mentions as "tribes," namely the Feng who were influential along the coast and inland southwest of Canton south to Hainan, the Ning who controlled the coast of the Gulf of Tongking and inland west of the Leizhou Peninsula, and the Chen family who controlled lands on the south bank of the Yu River. Attention is also given to less well-known groups, smaller ruling lineages whose members controlled smaller territories, such as the Pang, the Li, and the Yang.

HAN OR MAN?

Scholarly discussion in Chinese regarding this group of leaders, and of ethnohistory of the south of China in general, often assumes a division between

"Han" and "Man" or Chinese and barbaric foreigner as if it were concrete and definable based on ancestry, arguing that the portrayal of people from the Li-Lao ruling class as Li and Lao themselves in Tang texts was a case of mistaken identity because they were actually really only "Han" people who had taken on elements of "Man" or Li-Lao culture through living among the Li and Lao for long periods of time.[3]

There are three basic problems with this mode of discussion. The first is the idea that at the time there was any kind of static division between "Han" and "Man" to begin with. The idea of Han itself is an anachronism, having been rarely used in the Southern Dynasties or the early Tang to refer to anyone. As was discussed in chapter 3, the use of ethnonyms such as Man, Li, and Lao for certain groups of people in the Two Rivers Region served mainly as an indicator of perceived difference (and cultural inferiority) in the eyes of those who wrote about them. These were differences based not only on their behavior, but also on their administrative status and place of inhabitance. When writers no longer perceived difference, they would desist in their use of such ethnonyms, but because the cultural and political norms of those who were writing were not static themselves, different writers often expressed different judgments on the people of the same locale in different eras. The absence of a fixed distinction between Chinese and foreign others is obvious from collected descriptions of the great ruling families south of the Yu River. There was little consistency in the way writers applied names to members of the same family lineage, and even the names applied to individuals were not fixed over their lifetimes. The second problem is the habit of uncritically accepting at face value claims of northern or "Han" ancestry found in old Chinese genealogies. It has been shown that many such genealogies in the Two Rivers Region were the inventions of later generations who wished to hide their shameful barbaric ancestry.[4] This is particularly relevant for discussion of the Chen family, whose claim to northern ancestry is absent from the written record until the fifteenth century. The third and final problem is overemphasis on the importance of the paternal line in discussion of the great families to the exclusion of the maternal. Chinese texts seldom elaborate on maternal lineages, and consequently automatically omit half the story of the ancestry of the first generation, potentially three-quarters in the second, and so on. The Feng family is a notable exception to this because of the fame of their matriarch, Lady Xian. If they are counted among the ranks of the "southern-barbarized Chinese" (*Manhua Hanren*), this carries with it the assumption that the Chinese paternal line was a more important part of their identity than their maternal ancestry as Li and Lao, whereas their influence and status in their home region was surely more connected to her status and relationship to the Li and Lao than it was to those of their relatively unknown "Chinese" ancestor.

Each of the three great families discussed below originated in a different manner: the Feng were descended from a strategic marriage between a relative newcomer and a local chieftain and the Ning from a localized family of northern origin, whereas the Chen are most likely to have been of local extraction. Despite the diversity of their origins, all of the families belonging to this class shared several commonalities: they were born out of the centuries-long interaction between the imperial administrations and the local chieftains, they were all visibly close enough to the people they ruled to be described as bronze-drum owning Li-Lao chieftains of the *dong*, and some of their family members still led the life of *dong* chieftains. They also all at some time produced trusted servants of the Sui and Tang courts who were called on for military campaigns in the Korean Peninsula or places closer to home, and in return for their participation, the leaders of the families were given honors and positions at court. The outcome of their interactions with the Sui and Tang over the long term resulted in cultural change that removed some of them from the people they ruled and ended their effective rule over their home districts.

THE FENG OF GAOZHOU

The Feng family is the most well known of all the great families south of the Yu River. This is mainly due to the fame of its matriarch, Lady Xian, or Xian Furen, "Lady of the Land of Qiao" (*Qiaoguo furen*),[5] who has been appropriated over the years in premodern Chinese historiography as a loyal servant of the imperial dynasties, and more recently in Chinese national history as an example of a heroic minority leader who encouraged cooperation and peace between minority peoples and the Tang.[6] Lady Xian and the origins of the Feng family have already been given ample attention elsewhere in English,[7] so the following goes into detail only about her activities as they relate back to her Li-Lao ancestry and how this ancestry affected the status of her descendants. Lady Xian's biography describes her tribe as having over one hundred thousand households and states that over a thousand *dong* in Hainan and Dan'er had given her their allegiance.[8] From such descriptions, it is obvious that her leadership was based on her role as a member of the Li-Lao ruling class rather than as a bureaucrat employed from the imperial court.

Lady Xian was a native of Gaozhou and was described in the *Xin Tang shu* (New Book of the Tang) as the daughter of a great Yue ruling family.[9] She married the Chen governor of Gaoliang Feng Bao, son of Feng Rong, the former inspector of Luozhou, a province founded during the Dàtóng period (535–546) for the Liang. Successive strategic alliances with the Chen (through marriage), and then with the Sui and Tang courts, rewarded Lady Xian's descendants in the

Feng family line with material goods and an enlarged political domain, and gave the empires the ability to keep a large population in the lands south of the Yu River and southwest along the coast from Canton on their side without having to be involved in large-scale military conflict with them.

In Lady Xian's own lifetime (c. 512–c. 602), she and members of her family were awarded increasingly higher positions in government over an ever-expanding territory. Originally the land under the direct authority of the Feng was confined to the Gaozhou area, but in reward for her loyalty to the northern courts, members of Lady Xian's family were granted control over the northern end of the Leizhou Peninsula at Luozhou, and in 590 her son Feng Pu was made commander of Yaizhou on Hainan,[10] where a branch of her family continued to rule as a hereditary dynasty for the following two centuries.[11] Lady Xian's family was given the title "Defenders of Yangchun Commandery," and her grandsons Feng Ang and Feng Xuan held the posts of inspector of Gaozhou[12] and Luozhou, respectively.[13] Details of the influence Lady Xian had over other local chieftains in the Pearl River drainage area are apparent from her biography in the *Sui shu*: in late 590, after quelling an uprising by another Li commander known as Wang Zhongxuan who lived closer to Canton, Lady Xian took the Sui imperial envoy Pei Ju to visit four other Li commanders from the lands to the west and north, who were recorded as having met with Lady Xian and having taken her command "back to their tribes" (*buluo*),[14] a wording that shows that these people were perceived as belonging to the world of the *dong* chieftains rather than as administrators for the Sui.

Lady Xian's grandson Feng Ang is a fascinating figure and more records exist about him than any other of her descendants. The details of his life exhibit precisely the kind of ambiguity of the role between "people" and "Man" that is evident from the more scattered references to other local ruling families. At the beginning of the Renshou period of the Sui (601–605), in his guise as an ordinary local official, he became the magistrate of Songkang County (present-day Yangjiang). At this time, the Lao of five provinces, including Chaozhou and Chengzhou (close to present-day Wuzhou), rose in resistance, and Ang hastened to court requesting to be allowed to attack them. He was instructed to mobilize imperial troops from Jiangnan and local troops from Lingnan to carry out the attack, and after he had defeated them he was appointed to the governorship of Hanyang (now Wuhan), far outside his native district.[15] A few years later, Feng Ang went with Emperor Yang of the Sui to take part in the attack on Liaodong (Korea), holding the title of senior militant general over the period from 611 to 614. His positions and activities make him appear just like any other loyal Sui official, but others had a different way of viewing him. When Emperor Wen of the Sui sent Ang to go and discuss the layout of the Lao rebels with him, the court official senior supervisor Yang Su gasped in amazement at his abilities, exclaiming, "I had not expected that this man could be born among the Man and Yi."[16] Yang Su's comment was not based merely on a prejudice against southerners; the fact was that despite his ordinary position as governor of Hanyang, Ang still retained an alternate identity back in his home territory of Gaozhou as a chieftain (*qiuzhang*).[17] In the last year of the Sui (618), when the empire began to disintegrate, Feng Ang hastened back to the safety of his native country where he still held a great degree of influence. The *Xin Tang shu* reports that back on his home ground he was able to summon together many chieftains as well as an army of fifty thousand people.[18]

Like his grandmother, Feng Ang chose to cooperate with the imperial system and did not seem to have been interested in seeking complete political autonomy. In the fourth month of 618, before Tang rule was established at Chang'an, Ang had control over the districts of Cangwu, Gaoliang, Zhuyai, and Panyu, but soon made an alliance with Lin Shihong, who looked to be the prospective founder of a new dynasty.[19] Feng Ang's loyalty to Lin Shihong soon faltered, however. In 620, he moved against Gao Facheng of Panyu and Xian Baoche of Xinxing, two "rebel commanders" who had received orders from Lin Shihong to kill the remaining Sui officials in their respective areas. Ang defeated their forces once, but Xian Baoche's nephew Zhichen regrouped at Xinzhou to fight again. What won the final victory for Ang was the reputation he commanded among the people of the south. At the commencement of his second battle, he took off his helmet to show his face, shouting to the enemy forces, "Don't you recognize me?" at which point most of them dropped their weapons, stripped to the waist, and made obeisance to him.[20] After dispersing Xian Baoche and Zhichen's followers, he was able to capture them and other leaders, and in doing so he brought the lands of Panyu, Cangwu, and Zhuyai (Hainan) back under his own control, giving himself the title of area commander-in-chief (*zongguan*). In this period following the collapse of the Sui but before the Tang had consolidated enough power in the north to influence the politics of the Two Rivers Region, Feng Ang was effectively an autonomous ruler. An advisor well versed in the history of the Two Rivers Region made a suggestion to Ang to recognize this by taking a title. The advisor suggested the following:

> The last of the Sui has fallen, and all within the seas is in upheaval. Although the Tang has risen to meet the challenge, its authority has yet to spread to Nanyue and the region is still not yet at peace. You, my lord, have already overcome more than twenty provinces. That is much more than the nine commanderies of Zhao Tuo! You should request to be given the title of king of Nanyue.[21]

To this advice, Ang replied:

> We have lived here in Nanyue now for five generations, and only those of our own household are appointed as the local dignitaries. I have sons and daughters, silks and jades. It is no easy thing to be able to lead such luxurious life as this. I am always fearful that I will not be able to bear the burden of this and will let my inheritance be destroyed. The clothes and brocades of this province are already sufficient. What would I want with requesting anything else in addition? I won't hear of the title of King![22]

Although he did not choose to follow the example of the Qin general Zhao Tuo in proclaiming an independent kingdom, Feng Ang was still the last leader of the Two Rivers Region to openly proclaim allegiance to the new Tang Empire, and it was not until the seventh month of 622 that he finally did so, an action that was described in his biography as "surrendering the multitudes of Nanyue" to the Tang. After this, Tang emperor Gaozu divided Feng Ang's sphere of influence into the eight provinces of Gaozhou, Luozhou, Chunzhou, Bozhou, Yaizhou, Danzhou, Linzhou, and Zhenzhou,[23] and Ang received the titles of Supreme Pillar of State, Commander-in-Chief of Gaozhou and Luozhou, as well as the additional title of "Duke of the Princedom of Wu" (*Wuguo gong*), a title that was soon altered to the more geographically appropriate "Duke of the Princedom of Yue" (*Yueguo gong*). Emperor Gaozu also promoted Ang's sons Zhidai to the post of inspector of Chunzhou (present-day Yangchun in Guangdong) and Zhiyu to the post of inspector of East Hezhou (Dong Hezhou, a province that administered the larger part of the Leizhou Peninsula).[24] Such promotions and titles can be seen as a continuation of the policy of earlier dynasties of giving official titles to the members of local ruling families and recognizing their power within their own spheres of influence, but what made Feng Ang different from earlier local rulers from between the rivers was that he had also served an imperial dynasty as an official and soldier far from his native district. Through allying himself to the Tang, he and his family members gained control over a much larger territory than any of his ancestors had ruled, stretching from Canton westward along the coast to Hepu and south to Hainan.

After a few quiet years, Ang's loyalty to the Tang was brought into question at the beginning of the Zhenguan era (627–650), as the court received word that he had rebelled. Initially, Emperor Taizong summoned General Lin Mu and ordered him to lead the best troops from the Yangtze and Huai River regions southward to attack Ang, but he was dissuaded from this plan by an official named Wei Zheng, who remonstrated against military action, proposing instead to gain Ang's loyalty through virtuous means. As a result of this advice, Ang's son Zhidai was sent to court as an ambassador to the emperor.[25] Through this, the Tang court obtained a potential hostage by whom they could ensure Ang's loyalty, and Zhidai gained a paid post at court. To the

Sui, Feng Ang had been a trustworthy administrator and soldier outside his own district, but by the early years of the Tang he had become comfortably ensconced back in his home district with his own armed forces and the court was therefore reliant on his assent for peaceful control of the area. In the early days before Tang power was properly consolidated, the loyalty of a local leader such as Ang was a necessary expediency; the reasons behind Wei Cheng's remonstrance to the emperor against using military force to subdue Ang were not only because the reports of Ang's rebellion were unproven rumor, but also because it was not certain that the Tang troops would return victorious.[26]

In the words of Schafer, Feng Ang was "given the opportunity to prove his loyalty to the Tang"[27] in 631, when he led troops against the Lao people of two *dong* named Luo and Dou. As it turned out, this test of loyalty provided more benefits for Feng Ang than it did for the Tang court, as the following description shows:

> In the fifth year of the Zhenguan period (631), Ang came to court and was treated to many feasts and given many gifts. Suddenly the Lao of the Luo and Dou *dong* rebelled and Ang was ordered to lead 20,000 men to be the vanguard force to attack them. The bandits occupied strategic spots so they could not be attacked. Ang grasped his crossbow and told those around him, "As I use up all of my arrows, so shall you know if we are to win or lose" and he let off seven arrows in succession, striking seven people. The bandits all fled, and Ang released his soldiers to take advantage of this; they took over a thousand heads. For this it is noted that the emperor praised his merit, and before and after this bestowed on him uncountable rewards.[28]

At the same time, as he made war on smaller chiefdoms like the Luo and Dou *dong* in the name of the Tang, Ang was also eliminating potential competition in his own neighborhood and expanding his influence to the west, in addition to enriching himself with gifts from the Tang court.[29]

The *Xin Tang shu* records Ang's government in glowing terms: "He was good at government, and examining documents and was the best at catching wicked people. He humbly accepted his people's joyousness."[30] This agreeable description of Ang's administrative activities makes him out to be a loyal servant of the Tang, and yet descriptions of his lifestyle indicate that his relationship with the Tang court was also very much suited to his own purposes. Just like his famous grandmother, and many of the Li-Lao chieftains who preceded her, Ang made a decision to make an alliance with a northern empire. This did not result in a loss of his and his family's de facto power over their own region, but instead broadened and cemented it; in his own district, Feng Ang was more like a king than a governor. It was reported that he had armies of thousands of his own troops, controlled over two thousand *li* of territory (approximately 600 kilometers), and owned over ten thousand slaves.[31] Ang must have also been able to support many wives and concubines, as over his lifetime he managed to father thirty sons.[32] The awe in which he was held by ordinary people in his district and the reaction of local troops to the sight of his face are also testament to his great *mana* over the people of the area and his status as a powerful local chieftain. In the context of his own region, Tang administrative titles would have been merely ceremonial, as the power he wielded over his subjects was different from that held by the ordinary appointed governors to provinces in other parts of the Tang Empire. It was for these reasons that despite his years of loyalty and service to the Sui he was referred to regularly as a "chieftain" or "leader," and by Yang Su at court as a "Southern Man" (*Nan Man*). Significantly, his background and status resulted in his biography being relegated to the end chapters of the *Xin Tang shu* alongside the biographies of other non-Chinese rulers from the south.

Feng Ang's most famous son, Feng Zhidai, also received praise from the compilers of the *Xin Tang shu*, who recorded that he was brave and skilled in strategy, able to soothe crowds, devoted all his might to his official duties, and that chiefs and leaders (wording that refers again to Li and Lao chiefs and rulers, not to imperial bureaucrats) were all happy to be his subordinates.[33] Earlier in his life, Zhidai had a long residence at the capital serving the Sui Empire, and it was said that when he accompanied his father to Loyang, he led the best soldiers from his tribe to stand on night watch duty in the palace. When Emperor Yang, the last emperor of the Sui, was killed in a mutiny by imperial troops in 618, Zhidai hurriedly left the capital for his home district with the troops under his command. At that time, it was said that there were many robbers and bandits, that the roads over the passes were blocked, and that Zhidai had to frequently turn and fight while he made his advance southward. When he finally reached the pass at Gaoyuan, close to present-day Xinyi,[34] the Li commanders Zhidai was leading began to plot against him and held him captive, and it was only after his father Feng Ang arrived on the scene that Zhidai was permitted to leave with him. The significance of the location of Gaoyuan Pass is that it lay within the territory of the Luo and Dou *dong*, the same area that Feng Ang would be ordered to attack by the Tang thirteen years later in 631. Because some of the Li commanders who plotted against Feng Zhidai had originally been part of his retinue at Luoyang, it is probably the case that Feng Ang did not attack these two *dong* merely to subdue local resistance to the Tang, but that the attack was part of a longer local power struggle. Feng Ang's attack and successful defeat of the Luo and Dou *dong* was a conquest of local Li leadership who had previously exhibited questionable loyalty to his family. Later, when Zhidai attended the Tang court with his father, his meeting with the emperor is described as follows:

The Emperor rewarded them with gifts and promotions, making Zhidai Lesser Chief Minister for the Palace Garrison (*weiwei shaoqing*). Having heard of his soldiering skills the Emperor pointed at the clouds, asking "if there are rebels underneath this kind of cloud, could we attack them now?" To this Zhidai answered "The cloud is in the shape of a tree, and at the moment it is the hour of metal; the sharpness of metal overcomes the softness of wood, which means if we attack we will win." The Emperor was surprised at his response and advanced his rank to left-hand militant general (*zuowuwei jiangjun*). When he died he was given the posthumous title Commander-in-chief of Hongzhou.[35]

However, despite his relationship to the Tang court and his military honors, Feng Zhidai's biography sits with those of foreign peoples with his father's near the end of the *Xin Tang shu*.

The thirty years following Feng Ang's proclamation of loyalty to the Tan was the time of greatest influence for the Feng family, both at court and in their own territory. A year after Feng Ang's death in 649, the unquestioned supremacy of his branch of the family began to fade, as the Tang split Gaozhou into the three new provinces of Gaozhou, Enzhou, and Panzhou. In his study of the Xian and Feng families, Wang Xingrui has argued that this was an attempt to split up the concentrated power of a single member of the Feng family over such a large area.[36] Presumably the Tang had not dared to do this while Feng Ang was still alive. Ang's two sons Zhigui and Zhidai and his nephew Ziyou were made inspectors of each of the three new provinces, respectively,[37] so despite the split into smaller provinces, control of the larger area was still at least officially recognized as being in the hands of the Feng clan. Apart from Zhidai, Zhiyu, and Zhigui, Feng Ang's other sons whose names are recorded were Zhiji and Zhishi,[38] and a Tang official named Xu Jingzong married his daughter to one of these five, but it is unclear to whom.[39] By the time Feng Ang's grandson Feng Junheng died in the Shengli period (698–700) of the Tang, political power in the Gaozhou area had passed out of the hands of the Feng. Although Junheng's son was sent to Chang'an as an official, there was also an element of coercion and control on the part of the Tang, as this son was made a eunuch and was made to abandon the surname Feng, taking the name of Gao Lishi.[40]

Judging by their activities at court, the Feng appear to be loyal servants of the Sui and Tang who became increasingly acculturated to the norms of imperial bureaucratic and military life over the seventh century to a point when they were no longer viewed as barbaric by members of the imperial government, meaning they could marry into official families, meet with emperors, and were trusted enough to serve as palace guards. However, through this process of acculturation, the main branch of the family seems to have gradually lost its privileged position and influence in its home district, and by the beginning of the eighth century the Tang was no longer dependent on their cooperation for control of the lands between the Two Rivers. Other branches of the Feng family fared differently and continued to have influence over pockets of the country southwest of Canton. Even as late as the second half of the eighth century, some members of the family ruled as local leaders (rather than appointed administrators) southwest of Canton, and for even longer on Hainan, but it was never again that the power and influence of a single family member was spread over such a large area as it had been under Feng Ang and Lady Xian.

Although the main branch of the Feng family was increasingly involved with the Tang court, throughout the seventh century individual members of the Feng family continued to play the role of Li-Lao chieftains southwest of Canton. Records of the deeds of Feng Shihui and Feng Ziyou give us an indication of their status as chieftains of *dong*. Feng Shihui held the post of inspector of Gangzhou, a province administering the lands between Canton and Macau, and in the seventh month of 623 he rebelled against the Tang at Xinhui. Shihui's precise relationship to Feng Ang is unknown, but a Feng Cenweng was noted in Lady Xian's biography describing events four decades previously as a local leader of Gangzhou,[41] which suggests that Shihui belonged to a different branch of the family that had made its home in that province. The outcome of his rebellion was that inspector of Guangzhou Liu Gan attacked and defeated him, but then immediately restored him to his post of inspector.[42] His restoration to this administrative post after leading a rebellion suggests that it was either not possible or not prudent for the Tang to remove him from his position because of the power of his local connections, and that it was instead necessary to come to some agreement with him.

Feng Ang's nephew Ziyou flourished in the middle decades of the seventh century, and despite prolonged contact between his family and the Tang court and his investiture as inspector of Panzhou, he definitely belonged to the world of the Li chieftains rather than that of the Tang bureaucracy. Details of his life are related in Feng Ang's biography in the *Xin Tang shu* as follows:

> He was famed for his military prowess. During the Zhenguan (627–650) period he went to court, taking with him a barge of gold. During Gaozong's time [628–683] the royal scribe Xu Huan was sent to see his riches. When Huan reached the *dong*, Ziyou didn't come out to welcome him, but afterwards he led tens of his sons and younger brothers to beat bronze drums and line up around him and he then held Huan hostage and told him he was at fault. The Emperor dispatched Yang Jing as ambassador to examine the situation. When Jing arrived he resolved the problem through humble use of words, saying that it was Huan who was to blame for the trouble. Ziyou was so happy he gave him two hundred taels of gold and five hundred of silver. Jing would not accept it, so Ziyou said

"If you don't take this, then I shan't let you leave." So Jing took it and returned with his report, and the emperor commanded that it be accepted.[43]

This passage shows that members of Feng Ang's extended family were not nearly as close to the world of the Tang court as might be expected from Feng Ang's position as administrator and their own northern ancestry. Not only did his relative Ziyou live in and control a *dong*, he was also the owner of many bronze drums and had plenty of gold to give away, and thus resembled the descriptions of the *dulao* chieftains of earlier centuries. Early on, Ziyou seems to have treated the representatives of imperial authority with disdain, but later in his life he was a keen participant in the army that accompanied Cao Xuanjing in the name of the Tang to suppress the uprising of Lý Thúc Hiến in the Red River Plain in 687.[44] Even so, from the recorded details of Ziyou's life it is obvious that despite a northern ancestry and a military campaign for the Tang court, he was not considered an ordinary general or administrator. Ziyou is mentioned elsewhere as a "leader of Gaozhou" (*Gaozhou shouling*),[45] a "chief of Gaozhou" (*Gaozhou qiuchang*),[46] and a member of a great clan (*dazu*) of Guangzhou,[47] terms that confirm he was still functioning at home as a chieftain within the societal structure of the Li and Lao *dong*.

Aside from the gradual breakdown of their consolidated power through administrative reform, the eventual disappearance of the Feng as hereditary local rulers in the eighth century was also probably related to their involvement in later uprisings against the Tang. First, a leader from Guangzhou, Feng Renzhi, took part in the 728 uprising organized by a member of the Chen family against the Tang (discussed shortly), in which he took the title "King of Nanyue."[48] His involvement almost certainly had adverse consequences for his family's status in the eyes of the Tang and would have resulted in the deaths of many of his subjects.

A further uprising involving the Feng was in the 760s, in a period of wider unrest that lasted from 756 to 771.[49] The *Zhizhi tongjian* (Comprehensive Mirror of Government) records that the "bandit commander" (*zeishuai*) of Panyu, Feng Zhongdao, and rebel general Zhu Jishi of Gùizhou and others blocked off the *dong* and caused unrest that spread over ten provinces. The Tang army attacked them for successive years, but was unable to overcome them until they were finally defeated and killed by the combined force of generals Li Guan and Wang Hong in the third month of 771.[50] The motives for such uprisings are seldom noted in Chinese texts, but it is interesting that the last two members of the family involved in uprisings are again labeled "commander" or "bandit commander," indicating that they held de facto power over their people but were not recognized as legitimate leaders by the Tang. So even in the late eighth century there were members of the Feng family who retained positions of power outside the Tang administrative system, and were still connected to the world of the *dong*. It is reasonable to hypothesize that such friction between the Feng and the Tang came about because members of the Feng family felt aggrieved that the Tang was encroaching on their territory and prerogatives, and that they were increasingly being excluded from local administrative positions in their home area through replacement of their family members by officials appointed by the court, as was the customary practice in the other regions of the empire. Whatever the reasons for the rebellions, the consequence of their involvement was that the Feng ceased to be a local dynasty on the mainland and no they longer appear as local leaders in the Gaozhou area in records after the 770s.

THE NING FAMILY OF QINZHOU

To the west of the Feng territory, the Ning family controlled the land drained by the Nanliu and Qin Rivers from the late sixth century for at least one and a half centuries. It was this family that controlled the route through the Ghost Gate Pass to the Red River Plain, allowing the Tang access in 622. Schafer was convinced that the Ning were a local indigenous group,[51] which is not surprising because the same opinion was held by most of their contemporaries who wrote about them. The *Xin Tang shu* describes the Ning family in two separate entries, one as Lao of Nanping, a name for the upland country where the Two Rivers have their source to the west, and the other as Man of the Western Plains (*Xiyuan Man*), which referred to the flat country around the Zuojiang and Youjiang Rivers. The first entry explains that the family was "great leaders of Nanping"[52] and the second that they were the local strongmen (*hao*) of the lands south of Guangzhou and Rongzhou and west of Yongzhou (Nanning) and Gùizhou (modern Liuzhou).[53] In this book and other old texts, the members of the Ning family are ambiguous in status, appearing both in the role of literate and cultured officials and as Li-Lao chiefs like the Feng.

The most notable members of the family in the late sixth century exemplify this ambiguity. Details of Ning Mengli's (553–c. 601) life appear in the biography of a military official named Linghu Xi in the *Sui shu*: Mengli was said to have been born on the same day as the second Chen emperor Chen Shubao, and in Chen times he controlled the region along the South Sea (presumably the Gulf of Tongking). He was given the post of inspector of Anzhou as a pacification measure by the first Sui emperor after the conquest of the Chen Empire in 589.[54] The use of the verb *fu* in the *Sui shu* that I have translated as "pacification measure" suggests that the appointment was recognition of his de facto power over Anzhou rather than the result of an appointment by the court. When the Sui abolished provincial administrations in the newly conquered territories of the Chen Empire and replaced them with commanderies, they gave the name "Ningyue Commandery" to the territory around present-day Qinzhou and up the Qin River, but the Ning appear to have retained autonomous rule over the area.

In the *Sui shu* it was written that the appointment as inspector of Anzhou made Mengli arrogant so that he relied on his remote and strategic position to maintain his independence, and as a result would not go to pay homage to the emperor.[55] A later record suggests a different reason for Mengli's refusal to attend court: the propitious date of his birth apparently led him to delusions of grandeur and he believed that he should replace the last Chen emperor as the Son of Heaven, adding that the swamp miasmas of the region did an effective job of keeping the Sui troops out of his domain.[56] Linghu Xi managed to persuade him to change this attitude. Xi was the commander-in-chief of Gùizhou and oversaw the military affairs of fourteen provinces in the Two Rivers Region, probably all those to the west of Canton.[57] He came to befriend Mengli by writing to him and sending him medicine for his sick mother.[58] The *Sui shu* also relates how Mengli later came to be on friendly terms with the Sui court through his relationship to He Chou, a general sent to quell an uprising of various leaders in the Two Rivers Region in the last years of the Kaihuang Era (581–601):

> The inspector of Qinzhou, Ning Mengli led a host to meet [He Chou's] army. Initially Mengli had obstinately held out in his *dong* in the mountains and had the intention of rebellion, but by this time he had become fearful, and he requested that he might be able to visit court. He Chou considered his haste as an indication of his honesty and a sign that he had no intention of betrayal, and upon sending him back to his province [He Chou] made an agreement with him saying that he would be summoned to the capital within eight or nine months. He Chou returned and reported this to the throne, but the emperor was not pleased. However in the tenth month of that year Mengli died, and the emperor said to He Chou "You didn't bring Mengli with you before, and now he has died." He Chou replied "Mengli had an agreement with me, and if it is the case that he has now died, then we ought to summon his son to come and attend court. The Yue people are upright in character, so his son will surely come." Before, when Mengli was about to die, he had instructed his son Changzhen "I made an agreement with an official, and one must not lose the trust of officers of the state. Once I am buried, you must start the journey to the capital." Changzhen did as instructed and went to court. The emperor was delighted and said "this was only achievable through He Chou gaining the trust of the Man and Yi" and for this honour he bestowed upon He Chou the post of commander.[59]

It is already evident from these texts that Mengli had multiple identities. He held an administrative position as inspector of Anzhou (the name of this province was changed at the request of Linghu Xi to Qinzhou), and yet he lived in a *dong* in the mountains. It seems he was literate in Chinese, and yet He Chou called him a Yue person and the Sui emperor lumped him in with the Man and Yi of the south.[60]

Mengli's son Changzhen was a contemporary of Feng Ang and has a similarly ambiguous status that vacillates somewhere between an official and Li commander. In the first month of 605, he was sent in his official capacity as the inspector of Qinzhou to accompany General Liu Fang and Li Hun, governor of Huanzhou, on an unsuccessful expedition to plunder Linyi of its rare treasures.[61] Like Feng Ang, Ning Changzhen also led "several thousands of his tribe" on one of the Sui campaigns against Liaodong on the Korean Peninsula in the period from 611 to 614. As a reward for this, the second Sui emperor (Yang) summoned him to court and sent him home with the honorary titles of Chief Ceremonial Minister (*honglu qing*) and Commander-in-Chief of Pacification (*anfu dashi*) and appointed his relative Ning Xuan as governor of Hepu.[62] A few years later, during the same period of political turmoil in which Feng Ang had enjoyed autonomous rule between the downfall of the Sui and the consolidation of Tang power, Changzhen became the most influential leader in the west of the Two Rivers Region. As he heard of the fall of the Sui, he was said to have led several provinces and counties of Lingnan to give their allegiance to Xiao Xian, a descendant of the Liang royal house who at the time appeared to be the prospective new emperor, and who in 618 declared himself emperor of a restored (but ultimately short-lived) Liang empire.[63] In the same year, Xiao Xian sent an envoy to Qiu He, governor of Jiaozhi, who refused to recognize him as he was not yet aware that the Sui Empire had been overthrown. Xiao Xian had heard that the lands to the west of Linyi sent Qiu He a tribute of pearls, patterned rhinoceros horns, and golden treasures, and that He had become wealthy as a king from this. Desiring these precious things he ordered Ning Changzhen to lead a force of the Hundred Yue over the sea to attack Qiu He.[64]

In the campaign against Linyi in 605, Changzhen took part in leading a larger force of over ten thousand, but how many were directly under his control during the campaign against Qiu He in the Red River Plain is not mentioned. However, by the time of his attack on Jiaozhi it appears that he had his own standing army as well as the ships required for its transport to Jiaozhou. The size of his force also seems to have been comparable to that under the command of Qiu He for the defense of the Red River Plain, as Qiu He had to be talked out of surrendering to Changzhen by his administrative clerk Gao Shilian, who assured him that although Changzhen was leading many soldiers, they would be fatigued from the long journey and would not be able to keep up the fight for very long.[65] When referring to his attack on Jiaozhou, the *Jiu Tang shu* (Old Book of the Tang) refers to him as "Ning Changzhen of Qinzhou," but in the *Xin Tang shu* description of the same event he is called a "Li commander" (*Lishuai*). In the summer of 622, Ning Changzhen finally surrendered Yulin and Ningyue Commanderies to Tang general Li Jing and was given the title of commander-in-chief of Qinzhou.[66] Following in the footsteps of the Chen and the Sui, this recognition by the Tang was the third time that a Chinese dynasty left the district in the hands of a local leader whose power they legitimized through the bestowal of a title after an agreement of loyalty.

From 620 onward, the politics of Qinzhou are confused, and to make sense of them one must step back to consider events involving another branch of the Ning family who descended from Mengli's relative Ning Xuan. When the Tang came to power in the north, Ning Xuan sent an ambassador to announce his submission to the Tang, but died before the court received it.[67] His son Ning Chun was given the post of governor of Lianzhou—a small province near Hepu named after a newly conquered *dong*. In the fourth month of 623, Ning Chun went to fight a group of three leaders described as rebels who were members of the great families who lived to the east; these were Pang Xiaotai,[68] governor of Nanzhou (later Baizhou), Ning Daoming from Nanyuezhou, and Feng Ang's brother Feng Xuan (described here as a "commander") from Gaozhou. Their allied forces had already taken control of southern Hepu and were advancing to attack the province of Jiangzhou (near present-day Pubei) to the north before Ning Chun led his troops to rescue it.[69] Ning Daoming's family relationships are unclear; although it is not recorded that he was a member of the same Ning family, the rarity of the surname and its connection with the Hepu and Qinzhou areas make it more than likely that he was a relative. The next mention of him is in 626 as "Inspector Daoming," who was killed in a rebellion by a man of Yuezhou named Lu Nan. Within three years, Ning Daoming had shifted from a rebel in the eyes of the Tang to a holder of the inspectorate.[70] In this case the difference between rebel and inspector looks to have hinged upon whether one was acting in accordance with court wishes or otherwise.

Ning Daoming was not the only one to be classed as both governor and rebel. Returning to the story of Ning Changzhen, in 625 he is recorded as having begun an insurrection through his capture of Fengshan County (again, close to present-day Pubei). The man who led a force against him was none other than the former rebel Pang Xiaotai, now made inspector of Changzhou (another name for Baizhou), who now fought and routed the forces of Changzhen and of his own former ally Feng Xuan of Gaozhou.[71] Changzhen died the year after his rebellion in 626 and his son Ning Ju took over his post as protector.[72]

A military defeat followed by recognition and alliance through political investiture was not at all uncommon in dealings between the empires and leaders of the Li and Lao. In addition to Ning Daoming and Ning Changzhen, two examples have already been given: Chen Tan, the Dragon Galloping General of Hepu in the mid-fifth century who acquired his post after a military defeat, and Feng Shihui, who retained recognition of his government of Gangzhou after the defeat of his rebellion. In the case of Pang Xiaotai, the politics are even more confusing because after his rebellion he went into battle against people against whom he had previously fought as "rebels" themselves.

These confusing records of rebellion and restoration are almost certainly the results of imperial recognition of the local Li and Lao power structures, and the shifting alliances between the chieftains and the empires at this time probably have more to do with internal territorial conflicts among Li and Lao than they do with any desire to uphold imperial rule in the region. Military actions taken by the Li and Lao leadership could be portrayed as either rebellion or as the quelling of rebellion, depending on which chieftain was in favor with the Tang at the time. Certain actions of self-aggrandizement also conveniently doubled as obedience to imperial orders; for instance, a "commander" of Qinzhou named either Ning Shisong or Shijing was ordered by Li Hongjie who held the title of Duke of Qingping to "open up" the lands of the Yi and Lao and found the new province of Rangzhou to the west of Qinzhou in order to improve the overland connection to Jiaozhi in 637.[73] When considered in the light of the Feng expanding their influence over Hainan and the battles between the Ning, Feng, and Pang over control of the Baizhou area, it is likely that the foundation of Rangzhou was not carried out purely on the basis of obedience to an imperial order, but was also an excuse to expand the influence of the Ning to the southwest and attack competing *dong*.

If one relies solely on descriptions transmitted by the written word in the Chinese histories, the Ning appear to be a family of Li and Lao chieftains whose members had received Chinese education and military training, and members of their family look to have been given administrative posts either as an expedient tactic of placation of local chieftains, or as a reward for their services to the imperial courts. However, two stelae dating from the seventh century contradict the Ning's Li and Lao identity as recorded in the transmitted texts by showing that they were in fact not descended from the local Li and Lao chieftains at all, but were actually the descendants (in the male line at least) of migrants who had lived only a few generations in the south. These stelae were unearthed in the Qinzhou area and their inscriptions provide not only much information relating to the origins of the Ning family, but also the only evidence of how the Ning family (or indeed any people recorded as Li or Lao in Chinese texts) actually saw themselves. This image is radically different from that gleaned from descriptions penned by outsiders.[74]

The earlier inscription is from the memorial tablet for the tomb of Changzhen's younger brother Ning Xuàn, excavated in 1826, and bears the date of the fifth month of 609. The inscription explains that the Ning family had originally come from Jizhou,[75] and it has been suggested that their ancestors took refuge in the south when this province was lost by the Liu-Song to the northern Wei.[76] The inscription goes on to explain that the family came to the area when Emperor Wu of the Liang first appointed Ning Mengli's father, Ning Kui, as inspector of Dingzhou (present-day Guiping) and military overseer of nine provinces,[77] and that Emperor Xuanwu of the Chen[78] then appointed him to the post of inspector of Anzhou. The information contained in this stele paints a very different picture of the Ning family than that contained in the standard histories. The stele is inscribed in a flowery literary style and extols both Ning Xuàn's virtues and the depth of his learning. On the occasion of his visit to the Sui court in 594, the inscription notes that the emperor regarded Xuàn as a "descendent of gentlefolk," quite unlike his comments about "barbarians" recorded in the *Sui shu* concerning his brother Changzhen's visit to court—even though it is highly likely that they attended court together. Whoever composed Ning Xuàn's stele was careful to make a clear distinction between him and the uncivilized people he ruled over, noting that his "fame was broadcast to the Hundred Man" and that he "punished and regulated the customs of the Hundred Yue."

The contrast between the Ning family's own records carved in stone with those of the court transmitted in books is surprising. The Ning portray themselves as a family of civilized, capable rulers and loyal generals, but even though they believed themselves to be on a par with the scholar officials in the rest of the empire (and could prove it by examination when Ning Chun's grandnephew Ning Yuanti was ranked ninth presented scholar [*jinshi*] in the 689 examinations in Chang'an),[79] they still ended up being referred to as Lao chieftains in the transmitted texts. The inscription concerning Ning Xuàn's ancestry was made so close to the time it describes that it is unlikely to be fraudulent, meaning that it took only a generation of residence in the Qinzhou area to transform the Ning from a family of ordinary officials into Lao chieftains and Li commanders from the viewpoint of those at court. Like the Feng, the Ning had two faces, and no matter what efforts they made to present or prove themselves as civilized people, where they lived and the nature of their rule over those they governed ensured that they could never quite escape the stigma of barbarism as far as those in the capital were concerned.

Ning rule of Qinzhou ended in a similar manner to that of the Feng in Gaozhou, through a combination of administrative reforms that gradually split their power base followed by a final decisive military defeat. The balance of power between the rivers shifted, and the Ning, like the Feng, were no longer necessary to the Tang in securing rule of the lands between the Two Rivers and had become an impediment to rule by the appointed bureaucrats of an increasingly strong and centralized empire. The Tang began to increase their direct control of Ning territory after the death of Ning Changzhen, according to the geographical treatise in the *Jiu Tang shu*. After Xiao Xian's defeat in 622, Ningyue Commandery was first renamed Qinzhou Province, a third of the province was detached, and two counties in the east were given to a new province called Nantingzhou in the same year. This took a large chunk of territory out of Ning control and was presumably one of the background causes of Ning Changzhen's attack on Fengshan County in 625. Qinzhou had the special status of protectorate, which it lost a few years later in 628, perhaps as a punishment for Ning Changzhen's infractions.[80] After this time, the Tang appointed new administrators to these provinces from outside, and the Ning were given less important positions.[81] This was similar to the way the Tang broke down the Feng family's power base, first by rearranging and increasing the number of administrative units in the area where their power was most concentrated, and then gradually removing family members from power. Despite this, the Ning remained the local dignitaries in the Qinzhou area up until 706, when the "Man chieftain" Ning Chengji and his brothers demanded a daughter in marriage from Lady Cui, mother of the former Empress Wei, the second wife of Tang emperor Zhongzong who had been exiled to the south by Empress Wu and whose husband Wei Xuanzhen had already died in Qinzhou. When Lady Cui refused him, Chengji killed her and her four sons. Such an act of violence on a family closely connected to the Tang ruling house brought swift retaliation. The protector of Guangzhou, Zhou Rengui, received orders to attack Chengji and took a force of twenty thousand men to pursue him and his forces. After he was caught and killed, Rengui offered his head as a posthumous sacrifice at Lady Cui's grave, in addition to capturing and exterminating his whole family.[82] This marked the end of the Ning as the localized dynasty to the west of Hepu, and although other clans such as the Huang and Nong grew in influence to fill the power vacuum to the north and west of Qinzhou in the eighth century, no local family held Qinzhou itself again as a hereditary seat.[83]

THE CHEN OF SHUANGZHOU

The Chen were another influential family between the Two Rivers, and were at the peak of their power from the Sui to the mid-Tang. Like the Ning and Feng, they held dominion over a reasonably well-defined territory, and also like the Ning, writers were unsure whether to call them Li chieftains or inspectors and governors. Although the story of the Chen family is not nearly as cohesive as those of the Feng and Ning, and the surname is common enough for the different recorded individuals to have possibly come from different families, their shared place of origin and their status as both local chieftains and imperial administrators in the area points to a probable relationship between the different individuals who appear in the records at different times.

This Chen family was associated with Shuangzhou, a hilly province founded in the area of a preexisting *dong* only fifty years prior to the first mention of notable member of the family Chen Fozhi. Fozhi was recorded as a "bandit general" who joined Li commander Wang Zhongxuan in his siege of Guangzhou in late 590 and met his death at the hands of Feng Ang.[84] His descendants held other important positions in the area. His son Chen Longshu served as the inspector of Qinzhou, and was probably appointed to the area by the Tang in order to break the stranglehold of the Ning over the region. During the reign of Empress Wu (690–705), his grandson Chen Jiyuan served as a general for the Tang; his short biography in the *Jiu Tang shu* records him as a native of Kaiyang (a town in Shuangzhou) and that his ancestors had been chiefs of the land beyond the passes (that is, the Two Rivers Region) for generations.[85] Another notable Li person from the same district was named Chen Puguang, who in 621 was supposed to have founded a Buddhist temple containing a stone-carved Buddha near the present-day town of Huaide.[86]

Liao Youhua believes that the family arrived in the area from the north only during Liang times, based on Chen Fozhi's biography in the fifteenth-century gazetteer of the Ming Empire the *Daming yitongzhi* (Comphrehensive Gazetteer of the Ming), which states that his ancestors came from Yanling in what is now Henan.[87] This is a late text, but gives details of four generations of the Chen family at Shuangzhou, recording that they lived along the Shuang River and had inherited the post of Duke of Yongping Commandery (*Yongpingjun gong*) there for generations. The various posts held by members of the family are as follows: Chen Fozhi's father Chen Fanian was inspector of Xinzhou and Shizhou, both of which lay south of the Yu River and to the east and west of Shuangzhou. Fozhi himself served as inspector of Luozhou and Xihengzhou (present-day Hengyang in Hunan) during the Taijian era (569–583) of the Chen Empire, his son Longshu served the Tang as inspector of six provinces, beginning with his native Shuangzhou, then Nanfuzhou,[88] then at Jianzhou (present-day Jianzhou in northern Fujian), and then in three other provinces in the north of the Tang Empire.[89] The earliest inspectorates held by the first three generations of the Chen family were in provinces on the south bank of the Yu River in fairly close proximity to Shuangzhou.[90] This record of the four generations of Chens indicates a change in their status from a local family holding a hereditary post in their own district to a bureaucratic elite family whose members were appointed to positions in high levels of government far outside their own local sphere of influence. Although the connection of the family to the Li-Lao country and their rise up the administrative ladder to office in the capital are confirmed by earlier texts, there are several problems with the Ming text that cast doubt upon some of its claims regarding the ancestry of the Chen family.

Chen Fozhi was said to have been the governor of Nanjing in Fujian at the beginning of the Guangda period (567–569) of the Chen Empire, during which time he was said to have "trained the customs of the southern barbarians in filial piety and virtue," but this place name is a clear anachronism, as Nanjing did not exist until five hundred years later. The Ming text also mentions that Fozhi was enfeoffed as Duke of Anjing Commandery (*anjingjun gong*), but not only was there no place named Anjing during Chen times, the title of commandery duke (*jungong*) was also usually reserved for members of the imperial house and was unlikely to have been held by someone from the wild frontier of the Li-Lao country.[91] The Ming text also neglects to mention Chen Longshu's service as inspector of Qinzhou recorded in the *Jiu Tang shu*.

The Ming text completely contradicts the image of Chen Fozhi given in the earliest sources as a local "bandit leader" by portraying him as a respected official, great civilizer, and transformer of barbaric customs. Though it is conceivable that this difference in description is based on the difference in his relationships to the governments of two different empires, that is, between the actions of a successful official under the Chen Empire and those of a disaffected official who rebelled because he had not received a new posting under the new Sui regime, the various problems with the text suggest that the Ming text is not in fact a record of the Chen family history handed down from Sui times, and is more likely to represent an ancestry created at a later date by the descendants of the Chen who had risen to prestigious positions in order to conceal their barbarian connections. A northern ancestry for the Chen of Shuangzhou is possible, but highly suspect on account of its first appearance in such a late text full of so many inaccuracies.

There had been other Li-Lao leaders surnamed Chen in the lands south of the Yu River in earlier centuries, and although the surname Chen is too common to conclusively prove a relationship with the Chen of Shuangzhou, it seems very likely from the localities mentioned in connection with them that there is a family relationship. The first two of these have already been mentioned in the preceding chapters, but a few details are repeated here for the ease of distinguishing a pattern in their activities and geographical locale. First, there was Chen Tan of Hepu, alive during the Daming period of the Liu-Song (457–465).[92] His status was indicated by his title of great commander (*da shuai*) and his appearance in the section of the *Song shu* dealing with the affairs of the Southern Man. Less than a century later was Chen Wenche, the Li commander (*Li shuai*) who led an attack on Gaoyao Commandery. The location of the commandery he attacked and his ownership of a large bronze drum indicate almost certainly that he came from south of the Yu River and probably from close to Shuangzhou.[93] In addition to these two, in the last decade of the sixth century, a "leader" (*shouling*) of Cangwu named Chen Tán was a contemporary of Lady Xian and was mentioned in the list of tribal rulers who received her instructions.[94] Cangwu Commandery under the Sui controlled lands on both sides of the Yu River, and the territories of the south bank of the river were close to what later became Shuangzhou.

A century after Chen Fozhi, another local leader named Chen Xingfan emerged in Shuangzhou. Unlike Chen Fozhi's family, who went on to serve as officials elsewhere in the empire, Xingfan remained in Shuangzhou as a local ruler; he was variously described as a "Shuangzhou Man"[95] and a "Lao leader" (*Lao shouling*), but at the same time he held the official title of inspector of Shuangzhou.[96] In the third month of 728, he rebelled against the Tang, declaring himself emperor and leading an army to capture forty walled cities. He was accompanied by a "Lao of Guangzhou" named Feng Lin and another man named He Youlu who declared themselves respectively "King of Nanyue" (*Nanyue wang*) and "Great General who settles the Country" (*dingguo jiangjun*). Yang Sixu, a native of the nearby province of Luozhou,[97] took a force of one hundred thousand men to fight them and defeated them in the twelfth month, capturing and beheading Feng Lin and He Youlu, but Xingfan managed to escape two *dong* named Yunji and Panliao,[98] where Yang Sixu came to attack him, and eventually beheaded him along with a supposed sixty thousand of his followers, confiscating a great abundance of slaves, horses, gold, and jade.[99] The details of Chen Xingfan's life show that local traditions of leadership had still not disappeared in some areas south of the Yu River even a century after the foundation of provinces like Shuangzhou, and even though some Li and Lao held imperial administrative titles, this still did not imply that they were necessarily loyal servants of the court. Others surnamed Chen from the same province had risen to high positions in the Tang government over the years, but Xingfan retained his connections to and influence over the rulers of *dong* and was still capable of raising an army large enough to carry out a nine-month-long armed resistance against the Tang.

The Chen family's power base at Shuangzhou was one of the last areas where the Southern Dynasties had founded administrative units, and it lay close to the Yunkai Mountains and the heartland of the bronze drum country, so Yang Sixu's defeat of the Chen uprising struck a fatal blow at one of the last centers of Li-Lao society between the Two Rivers and led to the final destruction of the local ruling class just as Ma Yuan had destroyed the native rulers of the Red River Plain over seven centuries previously. The defeat also seems to have resulted in a mass depopulation. Although undoubtedly exaggerated, the total of sixty thousand people killed by Yang Sixu shows both the extent of Chen Xingfan's following and also offers a reason for the lack of any significant Li-Lao leadership by the Chen family, or indeed anyone else mentioned as Li commanders or Man chieftains in the region after this time. In the census made in the Kaiyuan period (742), the number of registered households in Shuangzhou was only 714,[100] a fraction of the 14,319 registered households recorded in the census made under the Sui over a century previously in Yongxi Commandery, an administrative unit that covered roughly the same territory as Shuangzhou.[101]

Whether some of those surnamed Chen in Shuangzhou were ultimately related or not, there is a still a constant thread of "barbaric" terminology used to refer to them over the centuries, and even if it is not stated directly, it is still suggested through the use of terms such as *leader* or *chief* instead of official titles, and *tribe* instead of *subjects* or *people*. Just like the Feng and Ning, those surnamed Chen who prospered under the Southern Dynasties and Sui had a multifaceted existence as either Li or Lao, or officials, and although proof of northern ancestry was to become important to their descendants later on, during their lifetimes it appears to have been of no relevance to their status as leaders of the Li and Lao, nor does it seem to have been important for the people who described them as Li chieftains.

OTHER LOCALIZED DYNASTIES

The Feng, Ning, and Chen were the most powerful of the Li and Lao ruling families in the Pearl River drainage area, but they were not the only ones. There are scattered records of similar people who represented lineages of less powerful rulers and share many of the characteristics of the three families described in this chapter.

Like the representatives of the three great families discussed, these people possessed Chinese surnames and power bases in specific districts, and sometimes worked as part of the imperial administrative system or served in the army, but at the same time they appear to have been the de facto rulers in their own localities and are frequently referred to by names that imply they are native rulers. The existence of these other families suggests that the three great families stand only as the most prominent representatives of a ruling class of chieftains-cum-bureaucrats that was widespread throughout the Two Rivers Region.

Some members of these families have already been mentioned earlier in connection with the Ning and Feng, as they were involved in alliances with both of these families. East of Hepu was a family surnamed Pang that produced Pang Jing the "rebellious commander" and native of the province of Luozhou who was a contemporary of Lady Xian.[102] He was probably related to the previously mentioned Governor Pang Xiaotai, who later died leading troops from Lingnan against the Koreans in 662 and came from the same district.[103] A family surnamed Li dwelled north of the Yu River at Gùizhou and Tengzhou. A Li Guanglue of Tengzhou is mentioned in the list of tribal leaders of Lingnan who met with Lady Xian,[104] and a Li of Gùizhou named Li Guangshi was said to have assembled hordes in rebellion at the end of the Kaihuang period of the Sui (581–601).[105] There was also a Li Guangdu who was protector of Nanyinzhou (present-day Gui County in Guangxi) in 624, [106] but had formerly served as governor of Yongping Commandery under the Sui.[107] He was mentioned along with Ning Chang-zhen and Feng Ang as one of the great leaders (*da shouling*) whom it was necessary for Tang general Li Jing to placate upon his entry into the Two Rivers Region.[108] Although the relationship between these three is unclear, the similarity in the names seems to point to a localized dynasty of Li people hired as officials in the lands to the north and west of present-day Wuzhou. Isolated records of individual Li commanders also probably stand for local lineages. Close to Canton lived the previously mentioned Li commander Wang Zhongxuan of Guangzhou, who led an uprising in 590.[109] To the east of Canton lived Li commander Yang Shilue, who controlled the two prov-inces of Xunzhou and Chaozhou, and surrendered them to the Tang in the first month of 622.[110]

There were undoubtedly many more of these small localized dynasties of Li and Lao whose rulers doubled as the governors of small provinces and counties. In certain areas, these dynasties survived into the late Tang. A tenth-century gazetteer records a family of Li people of Gùizhou with the surname Teng who were said to still be in possession of seals called "bamboo emis-sary seals" (*zhushifu*) and "bronze tiger tallies" (*tonghufu*) said to have been bestowed on their family by the Han.[111] Although the meaning of "bamboo emissary" is a mystery, tiger tallies are well-known emblems of military authority. These were bronze tiger figurines divided in half, with one half given to a troop commander or local official and the other kept by the gov-ernment in the capital; troops could only be called up or set in motion when the two halves were matched.[112] Another family with the surname of Lu in nearby Binzhou was in possession of not only "bronze tiger seals," but also silver seals and bronze tiger tallies with green ribbons that were said to have been the precious heirlooms of generations.[113] Binzhou was the approximate location of Lingfang, a county founded during the Western Han that had its own defender (*duwei*) or head of military forces.[114] The Teng and Lu families may well have been the descendants of the Wuhu or leaders who had contin-ued to rule their chiefdoms in the name of counties, or they may have been descendants of Chinese migrants sent to the area as administrators. Like the other families described here, although they might have been descendants of migrants from elsewhere, their ultimate origins were less important factors in deciding whether they would be described as Li or Lao than where they lived, the people they ruled, the manner in which they ruled them, and their relationship to the imperial administrative system.

THE END OF LI AND LAO LEADERSHIP

The story of the three great families and their eventual downfall and disappearance is the final stage in the development of the Li and Lao political structures south of the Yu River. By the foundation of the Sui Empire, the heads of these families were stronger and richer rulers than any of the Li-Lao rulers of previous centuries and they held consolidated power over many smaller *dong*. This new ruling class was produced through long-term interaction between the societies of the *dong* and the imperial administrative systems in combination with acculturation of northern migrants into local ways of life between the Two Rivers. The result is that it was impossible for outsiders to distinguish between families of purportedly northern origin such as the Ning, families of known mixed origin, such as the Feng, and families more likely to have been of local origin, such as the Chen. The question of who was actually a true Man (or Li or Lao) among these people becomes irrelevant in light of the fact that people could come to be considered Man, Li, or Lao as they acculturated to native customs and governmental practices. Like the smelting of copper coins to make drums, the acculturation of outsiders to Li and Lao norms of behavior implies that the attractions of the way the ordinary people of the Li-Lao *dong* on the imperial periphery conducted their affairs at certain times outweighed the attraction of the way things were done at the centers of imperial power.

From the texts, it appears that leaders of these families had, as individuals, mastered the art of being several different things to different people—to their subjects who still spoke Tai-Kadai languages they probably had a status similar to *dulao*, but to the imperial court in Jiankang or the governorship of Panyu they could be either Li commanders, chiefs, or governors depending on the relationships they had negotiated. As the balance of power shifted in favor of the large powerful centralized empire of the Tang in the late seventh century, these families were no longer considered useful, and over a period of eighty years their power was destroyed by a combination of administrative reforms and increased use of military force to quell resistance. Yang Sixu's defeat of the Chen and Feng forces was the final event that decimated local leadership in the heart of the bronze drum country. Although resistance to Tang rule between the rivers continued into the 750s and 760s, this was concentrated to the west and north along the upper reaches of the Youjiang, Zuojiang, and Zangke Rivers. The lands of the Li and Lao between Hepu and Canton no longer produced any leaders capable of disrupting Tang control.

The end of rule by great families such as the Feng, Chen, and Ning was also the end of the autonomous Li-Lao political structures that had developed out of the *dong* between the Two Rivers, although more powerful *dong* continued to exist north of the West River, and the term *dong* was still retained for small settlements of people who had evaded direct imperial rule. The presence of smaller groupings of Li and Lao people inhabiting villages and rural areas was still noted two centuries later in tenth- and eleventh-century geographies, but by this time they were leaderless peoples who dwelled on the fringes of Tang and Song provinces and counties.

The disappearance of the ruling class of Li commanders and Lao chieftains is demonstrated not only by its absence from the written record after the mid-eighth century, but also by the end of the Heger type II drum-casting tradition south of the Yu River, as the fragmentary communities of Li and Lao who remained in this region no longer produced leaders who were rich, powerful, or interested enough in such symbols of chieftainship to organize their production.

NOTES

1. SuS 82: 1a.

2. Schafer, *Vermilion Bird*, 69. Text Pinyinized.

3. Liao, *Lishi dilixue*, 253–58, refers to these people as "southern-barbarized Han people" (*manhua hanren*). Zheng and Tan refer to the Ning family as "Han people who were Yue-ized to a high degree." Zheng and Tan, *Zhuangzu lishi wenhua*, 480.

4. Invoking a northern ancestry as proof of one's ethnic status became particularly common in Guangdong during Ming times. See David Faure, "Becoming Cantonese, the Ming Dynasty Transition," in *Unity and Diversity—Local Cultures and Identities in China,* ed. David Faure and Tao Tao Liu (Hong Kong: Hong Kong University Press, 1996), 37–50. See also Su Guanchang's study of the invented ancestry of the Cen family of Guangxi (Su Guanchang 粟冠昌, "Guangxi tuguan minzu chengfen zaitan" 廣西土官民族成份再探, *Xueshu luntan* 學術論壇 2 [1981]: 83–86), and the example of the Wei family of Guangxi (mostly classed as Zhuang by the present government) who had invented a story of descent from Han general Han Xin 韓信 (Zheng and Tan, *Zhuangzu lishi wenhua*, 481).

5. There were various places by the name of Qiaoguo in what are now the northern Chinese provinces of Anhui and Henan, and Duke of Qiao (*Qiaoguo gong*) was one of the titles held by Lady Xian's husband Feng Bao, though precisely what relationship he had to these areas in the north is uncertain.

6. Wade, *The Lady Sinn*, 139–40. Wade is the most detailed and comprehensive source on Lady Xian available in English. In Chinese, the standard monograph is Wang Xingrui 王興瑞, *Xian furen yu fengshi chiazu—Sui Tang jian Guangdong*

nanbu diqu shehui lishi de chubu yanjiu 冼夫人與馮氏家族—隋唐間廣東南部社
會歷史的初步研究 (Beijing: Zhonghua shuju, 1984).

7. See Wade, *The Lady Sinn*. For her descendants on Hainan, see He Xi, "The
Past Tells It Differently: The Myth of Native Subjugation in the Creation of Lineage
Society in South China," in *Chieftains into Ancestors: Imperial Expansion and
Indigenous Society in South China*, ed. David Faure and Ho Ts'ui P'ing (Vancouver:
University of British Columbia Press, 2013), 138–70.

8. SuS 80: 4a. Wade, *The Lady Sinn*, believes that Hainan and Dan'er refer to
the Lingnan region as a whole, not merely to the island of Hainan.

9. XTS 110: 1a.

10. ZZTJ ch. 177: 5534.

11. Wang, *Xian furen*, 53–54.

12. ZZTJ ch. 177: 5533.

13. SuS 68: 10a.

14. SuS 80: 6b. These were Chen Tán of Cangwu, Feng Cenweng of Gangzhou
(probably a relation), Deng Matou of Lianghua (halfway between modern Hong Kong
and Canton), Li Guanglue of Tengzhou, and Pang Qing of Luozhou. The significance
of several of these people's surnames will become clear when they appear later in this
chapter.

15. XTS 110: 1a–b; ZZTJ ch. 179: 5589. The provincial seat of Chengzhou lay
on the Yu River near present-day Fengkai.

16. XTS 110: 1a; ZZTJ ch. 179: 5589.

17. ZZTJ ch. 179: 5589.

18. XTS 110: 1a.

19. ZZTJ ch. 185: 5790.

20. ZZTJ ch. 188: 5899–900; XTS 110: 1b. Although no texts mention the relationship, Xian Baoche and his nephew Zhichen were almost certainly related to Feng
Ang through his grandmother's marriage. Zhichen's surname is not mentioned in the
text, but because he was the son of Baoche's elder brother, it was probably Xian.

21. XTS 110: 1b.

22. Ibid.

23. Ibid. The first four provinces were on the coast southwest from Canton, and
the second four were on Hainan.

24. XTS 110: 1a.

25. XTS 110: 1b–2a.

26. Ibid.; ZZTJ ch. 192: 6038–39.

27. Schafer, *Vermilion Bird*, 62.

28. ZZTJ ch. 193: 6092.

29. There may also have been a strategic advantage for Feng Ang in the conquest
of the Luo and Dou *dong*. There was territorial competition between the Ning and
Feng clans for control of the Hepu area. Feng Ang's brother Feng Xuan was involved
in battles with the Ning clan who controlled the lands to the west of the Leizhou
Peninsula.

30. XTS 110: 2a.

31. JTS 109: 1b. One Tang *li* was equivalent to about a third of a kilometer.

32. XTS 110: 2a.

33. Ibid. The subsequent information about Zhidai is also from this source.

34. DMYTZ 81: 21a and DSFYJY ch. 104: 4297 both say that this was situated to the northeast of Xinyi. The Gaoyuan Pass was 100 *li* to the west of the Xinyi county seat, so it seems that they were returning home from the northwest, probably through the "Magic Trench" canal route.

35. XTS 110: 2a. Hongzhou is in present-day Jiangxi.

36. Wang, *Xian furen*, 51.

37. ZYGJ ch. 22: 234. Here he is described as one of three sons, but his name is written with the homophonous character *you* 游.

38. These two names appear in Wang, *Xian furen*, 51, but no source is given.

39. XTS 223a: 1b.

40. His biography can be found in JTS 184: 3a–4b and XTS 207: 2a–3b. Details about Feng Junheng are from a Tang stele, the text of which is recorded in ZYGJ ch. 16: 169–70.

41. See note 14.

42. ZZTJ ch. 190: 5969–70.

43. XTS 110: 2b.

44. Ibid.

45. JTS 67: 10b.

46. ZZTJ ch. 204: 6423.

47. JTS 190a: 8b.

48. JTS 8: 15a–b.

49. See Schafer, *Vermilion Bird*, 63–64.

50. ZZTJ ch. 224: 7217.

51. Schafer refers to the "Ning tribe" and calls Ning Changzhen a "converted aborigine."

52. XTS 222c: 18a.

53. XTS 222c: 17a.

54. SuS 56: 4b. The name *Nanhai* in this text I take to refer to the region along the South China Sea coast rather than the city of Canton, which also went by the name Nanhai. If Ning Mengli had managed to take and occupy such an important city, it would have certainly been recorded elsewhere.

55. SuS 56: 4b.

56. XTS 222c: 17a.

57. This I infer from the advice Xi gave to the throne on changing the names of five provinces scattered throughout the region (Anzhou to Qinzhou, Huangzhou to Fengzhou, Lizhou to Zhizhou, Dezhou to Huanzhou, and Dongning to Rongzhou) and the approximate number of provinces west of the Pearl River delta at the time; see SuS 56: 4b.

58. Ibid.

59. SuS 68: 9a–10b. Anzhou was renamed Qinzhou in 599 (SuS 31: 12a). It is likely that the other provinces were renamed at the same time.

60. ZZTJ ch. 178: 5553 refers to the same event but calls him a Li commander.

61. ZZTJ ch. 180: 5616; SuS 82: 2b.

62. XTS 222c: 18a. Hucker, *Dictionary of Official Titles*, 104, describes the latter title as "an occasional honorary designation granted to a southwestern aboriginal chief."

63. XTS 87: 1a–b.

64. JTS 59: 4b–5a. This is an interesting way to put it, as it shows that at the time, the people of the Red River Plain were not considered as part of the "Hundred Yue."

65. ZZTJ ch. 185: 5790.

66. ZZTJ ch. 190: 5949.

67. XTS 222c: 18b. ZZTJ ch. 190: 5951 counts him among a list of "bandit commanders" (*zeishuai*) and dates his surrender to the Tang in the fourth month of 622.

68. XTS 222c: 18a refers to the first leader as Pang Xiaogong 恭. This is most likely a mistake for the character *tai* 泰 used in all other works.

69. ZZTJ ch. 190: 5967; XTS 222c: 18a–b records the same event but mentions only the three names, Ning Daoming and two leaders from Gaozhou, Feng Xuan and Tan Dian.

70. ZZTJ ch. 191: 6003. Yuezhou was soon renamed Lianzhou. It is now the district of Hepu.

71. XTS 222c: 18a–b. Changzhou may have been a short-lived alternative to the name Baizhou because Pang Xiaotai is always mentioned elsewhere as holder of the inspectorate of Baizhou, the area known as Nanchang Commandery under the Sui. The character *chang* probably originated from the second character of this name.

72. XTS 222c: 18b; Zheng and Tan, *Zhuangzu lishi wenhua*, 488, note that this is incorrect, as the protectorate had already been abolished by that time.

73. TPHYJ 167: 14b–15a; JTS 41: 42a. Rangzhou lay in the vicinity of present-day Longzhou.

74. Yang Hao 楊豪, "Lingnan ningshi jiazu yuanliu xinzheng" 嶺南甯氏家族源流新證, *Kaogu* 考古 no. 3 (1989): 269–73, has the texts of the two stelae, but for dates and a more detailed interpretation see Zheng and Tan, *Zhuangzu lishi wenhua*, 477–83.

75. Present-day Jinan in northern China.

76. Zheng and Tan, *Zhuangzu lishi wenhua*, 422.

77. This would have been between 543 and 550, when Emperor Wu died. There were earlier written references to a possible member of the Ning family in 543 (LS 3: 26b) when the inspector of Luozhou Ning Jú was sent off to fight Lý Bốn in the Red River Delta. At that time, the inspector of Anzhou (later Qinzhou) was named Li Zhi. This suggests that the Ning family already had a presence in the area but were yet to gain control of Qinzhou.

78. There was not actually a Chen emperor with such a name, but there were two emperors named Wu 武 (reigned 557–559) and Xuan 宣 (reigned 569–582); perhaps both emperors had appointed Ning Kui with the same title.

79. GDTZ 44: 52b.

80. XTS 43a: 9a.

81. Zheng and Tan, *Zhuangzu lishi wenhua*, 486–87, provide the following information but do not provide a primary source. Ju's son Ning Daowu was the county magistrate of Xiāngzhou, a new province to the west of Qinzhou. Then he was made

the commander of Longzhou, and then was shifted off to Aizhou, to the south of the Red River Plain. His son Ning Qilan was given the lowly position of assistant magistrate (*zhubu*) in Shian and Guilin, both well outside the home territory of the Ning clan.

82. ZZTJ ch. 208: 6603–4.

83. Schafer, *Vermilion Bird*, 63, notes the four most important families in the 740s as the Huang, Nong, Zhou, and Wei. These families lived further to the north in the regions north and west of what is now Nanning.

84. SS 81: 6a; 7a.

85. JTS 188: 4a.

86. GDTZ 53: 52a. The inscription is at Longkan Grotto in Tanli Village, part of Pingtang town to the east of Luoding in Guangdong. The text uses the character *li* 里, meaning "village," in place of 俚.

87. Liao, *Lishi dilixue*, 256; DMYTZ 81: 16b.

88. This was founded in 621, and after many changes of name, the name Douzhou was settled on, taking after the Luo-Dou *dong* that lay somewhere in the province; see TPHYJ 163: 5a–6b.

89. These were Wanzhou, Puzhou, and Nanshizhou.

90. Yongping Commandery lay at the mouth of the Beiliu River as it joined the Yu River. Xinzhou and Shizhou lay to the east and west of present-day Wuzhou, respectively.

91. Hucker, *Dictionary of Official Titles*, 202, also notes that the title was only used from Tang to Yuan times, so its application twice to the sixth century is a suspicious anachronism. It is possible that the title Anjing could be construed as "pacifier of Jing" as well, but what place this Jing refers to is still unclear.

92. SS 97: 4a.

93. Liao, *Lishi dilixue*, 522, believes him to be related to the Chen family of Shuangzhou, which would seem to contradict his belief in the northern origins of the family during Liang times.

94. See note 14.

95. XTS 207: 2a.

96. JTS 8: 15a–b.

97. According to his biography (JTS 148: 2a), Yang Sixu was himself a native of Luozhou, to the east of Hepu, so his employment in dealing with uprisings between the Two Rivers may very well have been based on his local knowledge of the area.

98. ZZTJ ch. 219: 6781–82; JTS 184: 2b–3a; XTS 207: 1b–2a. These two names are probably Tai names. The characters *pan* and *yun* were pronounced (according to Pulleyblank, *Lexicon of Reconstructed Pronunciation*) as **ban* and **wun*, making it likely that they begin with the word *baan*, Tai for "village." For the meaning of such names beginning with similar-sounding characters, see Xu, *Yue jiang*, 205–6, and Li, *Dongtai yuyan*, 237–38, 298.

99. JTS 8: 15a–b.

100. TPHYJ 164: 2b.

101. SuS 31: 10a.

102. SuS 68: 10a. He is also mentioned as one of the tribal leaders who met with Lady Xian. See note 14.

103. XTS 3: 5b; JTS 82: 2b confirms that he came from Baizhou, which was in the same district as Luozhou.

104. See note 14.

105. SuS 68: 9b.

106. ZZTJ ch. 191: 5984.

107. JTS 59: 8a.

108. JTS 67: 2b.

109. SuS 65: 10b; ZZTJ ch. 177: 5532–33.

110. ZZTJ ch. 190: 5949.

111. TPHYJ 116: 11b. This work dates from the tenth century, but its contents may well have been culled from a Tang work.

112. This definition is from Graff, *Medieval Chinese Warfare*, 26. They were first mentioned in the *Shiji* for the year 177 BCE (SJ 10: 10b–11a). By the Tang, these had been replaced with tallies in the shape of a fish (see Graff, *Medieval Chinese Warfare*, 119), which suggests that the gift of the tiger-shaped tallies to the families predated the Tang.

113. TPHYJ 165: 7b.

114. HS 8b: 10b.

Conclusion

I have argued that the maintenance of local rulers in the area was the result of the Han Empire having bypassed the lands between the Two Rivers and concentrating its attention instead on the control of the Red River Plain and the major tributaries of the Pearl River system, thus leaving a large unconquered territory outside the control of the empire that was inhabited for the most part by small autonomous Li and Lao chiefdoms. Because they inhabited an area that the Chinese empires did not initially consider to be of great economic or strategic value, and because they were politically fragmented and difficult to conquer with a single military campaign, most of these chiefdoms were left to their own devices, but those in the vicinity of the Chinese imperial centers in the region began to be offered alliances, whereby they provided tribute products to the Chinese empires in exchange for undisturbed rule over their own people. After the disintegration of the Han Empire and the rise of its weaker successor states, it became clear to the imperial rulers at Jiankang that Li and Lao chiefdoms occupied an area of strategic importance on overland trade routes from Jiaozhou, one of their two important provinces in the south, and that they also had the economic benefits of gold and silver resources, as well trade items sought after by the people of the cities. By the time the Southern Dynasties came to realize the economic and strategic advantages of controlling these areas, they had more pressing problems with their rival northern empires and were plagued by internal instability. The resultant incapacity of the Southern Dynasties to march in and occupy the land between the Two Rivers encouraged them to engage in trade relationships with some of the chieftains of the Li and Lao in order to procure the items they desired, trading salt, iron, copper, and the prestige of recognition as legitimate rulers of their people in return for ivory, kingfisher feathers, gold, and silver.

These trade relationships were the major trigger for the growth in size and power of the Li and Lao chiefdoms, as the collection of the items sought after by outsiders required rule over large territories and the involvement of large groups of people, thus encouraging competition among chiefdoms for land and manpower. The bestowal of temporary Chinese administrative titles on chieftains between the Two Rivers that accompanied the trade relationships did not initially have the effect of drawing them into the Chinese administrative and cultural world, but instead had the opposite effect of strengthening local leadership. Leaders who could negotiate a trade relationship and gain a temporary appointment would have a powerful ally and would be immune from the small-scale military raiding by Chinese officials that became common from the fifth century onward. They would also be able to make their own military raids or conquests of other *dong* chiefdoms that did not enjoy such relationships with the empire without fear of retribution from their large and powerful ally.

Contrary to the commonly held beliefs of inevitable Sinification through trade and contact with the empires, the system of alliances practiced under the Southern Dynasties did not result in the acculturation of the Li and Lao leaders to Chinese norms of political behavior. The alliances had no stipulation other than the provision of trade goods, and as a result, Li and Lao leaders sought to display their prestigious positions in their own societies through the ownership of bronze drums, the symbols of authority more familiar to their own people, rather than the symbols of authority provided by the Chinese empires. The rise in wealth and power of the Li-Lao chieftains, in turn a result of economic and political contacts with the Chinese empires, spurred on the growth of the bronze drum casting tradition from the third century onward. The spread and popularity of the drum culture shows that over the four centuries between the end of the Han and the beginning of the Tang, aside from the increased adoption of Chinese surnames, contact with the Chinese usually had a "de-Sinifying" effect on the Li and Lao between the Rivers, and the local culture became so attractive to some migrants to the area who lived among them that some of them underwent a "Li-Lao-ification," marrying into local families, taking up local customs, and transforming into chieftains of *dong*.

The increase in size of *dong* chiefdoms was initially conducive to the autonomous political development of the Li and Lao. Whereas small fragmented polities of the first centuries CE had caused inconvenience to the Han Empire when they occasionally allied together, the large, militarily powerful chiefdoms that replaced them in the sixth century were too strong for the later Southern Dynasties to take on by force. In the long term, however, the increased power of local rulers over larger territories had the opposite effect, especially once the Tang Empire had consolidated its power and was in a better position to make deals on its own terms. The heads of large and powerful ruling clans were easier to negotiate with than dozens of tiny chiefdoms for the control of an area, and once they were sufficiently incorporated into the imperial system as bureaucrats and generals, it was easy for the Tang to break their hold on power over their own districts by reorganizing and fragmenting administrative units, using military force to defeat the small pockets of resistant peoples. This process occurred over the late seventh and eighth centuries and the end result was a final incorporation of Li and Lao districts into the imperial administrative system.

The fate of the Li and Lao under the Tang foreshadowed the future advance of Chinese empires further upstream into the lands where the Two Rivers have their source. Here the empires were to employ similar tactics, first coopting local leadership out of necessity then incorporating its more powerful members into the administrative system before eventually removing it from effective power once the balance of power was in their favor.

As for the Li and Lao south of the Yu River, small communities of them lingered at the edges of Tang and Song administrative units, some for three or four more centuries, some in more remote areas for as long as five centuries. After a long and gradual process of abandoning their language and forgetting their separate identity, by the eighteenth century, those who came across bronze drums when plowing fields or digging ditches no longer recognized them as the work of their own ancestors.

Glossary

Names are transliterated in Pinyin, with the exception of those in italics, which are in Sino-Vietnamese (Hán-Việt). Names in parentheses are alternative spellings, either in Pinyin or Sino-Vietnamese, that have not been used in the text but are provided for reference.

PERSONAL NAMES

Bao Gang 寶綱
Cao Xuanjing 曹玄靜
Chen 陳
Chen Baxian 陳霸先
Chen Boshao 陳伯紹
Chen Fanian 陳法念
Chen Fozhi 陳佛智
Chen Jiyuan 陳集原
Chen Longshu 陳龍樹
Chen Puguang 陳普光
Chen Shubao 陳叔寶
Chen Tán 陳坦
Chen Tan 陳檀
Chen Wenche 陳文徹
Chen Xingfan 陳行範
Cui 崔
Deng Matou 鄧馬頭
Deng Yue 鄧嶽
Du Cengming 杜僧明

Du Hongwen (*Đỗ Hoằng Văn*) 杜弘文
Du Huidu (*Đỗ Tuệ Độ*) 杜慧度
Du Tianhe 杜天合
Du Yuán 杜元
Du Yuan (*Đỗ Viện*) 杜瑗
Emperor Xiaowu 孝武
Emperor Xuan 宣 (reigned 569–583)
Emperor Xuanwu 宣武
Empress Dowager Deng 鄧太后
Fei Shen 費沈
Feng 馮
Feng Ang 馮盎
Feng Bao 馮寶
Feng Cenweng 馮岑翁
Feng Junheng 馮君衡
Feng Lin 馮璘
Feng Pu 馮僕
Feng Renzhi 馮仁智

Feng Rong 馮融
Feng Shihui 馮士翽
Feng Xuan 馮暄
Feng Zhidai 馮智戴 or Zhidai 智玳
Feng Zhigui 馮智戢
Feng Zhiji 馮智璣
Feng Zhishi 馮智式
Feng Zhiyu 馮智彧
Feng Zhongdao 馮崇道
Feng Ziyou 馮子猷
Gao Bao 高寶
Gao Facheng 高法澄
Gao Lishi 高力士
Gao Shilian 高士廉
Gu Bi 顧秘
Gu Yong 谷永
Han Kangbo 韓康伯
He Chou 何稠
He Youlu 何遊魯
Hou Jing 侯景
Hua Jiao 華皎
Huang 黃
Huang Wu 黃吳
Jiang Zhuang 姜壯
Lan Qin 蘭欽
Li 李
Li Bole 李百藥
Li Guan 李觀
Li Guangdu 李光度
Li Guanglue 李光略
Li Guangshi 李光仕
Li Hongjie 李宏節
Li Hun 李暈
Li Jing 李靖
Li Sidao 李思道
Li Xian 李賢
Li Zhi 李智
Liang Shuo 梁碩
Lin Mu 藺暮
Lin Shihong 林士弘
Linghu Xi 令狐熙

Liu An 劉安
Liu Fang 劉方
Liu Gan 劉感
Liu Mian 劉勔
Liu Mu 劉牧
Liu Yan 劉龑
Liu Yanyou 劉延祐
Liu Zhao 劉昭
Lu 陸
Lu Anxing 盧安興
Lü Dai 呂岱
Lu Ji 陸績
Lu Nan 盧南
Lu Xun 盧循
Lu Yin 陸胤
Lü Yu 呂瑜
Lu Yu 盧聳
Lý Bốn (Li Bi) 李賁
Lý Thúc Hiến (Li Shuxian) 李叔獻
Lý Tốn (Li Xun) 李遜
Lý Trương Nhân (Li Changren) 李長仁
Lý Phật Tử (Li Fozi) 李佛子
Lý Tư Thận (Li Sishen) 李思慎
Ma Jing 馬靖
Ma Yuan 馬援
Nanyue Wang 南越王
Ning 甯
Ning Changzhen 甯長真
Ning Chengji 甯承基
Ning Chun 甯純
Ning Daoming 甯道明
Ning Jú 甯巨
Ning Ju 甯據
Ning Kui 甯逵
Ning Mengli 甯猛力
Ning Qilan 甯岐嵐
Ning Shijing 甯師京 or Ning Shijing 甯師宋
Ning Xuan 甯宣
Ning Xuàn 甯贙

Ning Yuanti 甯原悌
Nong 農
Ouyang Wei 歐陽頠
Pang 龐
Pang Jing 龐靖
Pang Xiaotai 龐孝泰
Pei Ju 裴矩
Qian Bo 錢博
Qiu He 丘和
Ren Chuo 任逴
Ruan Fang 阮放
Ruan Fu 阮敷
Shen Huaiyuan 沈懷遠
Shen Jungao 沈君高
Shi Wei 士䲡
Shi Wu 士武
Shi Xie (*Sĩ Nhiếp*) 士燮
Shi Yi 士壹
Tai Kaizhi 戴凱之
Tan Daoji 檀道濟
Tan Dian 談殿
Tao Huang 陶璜
Tao Ji 陶基
Tao Kan 陶侃
Tao Shu 陶淑
Tao Sui 陶綏
Tao Wei 陶威
Teng 滕
Teng Dunzhi 滕遯之
Teng Kan 滕含
Teng Xiu 滕修
Triệu Âu (Zhao You) 趙嫗
Trưng (Zheng) 徵
Wang Hong 王翃
Wang Liang 王諒
Wang Shi 王式
Wang Zhongxuan 王仲宣
Wei Xuanzhen 韋玄貞
Wei Zheng 魏征
Wen Fangzhi 溫放之
Xi Guang 錫光
Xian 冼

Xian Baoche 冼寶徹
Xian Furen 冼夫人
Xian Zhichen 冼智臣
Xiao Ang 蕭昂
Xiao Li 蕭勵
Xiao Mai 蕭勱
Xiao Xian 蕭銑
Xiao Yu 蕭譽
Xiao Yuanjian 蕭元簡
Xiao Zi 蕭諮
Xu Daoqi 徐道期
Xu Huan 許瓛
Xu Jingzong 許敬宗
Xue Zong 薛綜
Xun Fazhao 荀法超
Xun Fei 荀斐
Xun Jiang 荀匠
Yan Han 顏含
Yang Ji 楊稷
Yang Jing 楊璟
Yang Ping 楊平
Yang Shilue 楊世畧
Yang Sixu 楊思勗
Yang Su 楊素
Yang Xiong 楊雄
Yu Yi 庾翼
Yu Yiqi 俞益期
Yuwenheitai 宇文黑泰
Zhang Fangzhi 張方直
Zhang Lian 張璉
Zhang Rong 張融
Zhang You 張游
Zhao Tuo (*Triệu Đà*) 趙佗
Zhao Yingqi 趙嬰齊
Zhou Rengui 周仁軌
Zhou Shixiong 周世雄
Zhou Wenyu 周文育
Zhu Fan 朱蕃
Zhu Jishi 朱濟時
Zhu Juan 朱儁
Zhu Wang 竹王
Zhu Yi 朱异

PLACE NAMES

Anchang 安昌
Anfu 安復
Anjin 安金
Anjing 安靖
Annan (An Nam) 安南
Anzhou 安州
Baizhou 白州
Beiliu 北流
Bianzhou 辯州
Binzhou 賓州
Boliang 百梁
Cangwu 蒼梧
Changsha 長沙
Changzhou 昌州
Chaoyang 潮陽
Chaozhou 潮州
Chéngzhou 澄州
Chengzhou 成州
Chunzhou 春州
Dahan 大漢
Dalian Dong 大廉洞
Dangzhou 黨州
Danzhou 儋州
Daqin 大秦
Dayu 大庾
Dayue 大越
Dezhou 德州
Dingliu 丁留
Dingzhou 定州
Dongguan 東官
Donghai 東海
Dong Hezhou 東合州
Dongning 東寧
Douzhou 竇州
Duanxi 端溪
Duanzhou 端州
Enzhou 恩州
Fengshan 封山
Fengxi 封溪
Fengzhou 峰州

Fuchang 富昌
Fuchun 夫阺
Futang 釜塘
Furen 夫任
Gangzhou 岡州, alternatively 崗州
Gaoliang 高涼
Gaoxing 高興
Gaoyao 高要
Gaoyuan 高源
Gaozhou 高州
Gongzhou 龔州
Guangxi 廣熙
Guangxin 廣信
Guangxing 廣興
Guangzhou 廣州
Gudang Dong 古黨洞
Guilin 桂林
Guimen Guan 鬼門關
Guiyang 桂陽
Gùizhou 桂州
Guizhou 貴州
Gusu 姑蘇
Haichang 海昌
Haifeng 海豐
Haining 海寧
Haiping 海平
Hanyang 漢陽
Heng County 橫縣
Héngzhou 橫州
Hengzhou 衡州
Hepu 合浦
Hézhou 合州
Hezhou 賀州
Houguan 侯官
Huazhou 化州
Huangzhou 黃州
Huanzhou (*Hoan Châu*) 驩州
Hongzhou 洪州
Huaide 懷德
Jiankang 建康

Jianling 建陵
Jiang xi 江西
Jiangzhou 姜州
Jianzhou 建州
Jiaozhi (*Giao Chỉ*) 交趾
Jiaozhou (*Giao Châu*) 交州
Jin'an 晉安
Jincheng 晉城
Jinfeng Mountain 金封山
Jin Gang 金岡
Jin Jiang 斤江
Jinkang 晉康
Jinnan Jiang 斤南江
Jinsang 進桑
Jinxing 晉興
Jingzhou 荆州
Jiude (*Cửu Đức*) 九德
Jiudejiu (*Cửu Đức Cửu*) 九德究
Jiuzhen (*Cửu Chân*) 九真
Jizhou 冀州
Kaiyang 開陽
Kangzhou 康州
Kunming 昆明
Laozhou 牢州
Leishui 類水
Leizhou 雷州
Lianjiang 廉江
Lianzhou 廉州
Liangde 梁德
Lianghua 梁化
Linchen 臨塵
Lingshan 靈山
Linqing 臨慶
Linyi (*Lâm Ấp*) 林邑
Linzhang 臨瘴, alternatively 臨漳
Lingfang 領方
Lingling 零陵
Lingluo 陵羅
Ling Qu 靈渠
Lingnan 嶺南
Linhe 臨賀
Lizhou 利州

Long Biên (Longbian) 龍編
Long Dong 籠洞
Longkan Grotto 龍龕岩洞
Longzhou 籠州
Longsu 隴蘇
Longxue Shan 龍穴山
Luanzhou 巒州
Luodou Dong 羅竇洞
Luozhou 羅州
Luy Lâu (Leilou) 贏樓
Luzhou 陸州
Lüzhu jing 綠珠井
Mê Linh (Miling) 麊泠
Nanba 南巴
Nanchang 南昌
Nandingzhou 南定州
Nan'enzhou 南恩州
Nanfuzhou 南扶州
Nanhai 南海
Nanfuzhou 南扶州
Nanhezhou 南合州
Nanjing 南靖
Nankang 南康
Nanliu 南流
Nanshizhou 南施州
Nanxuzhou 南徐州
Nanyinzhou 南尹州
Nanyue (*Nam Việt*) 南越
Ningpu 寧浦
Ningxin 寧新
Ningyue 寧越
Ningzhou 寧州
Panliao 盤遼
Panyu 番禺
Panzhou 番州
Panzhou 潘州
Puzhou 普州
Qianzhou 黔州
Qiaoguo 譙國
Qin Jiang 欽江
Qingping 清平
Qinzhou 欽州

Qìnzhou 勤州

Qiongzhou 瓊州

Qujiang 曲江

Quanzhou 泉州

Rangzhou 瀼州

Rinan (*Nhật Nam*) 日南

Rongcheng 戎城

Rongzhou 容州

Shaozhou 韶州

Shian 始安

Shijian 始建

Shiqi (*Thạch Kỳ*) 石碕

Shixing 始興

Shizhou 石州

Shu 蜀

Shuangzhou 雙州, alternatively 瀧州

Shuangtou Dong 雙頭洞

Shunzhou 順州

Sihui 四會

Siping 思平

Songchang 宋昌

Songkang 宋康

Songlong 宋隆

Songshou 宋壽

Songxi 宋熙

Suicheng 遂成

Suixi 遂溪

Tanquan 貪泉

Tengzhou 藤州

Tongan 同安

Tongling 銅陵

Tun shui 豚水

Tuojian 妥建

Wanzhou 萬州

Wuchun 吳春

Wuguo 吳國

Wuling 武陵

Wuping (*Vũ Bình*) 武平

Wuyang 舞陽

Wuzhou 武州

Xi Jiang 西江

Xiāngzhou 湘州

Xiangzhou 襄州

Xihengzhou 西衡州

Xinchang (*Tân Xương*) 新昌

Xinggu 興古

Xinjin 新淦

Xinhui 新會

Xinning 新寧

Xinxing 新興

Xinzhou 新州

Xiuzhou 繡州

Xuwen 徐聞

Xunzhou 循州

Xúnzhou 潯州

Yangchun 陽春

Yaizhou 崖州

Yanling 鄢陵

Yelang 夜郎

Yian 義安

Yingde 英德

Yinshan 銀山

Yinxue 銀穴

Yìzhou 義州

Yizhou 益州

Yongji 雍雞

Yongchang 永昌

Yongning 永寧

Yongping 永平

Yongxi 永熙

Yongzhou 邕州

Youjiang 右江

Yueguo 越國

Yuezhou 越州

Yulin 鬱林

Yulinzhou 鬱林州

Yunji 雲際

Yunkai 雲開

Yunwu 雲霧

Yushui 鬱水

Yuzhou 禹州

Zangke 牂柯

Zhangjiang 瘴江

Zhaoyi 招義

Zhizhou 智州
Zhongguo 中國
Zhongsu 中宿

Zhuguan 珠官
Zhuyai 朱崖
Zuojiang 左江

NAMES OF ETHNIC GROUPINGS

Ailao 哀牢
Chu 楚
Da Yue (*Đại Việt*) 大越
Dan 蜒
Di 狄
Dian 滇
Fuyan Yi 扶嚴夷
Hu 胡
Lai 倈
Lao 獠
Lao zei 獠賊
Laozi 獠子
Li 俚
Ma liu 馬流
Man 蠻
Man-Lao 蠻獠
Min Yue 閩越
Nan Man 南蠻

Nanping Lao 南平獠
Nanyue (*Nam Việt*) 南越
Piao 標 (Pao or Peu)
Rang 獽
Rong 戎
Shi or Zhi 狶
Tiyi 提佇
Wuling yi 五苓夷
Wuhu 烏滸
Xinan yi 西南夷
Xiyuan Man 西原蠻
Yi 夷
Yi 佁
Yi-Lao 夷獠
Yizei 夷賊
Yue (*Việt*) 越
Yueyi 越邑

CHINESE ADMINISTRATIVE TITLES

anfu dashi 安撫大使 commander-in-chief of pacification
cishi 刺史 inspector (of a province)
dingguo jiangjun 定國大將軍 Great General Who Settles the Country
duhu 督護 protector general
duwei 都尉 defender
furen 夫人 lady, an honorific title for women
gong 公 duke
honglu qing 鴻臚卿 Chief Ceremonial Minister
jungong 郡公 commandery duke
liumin duhu 流民督護 protector general of refugees
shilang 侍郎 deputy official
taishou 太守 governor (of a commandery)
weiwei shaoqing 衛尉少卿 Lesser Chief Minister for the Palace Garrison

Xijiang duhu 西江督護 Protector of the Western Rivers
zhubu 主簿 assistant magistrate
zongguan 總管 area commander-in-chief
zuo changshi 左常侍 senior attendant-in-ordinary
zuowuwei jiangjun 左武衛將軍 left-hand militant general

NAMES OF CHINESE ADMINISTRATIVE UNITS

chujun 初郡 proto-commandery
duhufu 督護府 protectorate
jimizhou 縻羈州 "halter and bridle" province
jun 郡 commandery
Lao jun 獠郡 Lao commandery

Li jun 俚郡 Li commandery
xian 縣 county
zhou 州 province
zuojun 左郡 left-hand commandery
zuoxian 左縣 left-hand county

NAMES OF ERAS

Daming 大明 (Song) 457–465
Dàtong 大通 (Liang) 527–529
Dàtóng 大同 (Liang) 535–546
Daye 大業 (Sui) 605–617
Jianwu 建武 (Han) 25–56
Kaihuang 開皇 (Sui) 581–601
Kaiyuan period 開元 (Tang) 713–742
Renshou 仁壽 (Sui) 601–605
Shengli 聖歷 (Tang) 698–700
Taijian era 太建 (Chen) 569–583

Taikang 太康 (Jin) 280–289
Taishi 泰始 (Song) 465–472
Taiyuan 太元 (Jin) 376–397
Tianjian 天監 (Liang) 502–520
Xingzhong 興中 (Qi) 501–502
Yongjia 永嘉 (Jin) 307–313
Yuanjia period 元嘉 (Song) 424–454
Yuanhui 元徽 (Song) 473–477
Zhenguan era 貞觀 (Tang) 627–650

MISCELLANEOUS CHINESE TERMS AND EXPRESSIONS

buluo 部落 tribe
buqu 部曲 troops
cizhu 棘竹 thorny bamboo (northern Chinese)
da shouling 大首領 great leader
daolao 倒老 variant of *dulao*, a Tai name for a chieftain
daonianzi 倒捻子 variant of *dunianzi*, a mangosteen
dashuai 大帥 great leader
dazu 大族 great clan
dong 洞 a *dong*, a non-Chinese political unit

dulao 都老 a Tai name for a chieftain, also *daolao*

dunianzi 都念子 a mangosteen

fengjianhua 封建化 feudalization

fu 撫 to placate, soothe, or pacify

fuliuteng 扶留藤 a name for betel leaf or *Piper betle*

gouwan 鉤挽, alternatively 鉤吻 the gelsemium vine, *Gelsemium elegans*

gouyuanzi 鉤緣子 the citron

gui 桂 cassia or cinammon

gui han lijun 歸漢里君 lord of the Li who returned to the Han

guzhongteng 古終藤 the cotton plant *Gossypium herbaceum*

hao 豪 strongman

huang 篁 a bamboo thicket

hudiaoshi 戶調式 household taxation system

hunu 狐弩 "fox crossbows"

jiaoteng 椒藤 *jiao* vine

jiaxiang 甲香 shell aromatic

jimi 縻羈 "halter-and-bridle" a type of administration by loose control

julang 枸桹 a kind of cotton tree

jushuai 渠帥 great commander

kaifa 開發 to develop

kaituo 開拓 to open up or develop

lak wai 笏圍 a hedge of thorny bamboo (Cantonese)

lan 欄 a stilt house, transliteration of a Tai word

le 勒 southern Chinese word for thorns

lezhu 笏竹 thorny bamboo (southern Chinese)

li hu 俚戶 Li households

Lishuai 俚帥 Li commander

liuren ying 流人營 refugee encampment

liuyu 流寓 refugees

Manhua Hanren 蠻化漢人 "southern-barbarized Han people"

min 民 subjects, commonfolk

minzu 民族 a nationality or ethnic group

mumian 木棉 the cotton tree *Bombax malabaricum*

Nan zei 南賊 bandits of the south

ping 平 to pacify, a euphemism for attacking and subduing

ping li dong 平俚洞 to pacify the Li *dong*

qiuzhang 酋長 chieftain

ran 蚺, alternatively 髯 a python

ren 人 person

ronghe 融合 to mix together

shaoshu minzu 少數民族 minority nationality or ethnicity

sheng fan 生蕃 "raw" barbarians

shouling 首領 leader
shu fan 熟蕃 "cooked" barbarians
shuguo 屬國 dependent state
tonggu wang 銅鼓王 the king bronze drum
tonghufu 銅虎符 bronze tiger tally
wushu 五銖 a type of coin
xiangli qiuhao 鄉里酋豪 village chieftains
yege 冶葛 the gelsemium vine, *Gelsemium elegans*
yiguo zhi ren 異國之人 people of different countries
yinshou 印綬 seals and ribbons
zeishuai 賊帥 bandit leader
zhushifu 竹使符 bamboo emissary seal
zushu wenti 族屬問題 ethnic identity problems

Bibliography

ABBREVIATIONS USED IN CITATIONS
OF PRIMARY SOURCES

BHL	*Beihu lu*	北戶錄
BLJYZ	*Bu Liang Jiangyu zhi*	補梁疆域志
BQS	*Bei Qi shu*	北齊書
BWZ	*Bowu zhi jiaozhu*	博物志校注
CS	*Chen shu*	陳書
CXJ	*Chuxue ji*	初學記
DMYTZ	*Daming yitongzhi*	大明一統志
DSFYJY	*Dushi fangyu jiyao*	讀史方輿紀要
GDTZ	*Guangdong tongzhi*	廣東通志
GHYHZ	*Guihai yuheng zhi jiaobu*	桂海虞衡志校補
GXTZ	*Guangxi tongzhi*	廣西通志
GZ	*Guang zhi*	廣志
GZJ	*Guangzhou ji*	廣州記
HHS	*Hou Han shu*	後漢書
HNZ	*Huainanzi*	淮南子
HS	*Han shu*	漢書
HYGZ	*Huayang guo zhi*	華陽國志
JAJ	*Jian'an ji*	建安記
JS	*Jin shu*	晉書
JTS	*Jiu Tang shu*	舊唐書
JYYNYWZ	*Jingyang yinan yiwuzhi*	荊楊以南異物志
JZYWC	*Jiaozhou yiwu zhi*	交州異物志
LBLY	*Lingbiao luyi*	嶺表錄異
LS	*Liang shu*	梁書
LWDD	*Ling wai daida jiaozhu*	嶺外代答校注
LYJ	*Linyi ji*	林邑記
LZTJJZ	*Liuzutan ching jianzhu*	六祖壇經箋註
NFCWZ	*Nanfang caowu zhuang*	南方草物狀

NQS	*Nan shu*	南齊書
NS	*Nan shi*	南史
NYZ	*Nanyue zhi*	南越志
NZBJYWZ	*Nanzhong bajun yiwu zhi*	南中八郡異物志
NZYWZ	*Nanzhou yiwu zhi*	南州異物志
QMYS	*Qimin yaoshu*	齊民要術
QSW	*Quan Sui wen*	全隋文
SGZ	*San guo zhi*	三國志
SJZ	*Shui jing zhu jiao*	水經注校
SS	*Song shu*	宋書
SuS	*Sui shu*	隋書
SWJZ	*Shuowen jiezi*	說文解字
TD	*Tongdian*	通典
TPHYJ	*Taiping huanyu ji*	太平寰宇記
TPYL	*Taiping yulan*	太平御覽
WLDLZ	*Wulu dili zhi*	吳錄地理志
WS	*Wei shu*	魏書
WX	*Wen xuan*	文選
XTS	*Xin Tang shu*	新唐書
XXBC	*Xinxiu bencao*	新修本草
YDJS	*Yudi jisheng*	輿地紀勝
YHJXTZ	*Yuanhe junxian tuzhi*	元和郡縣圖志
YTKC	*Yudi guangji*	輿地廣紀
YWLJ	*Yiwen leiju*	藝文類聚
ZP	*Zhu pu*	竹譜
ZYGJ	*Zhang yan gong ji*	張燕公集
ZZTJ	*Zizhi tongjian*	資治通鑑

PRIMARY SOURCES IN CHINESE

An asterisk indicates a work no longer fully extant that has been quoted in later books.

Bei hu lu 北戶錄 (Records from the North-Facing Window). Duan Gonglu 段公路 (ca. 875). Congshu jicheng edition. Shanghai: Shangwu yinshuguan, 1936.

Bei Qi shu 北齊書 (Book of Northern Qi). Li Bole 李百樂 (565–648). Bona edition. Taipei: Taiwan shangwu yinshuguan, 1983.

Bei shi 北史 (History of the Northern Dynasties). Li Yanxiu 李延壽 (ca. 659). Bona edition. Taipei: Taiwan shangwu yinshuguan, 1983.

Bowu zhi jiao zhu 博物志校注 (Commentary on the Wide Gleanings). Zhang Hua 張華 (232–300). Modern commentary by Fan Ning 范寧. Beijing: Zhonghua shuju, 1980.

Bu Liang jiangyu zhi 補梁疆域志 (Additions to Liang Administrative Geography). Hong Yisun 洪齮孫 (1804–1859). Contained in *Ershiwu shi bubian* 二十五史補篇, 5; 1–71. Shanghai: Kaiming shudian, 1937.

Chen shu 陳書 (Book of the Chen). Yao Silian 姚思廉 (557–637). Bona edition. Taipei: Taiwan shangwu yinshuguan, 1983.

Chuxue ji 初學記 (Materials for Elementary Instruction). Xu Jian 徐堅 (659–729). Kong Guang Dao edition, 1873.

Da Ming yitongzhi 大明一統志 (Unified Gazetteer of Great Ming). Compiled by Wei Junmin 魏俊民 (b. 1370) et al. 1461 edition. Taipei: Wenhai chubanshe, 1963.

Du shi fangyu jiyao 讀史方輿紀要 (Essentials of Geography for Reading History). Gu Zuyu 顧祖禹 (1624–1680). Beijing: Zhonghua shuju, 1955.

Guangdong tongzhi 廣東通志 (Complete Gazetteer of Guangdong). Hao Yulin 郝玉麟 and Lu Zengyu 魯曾煜. Siku quanshu edition. In *Yinying wenyuange siku quanshu* 印影文淵閣四庫全書 (1,500 vols.). Taipei: Taiwan shangwu yinshuguan, 1983–1986.

Guangxi tongzhi 廣西通志 (Complete Gazetteer of Guangxi). Xie Qigun 謝啓昆 (1737–1802). 1801 edition.

Guangyun 廣韻 (Comprehensive Rhymes). Chen Pengnian 陳彭年 (1008). Zecuntang edition, 1704.

*Guang zhi 廣志 (Annals of Guang). Guo Yigong 郭義恭 (Liu-Song 420–479).

*Guangzhou ji 廣州記 (Record of Guangzhou). Gu Wei 顧微 (Jin 265–420).

*Guangzhou ji 廣州記 (Record of Guangzhou). Pei Yuan 裴淵 (Eastern Jin 317–420).

Guihai yuheng zhi jiaobu 桂海虞衡志校補 (Commentated Annals of the Overseer of Forestry and Fishing between Guilin and the Sea). Fan Chengda 范成大 (1126–1193). Modern commentary by Qi Zhiping 齊治平. Nanning: Guangxi minzu chubanshe, 1984.

*Gujin zhu 古今注 (Commentaries on the Ancient and Modern). Cui Bao 崔豹 (fourth century).

Han shu 漢書 (Book of the Han). Ban Gu 班固 (32–92 CE). Bona edition. Taipei: Taiwan shangwu yinshuguan, 1983.

Hou Han shu 後漢書 (Book of the Later Han). Fan Ye 范曄 (398–446). Bona edition. Taipei: Taiwan shangwu yinshuguan, 1983.

Huainanzi 淮南子. Liu An 劉安 (179–122 BCE). Gusuju wentang edition, 1804.

Huayang guo zhi 華陽國志 (Records of the Lands to the South of Mt. Hua). Chang Qu 常璩 (ca. 339). Jinan: Jilu shushe, 2009.

*Jian'an ji 建安記 (Records of Jian'an). Xiao Zikai 蕭子開 (Liang 502–557).

*Jiaozhou ji 交州記 (Records of Jiaozhou). Liu Xinqi 劉欣期 (Jin 265–420).

*Jiaozhou yiwu zhi 交州異物志 (Annals of the Foreign Things of Jiaozhou; alternative title *Nanyi yiwu zhi* 南裔異物志). Yang Fu 楊孚 (late first century).

*Jingyang yinan yiwuzhi 荆楊以南異物志 (Annals of the Foreign Things from the Lands South of Jingzhou and Yangzhou). Xue Ying 薛瑩 (mid-third century).

*Jingzhou ji 荆州記 (Records of Jingzhou). Sheng Hongzhi 盛宏之 (Liu-Song 420–479).

Jin shu 晉書 (Book of the Jin). Fang Xuanling 房玄齡 (578–648). Bona edition. Taipei: Taiwan shangwu yinshuguan, 1983.

Jiu Tang shu 舊唐書 (Old Book of the Tang). Liu Xu 劉昫 (897–946). Bona edition. Taipei: Taiwan shangwu yinshuguan, 1983.

Liang shu 梁書 (Book of the Liang). Yao Cha 姚察 (533–606) and Yao Silian 姚思廉 (d. 637). Bona edition. Taipei: Taiwan shangwu yinshuguan, 1983.

Lingbiao luyi 嶺表錄異 (Records of the Foreign from the Outer Side of the Passes). Liu Xun 劉恂 (tenth century). Cungshu jicheng edition. Shanghai: Shangwu yinshuguan, 1936.

Lingwai daida jiaozhu 嶺外代答校注 (Commentary on the Answered Questions from South of the Passes). Zhou Qufei 周去非 (twelfth century). Modern commentary by Yang Wujuan 楊武泉. Beijing: Zhonghua shuju, 1999.

Linh Nam Chich Quái liệt truyện (Array of Strange Tales from South of the Passes; Chinese *Lingnan zheguai liezhuan* 嶺南摭怪列傳). Trần Thế Pháp 陳世法 (Chinese Chen Shifa) (fifteenth century). Taipei: Taiwan xuesheng shuju, 1992.

Linyi ji 林邑記 (Record of Linyi). Author unknown (date unknown, c. 200–499 CE).

Liuzutan jing jianzhu 六祖壇經箋註 (Commentary on the Platform Sutra). Hui Neng 慧能 (638–713). Taipei: Weixin shuju, 1969.

Nan Qi shu 南齊書 (Book of the Southern Qi). Xiao Zixian 蕭子顯 (489–537). Bona edition. Taipei: Taiwan shangwu yinshuguan, 1983.

Nan shi 南史 (History of the Southern Dynasties). Li Yanxiu 李延壽 (ca. 659). Bona edition. Taipei: Taiwan shangwu yinshuguan, 1983.

Nanfang caomu zhuang 南方草木狀 (Compendium of Plants and Trees of the South). Qi Gan 嵇含 (fourth century). Contained in Li Hui-lin, *Nan-fang ts'ao-mu chuang: A Fourth-Century Flora of Southeast Asia,* 139–46. Hong Kong: Hong Kong University Press, 1979.

Nanfang caowu zhuang 南方草物狀 (Compendium of Plants of the South). Xu Zhong 徐衷 or Xu Biao 徐表 (third–fourth century).

Nanyue zhi 南越志 (Annals of Nanyue). Shen Huaiyuan 沈懷遠 (ca. mid-fifth century).

Nanzhong bajun yiwu zhi 南中八郡異物志 (Annals of Strange Things from the Eight Commanderies in the South). Unknown author.

Nanzhou yiwu zhi 南州異物志 (Annals of Oddities from the Southern Provinces). Wan Zhen 萬震 (Three Kingdoms Wu 222–280).

Qimin yaoshu 齊民要術 (Techniques Essential for the Subsistence of the Common People). Jia Sixie 賈思勰 (sixth century).

Quan Sui wen 全隋文 (Complete Writings of the Sui). Compiled by Yan Kejun 嚴可均 (1762–1843). Fuwenzhai edition.

San guo zhi 三國志 (Annals of the Three Kingdoms). Chen Shou 陳壽 (233–297). Bona edition. Taipei: Taiwan shangwu yinshuguan, 1983.

Shi ji 史記 (Records of the Historian). Sima Qian (ca. 145–ca. 86 BCE). Bona edition. Taipei: Taiwan shangwu yinshuguan, 1983.

Shu yi ji 述異記 (Records of the Relation of Oddities). Ren Fang 任昉 (Liang 502–557).

Shui jing zhu jiao 水經注校 (Commentary on the River Classic). Wang Guowei 王國維 (1877–1927). Commentary on original work by Li Daoyuan (d. 527). Taipei: Xinwenfeng chuban gongsi, 1986.

Shuowen jiezi 說文解字. Xu Zhen 許慎 (d. ca. 120). 1873 Fuwenzhai edition. Beijing: Zhonghua shuju, 2002.

Song shu 宋書 (Book of the Song). Shen Yue 沈約 (441–513). Bona edition. Taipei: Taiwan shangwu yinshuguan, 1983.

Sui shu 隋書 (Book of the Sui). Wei Zheng 魏徵 (581–643). Bona edition. Taipei: Taiwan shangwu yinshuguan, 1983.

Taiping guangji 太平廣記 (Wide Gleanings of the Taiping Period). Li Fang 李昉 (922–996). Beijing: Zhonghua shuju, 1961.

Taiping huanyu ji 太平寰宇記 (Gazetteer of the World during the Taiping Period). Le Shi 樂史 (930–1007). 1793 edition. Taipei: Wenhai chubanshe, 1993.

Taiping yulan 太平御覽 (Imperially Reviewed Encyclopedia of the Taiping Period). Li Fang 李昉 (925–996). Song edition. Beijing: Zhonghua shuju, 1998.

Tong dian 通典 (Encyclopedic History of Institutions). Du You 杜佑 (735–812). Shanghai: Shangwu yinshuguan, 1936.

Việt Sử Lược 越史略 (An Abridged History of Việt; Chinese *Yue shi lue*). Anonymous (thirteenth century). Translation and commentary by Trần Quốc Vượng. Huế: Nhà xuất bản thuận hóa.

Wei shu 魏書 (Book of the Wei). Wei Shou 魏收 (506–572). Bona edition. Taipei: Taiwan shangwu yinshuguan, 1983.

Wen Xuan 文選 (Selected Writings). Compiled by Xiao Tong 蕭統 (501–531). Commentary by Li Shan 李善 (d. 689). Hong Kong: Shangwu yinshuguan, 1960.

Wulu dili zhi 吳錄地理志 (Geographical Gazetteer from the Records of Wu). Zhang Bo 張勃 (Three Kingdoms Wu 222–280).

Xin Tang shu 新唐書 (New Book of the Tang). Ouyang Xiu 歐陽修 (1007–1072). Bona edition. Taipei: Taiwan shangwu yinshuguan, 1983.

Xinxiu Bencao 新修本草 (Newly Amended *Materica Medica*). Su Jingdeng 蘇敬等 (ca. 657). Hefei: Anhui kexue jishu chubanshe, 2004.

Yiwen leiju 藝文類聚 (Collection of Literature Arranged by Categories). Ouyang Xun 歐陽詢 (557–641). Zhaoxing edition.

Yuanhe junxian tuzhi 元和郡縣圖志 (Illustrated Administrative Gazetteer of the Yuanhe Period). Li Jifu 李吉甫 (758–814). Beijing: Zhonghua shuju, 1983.

Yudi guangji 輿地廣記 (Wide Gleanings from Imperial Geography). Ouyang Min 歐陽忞 (fl. 1111–1121). 1812 edition. Taipei: Wenhai chubanshe, 1962.

Yudi jisheng 輿地紀勝 (Famous Places of the Empire). Wang Xiangzhi 王象之 (*chin shih* 1196). 1849 edition. Taipei: Wenhai chubanshe, 1962.

Zhang Yan Gong ji 張燕公集 (Collected Writings of Duke Zhang Yan). Zhang Yue 張說 (667–730). Congshu jicheng edition. Shanghai: Shangwu yinshuguan, 1936.

Zhu pu 竹譜 (Manual of Bamboo). Tai Kaizhi (Eastern Jin 317–420). Siku quanshu edition. In *Yinying wenyuange siku quanshu* 印影文淵閣四庫全書 (1,500 vols.). Taipei: Taiwan shangwu yinshuguan, 1983–1986.

Zizhi tongjian 資治通鑑 (Comprehensive Mirror for Aid in Government). Sima Guang 司馬光 (1019–1086). Beijing: Zhonghua shuju, 1956.

SECONDARY SOURCES

Allard, Francis. "Interaction and Social Complexity in Lingnan during the First Millennium BC." *Asian Perspectives* 33 (1994): 309–26.

————. "Frontiers and Boundaries: The Han Empire from Its Southern Periphery." In *Archaeology of Asia*, edited by Miriam T. Stark, 234–54. Malden, MA: Blackwell Publishing, 2006.

Aurousseau, Leonard. "La première conquête chinoise des pays annamites (IIIe siècle avant notre ère)." *Bulletin de l'École française d'Extrême-Orient* 23 (1923): 245–64.

Axtell, James. "Ethnohistory: An Historian's Viewpoint." *Ethnohistory* 26, no. 1 (1979): 1–13.

Bai Yaotian 白耀天. "Li lun" 俚論. *Guangxi minzu yanjiu* 廣西民族研究 no. 4 (1990): 28–38.

————. "Li lun (xu)" 俚論 (續). *Guangxi minzu yanjiu* no. 5 (1990): 52–64.

————. "Jin zhi Jinxingjun kao" 晉置晉興郡時間考. *Guangxi difangzhi* no. 1 (1997): 46–49.

Barker, David G., and Tracy M. Barker. "The Distribution of the Burmese Python, *Python molurus bivittatus*." *Bulletin of the Chicago Herpetological Society* no. 43 (2008): 33–38.

Barlow, Jeffrey G. "Culture, Ethnic Identity, and Early Weapons Systems: The Sino-Vietnamese Frontier." In *East Asian Cultural and Historical Perspectives* and *Society/Culture and Literatures*, edited by Steven Tötösy de Zepetnek and Jennifer W. Jay, 1–15. Edmonton: University of Alberta, Research Institute for Comparative Literature and Cross-Cultural Studies, 1997.

Bayard, Donn. "North China, South China, Southeast Asia, or Simply Far East?" *Journal of the Hong Kong Archaeological Society* 6 (1975): 71–79.

Beckwith, Christopher I. *Empires of the Silk Road: A History of Central Eurasia from the Bronze Age to the Present*. Princeton, NJ: Princeton University Press, 2009.

Beemer, Bryce. "Southeast Asian Slavery and Slave-Gathering Warfare as a Vector for Cultural Transmission: The Case of Burma and Thailand." *Historian* 71, no. 3 (2009): 481–506.

Bielenstein, Hans. "The Census of China during the Period 2–742 A.D." *Bulletin of the Museum of Far Eastern Antiquities* 19 (1947): 125–63.

————. "Chinese Historical Demography A.D. 2–1982." *Bulletin of the Museum of Far Eastern Antiquities* 59 (1967): 1–288.

Bộ Giáo Dục and Đào Tạo. *Lịch Sử 6*. Hanoi: Nhà Xuất Bản Giáo Dục, 2006.

Buttinger, Joseph. *The Smaller Dragon: A Political History of Vietnam*. New York: Praeger, 1958.

Calò, Ambra. *The Distribution of Bronze Drums in Early Southeast Asia: Trade Routes and Cultural Spheres*. Oxford: Archaeopress, 2009.

Chen Dayuan 陳大遠. "Guangdong Luoding xian faxian jiaozang tongqian" 廣東羅定縣發現窖藏銅錢. *Kaogu* 考古 no. 3 (1992): 282–83.

Chin, James K. "Ports, Merchants, Chieftains and Eunuchs: Reading Maritime Commerce of Early Guangdong." In *Guangdong: Archaeology and Early Texts*, edited by Shing Muller, Thomas Hollmann, and Putao Gui, 217–40. Wiesbaden: Harrassowitz Verlag, 2004.

Churchman, Catherine. "Where to Draw the Line: The Chinese Southern Frontier in the Fifth and Sixth Centuries." In *China's Encounters in the South and Southwest:*

Reforging the Fiery Frontier over Two Millennia, edited by James A. Anderson and John K. Whitmore, 59–77. Leiden: Brill, 2015.

Churchman, Michael. "Before Chinese and Vietnamese in the Red River Plain: The Han–Tang Period." *Chinese Southern Diaspora Studies* 4 (2010): 25–37. http://csds.anu.edu.au/volume_4_2010/04-2_Churchman_2010.pdf.

———. "The People in Between, the Li and Lao from the Han to the Sui." In *The Tongking Gulf through History*, edited by Nola Cooke, Li Tana, and James A. Anderson, 67–86. Philadelphia: University of Pennsylvania Press, 2011.

Condaminas, Georges. *From Lawa to Mon, from Saa' to Thai: Historical and Anthropological Aspects of Southeast Asian Social Spaces*. Translated by Stephenie Anderson, Maria Magannon, and Gehan Wijeyewardene. Edited by Gehan Wijeyewardene. Canberra: Department of Anthropology, Research School of Pacific Studies, Australian National University, 1990.

Cooke, Nola. *Colonial Political Myth and the Problem of the Other: French and Vietnamese in the Protectorate of Annam*. PhD thesis, Australian National University, 1991.

Đào Duy Anh. *Đất nước Việt Nam qua các đời nghiên cửu địa lý học lịch sử Việt Nam*. Huế: Thuận Hóa, 1994.

———. *Lịch Sử Cổ Đại Việt Nam*. Hanoi: Nhà Xuất Bản Văn Hoá Thông Thin, 2005.

———. *Lịch Sử Việt Nam tư Nguồn Gốc đến Thế Kỷ XIX*. Hanoi: Nhà Xuất Bản Văn Hoá Thông Thin, 2006.

de Beauclair, Inez. "The Keh Lao of Kweichow and Their History According to the Chinese Records." *Studia Serica* no. 5 (1946): 1–44.

de Crespigny, Rafe. *Generals of the South: The Foundation and Early History of the Three Kingdoms State of Wu*. Canberra: Faculty of Asian Studies, Australian National University, 1990.

de Rhodes, Alexandre. *Dictionarium Annamiticum Lusitanum, et Latinum ope Sacrae Congregationis de propaganda fide*. Rome, 1651.

Di Cosmo, Nicola. *Ancient China and Its Enemies: The Rise of Nomadic Power in East Asian History*. Cambridge: Cambridge University Press, 2002.

Dikötter, Frank. *The Discourse of Race in Modern China*. Stanford, CA: Stanford University Press, 1992.

Eberhard, Wolfram. *The Local Cultures of South and East China*. Translated by A. Eberhard. Leiden: E. J. Brill, 1968.

Elvin, Mark. *The Retreat of the Elephants—An Environmental History of China*. New Haven, CT: Yale University Press, 2004.

Fang Guoyu 方國瑜. *Zhongguo xinan lishi dili kaoshi* 中國西南歷史地理考釋. Taipei: Taiwan shangwu yinshuguan, 1987.

Fang Zhiqin 方志欽 and Zuyuan Jiang 蔣祖緣, eds. *Guangdong tongshi (Gudai shangce)* 廣東通史 (古代上冊). Guangzhou: Guangdong gaodeng jiaoyu chubanshe, 1996.

Faure, David. "Becoming Cantonese, the Ming Dynasty Transition." In *Unity and Diversity—Local Cultures and Identities in China*, edited by David Faure and Tao Tao Liu, 37–50. Hong Kong: Hong Kong University Press, 1996.

———. "The Yao Wars in the Mid-Ming and Their Impact on Yao Ethnicity." In *Empire at the Margins: Culture, Ethnicity and Frontier in Early Modern China*, edited by Pamela Kyle Crossley et al., 171–89. Berkeley: University of California Press, 2006.

Feng Mengqin 馮孟欽. "Guangdong Liren yicun de kaoguxue guancha" 廣東俚人遺存的考古學觀察. In *Baiyue yanjiu* 百越研究, edited by Baiyue minzu shi yanjiuhui 百越民族史研究會, 1: 216–30. Nanning: Guangxi kexue jishu chubanshe, 2007.

FitzGerald, Charles Patrick. *The Southern Expansion of the Chinese People.* Canberra: Australian National University Press, 1972.

Fiskesjø, Magnus. "On the 'Raw' and the 'Cooked' Barbarians of Imperial China." *Inner Asia* no. 1 (1999): 139–36.

Gao Mingqian 高明乾. *Zhiwu gu Hanming tukao* 植物古漢圖考. Zhengzhou: Daxiang chubanshe, 2006.

Gotō Kimpei 後藤均平. *Betonamu kyūgoku kōsōshi* ベトナム救国抗争史. Tokyo: Shin jinbutsu ōrai sha, 1975.

Graff, David A. *Medieval Chinese Warfare 300–900.* Abingdon: Routledge, 2002.

Hall, Kenneth R. "Economic History of Early Times." In *Cambridge History of Southeast Asia,* Volume One, Part One, edited by Nicholas Tarling, 197–275. Cambridge: Cambridge University Press, 2008.

Han, Xiaorong. "Who Invented the Bronze Drum? Nationalism, Politics, and a Sino-Vietnamese Archaeological Debate of the 1970s and 1980s." *Asian Perspectives* 43, no. 1 (2004): 7–33.

Han Zhenhua 韓振華. *Zhufan zhi zhubu* 諸蕃志注補. Center of Asian Studies Occasional Papers and Monographs no. 134, vol. 2. Hong Kong: Center of Asian Studies, University of Hong Kong, 2000.

Harrell, Stevan. "Civilizing Projects and the Reaction to Them." In *Cultural Encounters on China's Ethnic Frontiers,* edited by Stevan Harrell, 3–36. Seattle: University of Washington Press, 1995.

He Xi. "The Past Tells It Differently: The Myth of Native Subjugation in the Creation of Lineage Society in South China." In *Chieftains into Ancestors: Imperial Expansion and Indigenous Society in South China,* edited by David Faure and Ho Ts'ui P'ing, 138–70. Vancouver: University of British Columbia Press, 2013.

Heger, Franz. *Alte Metalltrommelen aus Südostasien.* Leipzig: K. W. Hiersemann, 1902.

Herman, John E. *Amid the Clouds and Mist: China's Colonization of Guizhou 1200–1700.* Harvard East Asian Monographs 293. Cambridge, MA: Harvard University Press, 2007.

Higham, Charles. *The Bronze Age of Southeast Asia.* New York: Cambridge University Press, 1996.

Hoàng Triều Ân, ed. *Từ Điên Chữ Nôm Tày.* Hanoi: Nhà Xuất Bản Khoa Học Xã Hội, 2003.

Holcombe, Charles. "Early Imperial China's Deep South: The Viet Regions through Tang Times." *T'ang Studies* nos. 15–16 (1997): 125–56.

———. *The Genesis of East Asia: 221 B.C.–A.D. 907.* Honolulu: University of Hawai'i Press, 2001.

Holm, David. *Killing a Buffalo for the Ancestors: A Zhuang Cosmological Text from Southwest China.* DeKalb: Southeast Asia Publications, Center for Southeast Asian Studies, Northern Illinois University, 2003.

———. *Recalling Lost Souls—The Baeu Rodo Scriptures: Tai Cosmogonic Texts from Guangxi in Southern China.* Bangkok: White Lotus, 2004.

Holmgren, Jennifer. *Chinese Colonisation of Northern Vietnam: Administrative Geography and Political Development in the Tongking Delta, First to Sixth Centuries A.D.* Canberra: Australian National University Press, 1980.

Hu Shaohua 胡紹華. *Zhongguo nanfang minzu shi yanjiu* 中國南方民族史研究. Beijing: Minzu chubanshe, 2004.

Hu Shouwei 胡守為. *Lingnan gushi* 嶺南古史. Shaoguan: Guangdong renmin chubanshe, 1999.

Huang Xingqiu 黃興球. *Zhuangtaizu fenhua shijian kao* 壯泰族分化時間考. Beijing: Minzu chubanshe, 2008.

Huang Zengqing 黃增慶. "Zhuangzu gudai tonggu de zhuzao gongyi" 壯族古代銅鼓的鑄造工藝. *Guangxi minzu xueyuan xuebao* 1 (1984): 41–47.

Hucker, Charles O. *A Dictionary of Official Titles in Imperial China.* Stanford, CA: Stanford University Press, 1986.

Jackson, Beverly. *Kingfisher Blue: Treasures of an Ancient Chinese Art.* Berkeley, CA: Ten Speed Press, 2001.

Janse, Olov Robert Thule. *Archaeological Research in Indo-China.* 3 vols. Cambridge, MA: Harvard University Press, 1947–1958.

Jiang Tingyu 蔣廷瑜. "Yueshi tonggu de chubu yanjiu" 粵式銅鼓的初步研究. In *Gudai tonggu xueshu taolunhui lunwenji* 古代銅鼓學術討論會論文集, 139–51. Beijing: Wenwu chubanshe, 1982.

Jiangsu yixueyuan 江蘇醫學院, ed. *Zhongyao dacidian* 中藥大辭典. 3 vols. Hong Kong: Shangwu yinshuguan, 1978–1979.

Katakura Minoru 片倉穣. "Chūgoku shihaika no betonamu—Chūgoku shoōchō no shūdatsu ni kansuru shironteki kōsatsu" 中国支配下のベトナム—中国諸王朝の収奪に関する試論的考察. *Rekishigaku kenkyū* 歴史学研究 380 (1972): 17–26; 381 (1972): 28–35.

Kawahara Masahiro 河原正博. *Kan minzoku Kanan hattenshi kenkyū* 漢民族華南發展史研究. Tokyo: Yoshikawa Kōbunkan, 1984.

Kempers, Bernet. *The Kettledrums of Southeast Asia: A Bronze Age World and Its Aftermath.* Rotterdam: A. A. Balkema, 1988.

Kieser, Annette. "Nur Guangdong ist ruhig und friedlich; Grabkult und Migration während der Sechs Dynastien im heutigen Guangdong." In *Guangdong: Archaeology and Early Texts (Zhou-Tang)*, edited by Shing Müller, Thomas O. Höllmann, and Putao Gui, 101–24. South China and Maritime Asia Series vol. 13. Wiesbaden: Harrassowitz Verlag, 2004.

Leach, Edmund. *Political Systems of Highland Burma: A Study of Kachin Social Structure.* London: Athlone Press, 1970.

Lehman, F. K. "Who Are the Karen, and If So, Why? Karen Ethnohistory and a Formal Theory of Ethnicity." In *Ethnic Adaptation and Identity: The Karen on the Thai Frontier with Burma*, edited by Charles F. Keyes, 215–53. Philadelphia: Institute for the Study of Human Issues, 1979.

Lemoine, Jacques. "What Is the Actual Number of the (H)mong in the World?" *Hmong Studies Journal* 6 (2005): 1–8. http://hmongstudies.org/LemoineHSJ6.pdf.

Lê Văn Quán. *Nghiên Cứu về Chữ Nôm.* Hanoi: Nhà Xuất Bản Khoa Học Xã Hội, 1981.

Liang Min 梁敏 and Zhang Junru 張均如. *Biaohua yanjiu* 標話研究. Beijing: Zhongyang minzu daxue chubanshe, 2002.

Liao Youhua 廖幼華. *Lishi dilixue de yingyong: Lingnan diqu zaoqi fazhan zhi tantao* 歷史地理學的應用: 嶺南地區早期發展之探討. Taipei: Wenjin chubanshe, 2004.

Li Fang-kuei. *A Handbook of Comparative Tai.* Honolulu: University Press of Hawai'i, 1977.

Li Huilin. *Nan-fang ts'ao-mu chuang—A Fourth Century Flora of Southeast Asia.* Hong Kong: Hong Kong University Press, 1979.

Li Jinfang 李錦芳. *Dongtai yuyan yu wenhua* 侗台語言與文化. Beijing: Minzu chubanshe, 2002.

Li Longzhang 李龍章. *Lingnan diqu chutu jingtongqi yanjiu* 嶺南地區出土青銅器研究. Beijing: Wenwu chubanshe, 2006.

Li Minzhan 李明湛. "Jiangmen Enping jingxian daxing Donghan tonggu gumian zhijing chao yi mi" 江門恩平驚現大型東漢銅鼓 鼓面直徑超一米. News.china.com article sourced from *Jiang men ribao* 江門日報, September 15, 2009. http://news.china.com/zh_cn/history/all/11025807/20090915/15639778.html.

Li Xulian 李旭練. *Laiyu yanjiu* 俍語研究. Beijing: Zhongyang minzu daxue chubanshe, 1999.

Li Xipeng 李錫鵬. "Xinhui chutu de gu qianbi" 新會出土的古錢幣. In *Zhongguo kaogu jicheng (Huanan juan)* 中國考古集成 (華南卷), 3: 2234–39. Zhengzhou: Zhongzhou guji chubanshe, 2005.

Liebermann, Victor. *Strange Parallels: Southeast Asia in a Global Context, c. 800–1830.* Cambridge: Cambridge University Press, 2003.

Lin Fushi 林富士. "Pinlang ru Hua kao" 檳榔入華考. *Lishi yuekan* 7 (2003): 94–100.

Luo Xianglin 羅香林. *Baiyue yuanliu yu wenhua* 百越源流與文化. Taipei: Zhonghua shuju, 1955.

Lombard, Denys. "Another 'Mediterranean' in Southeast Asia." Translated by Nola Cooke. *Chinese Southern Diaspora Studies* 1 (2007): 3–9. http://csds.anu.edu.au/volume_1_2007/Lombard.pdf.

Loewe, Michael. "Guangzhou: The Evidence of the Standard Histories from the Shi ji to the Chen shu, a Preliminary Survey." In *Guangdong, Archaeology and Early Texts,* edited by Shing Müller, Thomas O. Hollman, and Putao Gui, 51–80. Wiesbaden: Harrassowitz Verlag, 2004.

Lü Shipeng 呂士朋. *Beishu shidai de Yuenan* 北屬時代的越南. Hong Kong: New Asia Research Institute, Chinese University of Hong Kong, 1964.

Luo, Yongxian. "Expanding the Proto-Tai Lexicon—A Supplement to Li (1977)." *Mon-Khmer Studies* 27 (1997): 271–98.

Matsumoto Nobuhiro 松本信廣. *Indoshina no minzoku to bunka* 印度支那の民族と文化. Tokyo: Iwanami shoten, 1942.

MacKinnon, John, and Karen Phillips. *A Field Guide to the Birds of China.* Oxford: Oxford University Press, 2000.

Maspero, Henri. "Le Protectorat général d'Annam sous les T'ang: Essai de géographie historique." *Bulletin de l'École française d'Extrême-Orient* 10 (1910): 539–682.

Meacham, William. "On Chang's Interpretation of South China Prehistory." *Journal of the Hong Kong Archaeological Society* no. 7 (1976–1978): 101–9.

————. "Is an Anthropological Definition of the Ancient Yue Possible?" In *Lingnan gu yuezu wenhua lunwenji* 嶺南古越族文化論文集 (Collected Essays on the Culture of the Ancient Yue People in South China), edited by Chau Hing-wa, 140–54. Hong Kong: Urban Council, 1993.

Meng Wentong 蒙文通. *Yueshi congkao* 越史叢考. Beijing: Renmin chubanshe, 1983.

Meyer, Bernard F., and Theodore F. Wempe. *The Student's Cantonese Dictionary.* Hong Kong: Catholic Truth Society, 1947.

Mulholland, Jean. *Herbal Medicine in Paediatrics: Translation of a Thai Book of Genesis Faculty of Asian Studies Monographs New Series: New Series No. 14.* Canberra: Faculty of Asian Studies, Australian National University, 1989.

Murphy, John C., and Robert W. Henderson. *Tales of Giant Snakes: A Historical Natural History of Anacondas and Pythons.* Malabar, FL: Krieger Publishing Company, 1997.

Nguyen Duy Hinh. "The Birth of the First State in Vietnam." In *Southeast Asian Archaeology at the XV Pacific Science Congress,* edited by Donn Bayard, 183–87. Dunedin: University of Otago Studies in Prehistoric Anthropology, 1984.

Nguyen Khac Vien. *Vietnam: A Long History.* Hanoi: Foreign Languages Publishing House, 1987.

Nguyen Kim Dung, I. C. Glover, and M. Yamagata. "Excavations at Tra Kieu and Go Cam, Quang Nam Province, Central Viet Nam." In *Uncovering Southeast Asia's Past—Selected Papers from the 10th Conference of the European Association of Southeast Asian Archaeologists*, edited by E. A. Bacus, I. C. Glover, and V. C. Pigott, 216–31. Singapore: National University of Singapore Press, 2006.

Nguyễn Ngọc San. *Tìm Hiểu Tiếng Việt Lịch Sử.* Hanoi: Nhà Xuất Bản Đại Học Sư Phạm, 2000.

Nishimura Masanari 西村昌也. "Hokubu vietonamu dōko wo meguru minzokushi-teki shiten kara no rikai" 北部ヴィエトナム銅鼓をめぐる民族史的視点からの理解. *Tōnan ajia kenkyū* 東南アジア研究 46, no. 1 (2008): 3–42.

————. "Kōka deruta no jōkaku iseki, Lũng Khê jōshi wo meguru shin ninshiki to mondai" 紅河デルタの城郭遺跡, Lũng Khê 城址をめぐる新認識と問題. *Tōnan ajia rekishi to bunka* 東南アジア歴史と文化 30 (2001): 46–69.

————. "Settlement Patterns on the Red River Plain from the Late Prehistoric Period to the Tenth Century AD." *Indo-Pacific Prehistory Association Bulletin* no. 25 (2007): 99–107.

Norman, Jerry, and Tsu-lin Mei. "The Austroasiatics in Ancient South China, Some Lexical Evidence." *Monumenta Serica* 32 (1976): 274–301.

O'Harrow, Stephen. "Men of Hu, Men of Han, Men of the Hundred Man: The Biography of Si Nhiep and the Conceptualization of Early Vietnamese Society." *Bulletin de l'Ecole Francaise d'Extreme-Orient* no. 75 (1986): 249–66.

Okada Kōji 岡田宏二. *Zhongguo Huanan minzu shehui shi yanjiu* 中國華南民族社會史研究. Translated by Zhao Lingzhi 趙令志 and Li Delong 李德龍. Beijing: Minzu chubanshe, 2002.

Ostapirat, Weera. "Proto Kra." *Linguistics of the Tibeto-Burman Area* 23, no. 1 (2000): 1–251.

Papin, Philippe. "Géographie et politique dans le Viêt-Nam ancien." *Bulletin de l'École française d'Extrême-Orient* 87, no. 2 (2000): 609–28.

Pelley, Patricia. *Postcolonial Vietnam: New Histories of the National Past.* Durham, NC: Duke University Press, 2002.

Pelliot, Paul. *Notes on Marco Polo: Ouvrage Posthume.* 3 vols. Paris: Imprimerie Nationale, 1957–1973.

Peng Fengwen 彭豐文. "Nanchao lingnan minzu zhengce xintan" 南朝嶺南民族政策新探. *Minzu yanjiu* 民族研究 5 (2004): 93–100.

———. "Xijiang duhu yu Nanchao Lingnan kaifa" 西江督護與南朝嶺南開發. *Guangxi minzu yanjiu* 廣西民族研究 2, no. 76 (2004): 62–67.

Peters, Heather. *Tattooed Faces and Stilt Houses: Who Were the Ancient Yue?* Sino-Platonic Papers no. 17. Philadelphia: Department of Oriental Studies, University of Pennsylvania, 1990.

Phạm Đức Dương. *Văn hóa Việt Nam trong Bối Cảnh Đông Nam Á.* Hanoi: Nhà Xuất Bản Khoa Học Xã Hội, 2000.

Pham Huy Tong, ed. *Dong Son Drums in Vietnam.* Hanoi: Vietnam Social Science Publishing House, 1990.

Phan, John D. "Re-Imagining 'Annam': A New Analysis of Sino–Viet–Muong Linguistic Contact." *Chinese Southern Diaspora Studies* 4 (2010): 3–24. http://csds.anu.edu.au/volume_4_2010/03-1_Phan_2010.pdf.

Pittayaporn, Pittayawat. "Layers of Chinese Loanwords in Proto-Southwestern Tai as Evidence for the Dating of the Spread of Southwestern Thai." *MANUSYA: Journal of Humanities,* Special Issue no. 20 (2014): 47–68.

Ptak, Roderich. "The Gulf of Tongking: A Mini-Mediterranean?" In *The East Asian "Mediterranean": Maritime Crossroads of Culture, Commerce and Human Migration,* edited by Angela Schottenhammer, 53–73. Wiesbaden: Harrassowitz Verlag, 2008.

Pulleyblank, Edwin G. "The Chinese and Their Neighbours in Prehistoric and Early Historic Times." In *The Origins of Chinese Civilization,* edited by David N. Keightley, 411–66. Berkeley: University of California Press, 1983.

———. *Lexicon of Reconstructed Pronunciation in Early Middle Chinese, Late Middle Chinese and Early Mandarin.* Vancouver: University of British Columbia Press, 1991.

———. *Middle Chinese: A Study in Historical Phonology.* Vancouver: University of British Columbia Press, 1984.

Reid, Anthony. *Southeast Asia in the Age of Commerce 1450–1680: Volume One—The Lands below the Winds.* New Haven, CT: Yale University Press, 1988.

Reynolds, Susan. "Medieval *Origines Gentium* and the Community of the Realm." *History* 68, no. 224 (1983): 375–90.

Reza A. H. M. A., M. M. Feeroz, M. M. Islam, and M. M. Kabir. "Status and Density of Kingfishers (Family: Alcedinidae, Halcyonidae and Cerylidae) in the Sundarbans Mangrove Forest, Bangladesh." *Bangladesh Journal of Life Sciences* 15, no. 1 (2003): 55–60.

Richards, L. *Comprehensive Geography of the Chinese Empire and Dependencies, translated into English, revised, and enlarged by M. Kennelly.* Shanghai: T'u se wei Press, 1908.

Ruey Yih-fu 芮逸夫. "Laoren kao" 僚人考. *Guoli zhongyang yanjiuyuan, lishi yuyan yanjiusuo qikan* 國立中央研究院歷史語言研究所期刊 28 (1957): 727–71.

Sagart, Laurent. "The Expansion of Setaria Farmers in East Asia—A Linguistic and Archaeological Model." In *Past Human Migrations in East Asia: Matching Archaeology, Linguistics and Genetics*, edited by Alicia Sanchez-Mazas, 133–81. Routledge Studies in the Early History of Asia vol. 5. London: Routledge, 2008.

Salemink, Oscar. *The Ethnography of Vietnam's Central Highlanders: A Historical Contextualization 1850–1990*. Honolulu: University of Hawai'i Press, 2003.

———. "A View from the Mountains: A Critical History of Lowlander-Highlander Relations in Vietnam." In *Opening Boundaries: Upland Transformations in Vietnam*, edited by Thomas Sikor, Nghiem Phuong Tuyen, Jennifer Sowerwine, and Jeff Romm, 27–50. Singapore: National University of Singapore Press, 2011.

Schafer, Edward H. "The Pearl Fisheries of Ho-p'u." *Journal of the American Oriental Society* 74, no. 4 (1952): 155–68.

———. *The Vermilion Bird: T'ang Images of the South*. Berkeley: University of California Press, 1967.

Schafer, Edward H., and Benjamin E. Wallacker. "Local Tribute Products of the T'ang Dynasty." *Journal of Oriental Studies* no. 4 (1957): 213–48.

Schneider, Paul. *Dictionnaire historique des idéogrammes Vietnamiens*. Nice: Université de Nice-Sophia Antipolis, Unité de recherches interdisciplinaires sur l'Asie du sud-est, Madagascar et les îles de l'océan Indien, 1992.

Scott, James. *The Art of Not Being Governed: An Anarchist History of Upland Southeast Asia*. New Haven, CT: Yale University Press, 2009.

Shorto, Harry. *A Mon-Khmer Comparative Dictionary*. Edited by Paul Sidwell. Canberra: Pacific Linguistics, Research School of Pacific and Asian Studies, 2006.

Solheim, Wilhelm J. II. "Prehistoric South China: Chinese or Southeast Asian?" *Computational Analyses of Asian and African Languages* (Tokyo) no. 22 (1984): 13–20.

Spencer, Joseph Earle. *Asia, East by South: A Cultural Geography*. New York: J. Wiley, 1954.

Su Delin 粟德林. *Zhongguo yaowu dacidian* 中國藥物大辭典. 2 vols. Beijing: Zhongguo yiyao keji chubanshe, 1991.

Su Guanchang 粟冠昌. "Guangxi tuguan minzu chengfen zaitan" 廣西土官民族成份再探. *Xueshu luntan* 學術論壇 no. 2 (1981): 83–86.

Tan Qixiang 譚其驤, ed. *Zhongguo lishi dituji* 中國歷史地圖集. 8 vols. Beijing: Zhongguo ditu chubanshe, 1982–1987.

Tapp, Nicolas. *The Hmong of China: Context, Agency, and the Imaginary*. Leiden: Brill, 2001.

Taylor, Keith W. *The Birth of Vietnam*. Berkeley: University of California Press, 1983.

———. "The Early Kingdoms." In *Cambridge History of Southeast Asia,* Volume One, Part One, edited by Nicholas Tarling, 137–82. Cambridge: Cambridge University Press, 2008.

———. "On Being Muonged." *Asian Ethnicity* 2, no. 1 (2001): 25–34.

———. "Surface Orientations in Vietnam: Beyond Histories of Nation and Region." *Journal of Asian Studies* 8, no. 4 (1998): 949–78.

Trần Quốc Vượng. "Từ Truyền Thuyết Ngôn Ngữ đến Lịch Sử." In *Hùng Vương Dựng Nước*, edited by Viên Khảo Cổ Học Hanoi, 1: 148–53. Hanoi: Nhà Xuất Bản Khoa Học Xã Hội, 1970.

———. "Traditions, Acculturation, Renovation: The Evolutional Pattern of Vietnamese Culture." In *Southeast Asia in the 9th to 14th Centuries*, edited by David G. Marr and A. C. Milner, 271–78. Singapore: Institute of Southeast Asian Studies, 1986.

———. "Truyền thống văn hóa Việt Nam trong Bối Cảnh Đông Nam Á và Đông Á." In *Văn Hóa Việt Nam Tìm Tòi và Suy Ngẫm*, 7–16. Hanoi: Nhà Xuất Bản Văn Học, 2003.

Trần Quốc Vượng and Hà Văn Tấn, eds. *Lịch Sử Chế Độ Phong Kiến Việt-Nam*, vol. 1. Hanoi: Nhà xuất bản giáo dục, 1960.

Turton, Andrew. "Introduction to *Civility and Savagery*." In *Civility and Savagery: Social Identity in Tai States*, edited by Andrew Turton, 1–29. Richmond, Surrey: Curzon, 2000.

Ungar, Esta S. "From Myth to History: Imagined Polities in 14th Century Vietnam." In *Southeast Asia in the 9th to 14th Centuries*, edited by David Marr and A. C. Milner, 117–38. Singapore: Institute of Southeast Asian Studies, 1986.

van Schendel, Willem. "Geographies of Knowing, Geographies of Ignorance: Jumping Scale in Southeast Asia." In *Locating Southeast Asia: Geographies of Knowledge and Politics of Space*, edited by Paul Kratoska, Remco Raben, and Henk Schulte Nordholt, 275–307. Singapore: Singapore University Press, 2005.

Viện khảo cổ học, ed. *Hùng Vương Dựng Nước*. 4 vols. Hanoi: Nhà Xuất Bản Khoa Học Xã Hội, 1970–1974.

———, ed. *Những Phát Hiện Mới về Khảo Cổ Học*. Hanoi: Nhà Xuất Bản Khoa Học Xã Hội, 1972–2009.

von Falkenhausen, Lothar. "The Use and Significance of Ritual Bronzes in the Lingnan Region during the Eastern Zhou Period." *Journal of East Asian Archaeology* 3, nos. 1–2 (2001): 193–236.

Wade, Geoff. "The Lady Sinn and the Southward Expansion of China in the Sixth Century." In *Guangdong: Archaeology and Early Texts*, edited by Shing Muller, Thomas Hollmann, and Putao Gui, 125–50. South China and Maritime Asia Series vol. 13. Wiesbaden: Harrassowitz Verlag, 2004.

———. "The Southern Chinese Borders in History." In *Where China Meets Southeast Asia: Social and Cultural Change in the Border Region*, edited by G. Evans, C. Hutton, and K. E. Kuah, 28–50. Singapore: Institute of Southeast Asian Studies, 2000.

Wan Fubin 萬輔彬, Fang Minghui 房明惠, and Wei Dong-ping 韋冬蘋. "Yuenan tonggu zai renshi yu tonggu fenlei xinshuo" 越南東山銅鼓再認識與銅鼓分類新說. *Guangxi minzu xueyuan xuebao (zhexue shehui kexueban)* 廣西民族學院學報 (哲學社會科學版) 25, no. 6 (2003): 77–83.

Wang Guichen 王貴忱 and Wang Dawen 王大文. "Cong gudai zhongwai huobi jiaoliu kan Guangzhou haishang sizhou zhi lu" 從古代中外貨幣交流看海上絲綢之路. In *Zhongguo kaogu jicheng (Huanan juan)* 中國考古集成 (華南卷), 2: 1067–73. Zhengzhou: Zhongzhou guji chubanshe, 2005.

Wang Gungwu. "The Nan-Hai Trade: A Study of the Early History of Chinese Trade on the South China Sea." In *Southeast Asia-China Interactions*, edited by Geoff Wade, 51–166. Singapore: National University of Singapore Press, 2007. Originally published in *Journal of the Malayan Branch of the Royal Asiatic Society* 31, no. 2 (1957): 1–135.

Wang Jia 王佳. "Zhouheng tonggu nishen bao guojia yiji wenwu—shen gaodu guan quanguo" 周亨銅鼓擬申報國家一級文物 身高度冠全國. Huaxia. com news article sourced from Nanfang ribao 南方日報, August 7, 2009. http://big5.huaxia.com/zhwh/whbh/2009/08/1525896.html.

Wang Jun 王均, ed. *Zhuangdong yuzu yuyan jianzhi* 壯侗語族語言簡志. Beijing: Minzu chubanshe, 1984.

Wang Kerong 王克榮, Qiu Zhonglun 邱鍾侖, and Chen Yuanzhang 陳遠璋. *Guangxi zuo jiang yanhua* 廣西左江巖畫. Beijing: Wenwu chubanshe, 1988.

Wang Wenguang 王文光, ed. *Zhongguo nanfang minzu shi* 中國南方民族史. Beijing: Minzu chubanshe, 1999.

Wang Wenguang 王文光 and Li Xiaobin 李曉斌. *Baiyue minzu fazhan yanbian shi: Cong yue, lao tao zhuangdong yuzu ge minzu* 百越民族發展演變史: 從越, 僚到壯侗語族各民族. Beijing: Minzu chubanshe, 2007.

Wang Xingrui 王興瑞. *Xian furen yu Fengshi chiazu—Sui Tang jian Guangdong nanbu diqu shehui lishi de chubu yanjiu* 冼夫人與馮氏家族—隋唐間廣東南部地區社會歷史的初步研究. Beijing: Zhonghua shuju, 1984.

White, Richard. *The Middle Ground: Indians, Empires, and Republics in the Great Lakes Region, 1650–1815*. New York: Cambridge University Press, 1991.

Wiens, Harold J. *China's March toward the Tropics*. Hamden: Shoe String Press, 1954.

Wolters, O. W. *History, Culture and Region in Southeast Asian Perspectives*. Revised edition. Ithaca, NY: Southeast Asia Program, Cornell University, 1999.

Wu Yongzhang 吳永章. "Nanchao Lingnan li lao kai lun" 南朝嶺南俚獠概論. In *Baiyue minzu yanjiu* 百越民族研究, edited by Peng Shifan 彭適凡, 234–42. Nanchang: Jiangxi jiaoyu chubanshe, 1990.

Xu Haiou 許海鷗. "Wachu tonggu bei er wumai cunmin qianyuan shuhui jiao guojia" 挖出銅鼓被兒誤賣 村民千元贖回交國家. *Nanguo ribao* 南國日報 (April 9, 2011): 9.

Xu Hengbin 徐恆彬. "Liren ji qi tonggu kao" 俚人及其銅鼓考. In *Gudai tonggu xueshu taolunhui lunwenji* 古代銅鼓學術討論會論文集, 152–58. Beijing: Wenwu chubanshe, 1982.

Xu Songshi 徐松石. *Yuejiang liuyu renmin shi* 粵江流域人民史. Shanghai: Zhonghua shuju, 1939.

Yan Gengwang 嚴耕望. *Zhongguo difang xingzheng zhidu shi* 中國地方行政制度史. 4 vols. Taipei: Zhongyang yanjiuyuan lishi yuyan yanjiusuo, 1963.

Yang Hao 楊豪. "Lingnan ningshi jiazu yuanliu xinzheng" 嶺南甯氏家族源流新證. *Kaogu* 考古 no. 3 (1989): 269–73.

Yang Shaoxiang 楊少祥. "Shilun hepu xuwengang de xingshuai" 試論合浦徐聞港的興衰. In *Zhongguo kaogu jicheng (Huanan juan)* 中國考古集成 (華南卷), 2: 1498–501. Zhengzhou: Zhongzhou guji chubanshe, 2005.

Yao Shun'an 姚舜安. "Beiliu xing tonggu zhuzao yizhi chutan" 北流型銅鼓鑄造遺址初探. *Kaogu* no. 6 (1988): 558–61.

Yao Shun'an 姚舜安, Wan Fubin 萬輔彬, and Jiang Tingyu 蔣廷瑜, eds. *Beiliu xing tonggu tanmi* 北流型銅鼓探秘. Nanning: Guangxi renmin chubanshe, 1990.

Yao Shun'an 姚舜安, Jiang Tingyu 蔣廷瑜, and Wan Fubin 萬輔彬. "Lun lingshan xing tonggu" 論靈山型銅鼓. *Kaogu*考古 no. 10 (1990): 929–43.

Yoshikai Masato 吉開將人. "Dōko saihen no jidai—issennenki no betonamu, minamichūgoku" 銅鼓"再編"の時代—一千年期のベトナム、南中國. *Tōyō Bunka* 東洋文化 78 (1998): 199–218.

———. "Rekishi sekai to shite no ryōnan—hokubu betonamu; sono kanōsei to kadai" 歴史世界としての嶺南 北部ベトナム—その可能性と課題. In *Tōnan ajia rekishi to bunka* 東南アジア歴史と文化 no. 31 (2002): 79–95.

———. "Shirushi kara miru nanetsu sekai (zenpen; chūhen; kōhen)—ryōnan kodai sekiin kō" 印からみた南越世界 (前篇;中篇;後篇)—嶺南古璽印考. *Tōyō bunka kenkyūjo kiyō* 東洋文化研究所紀要 no. 136 (1998): 89–135; no. 137 (1999): 1–45; no. 139 (2000): 1–38.

Zhang Junru 張均如, ed. *Zhuangyu fangyan yanjiu* 壯語方言研究. Chengdu: Sichuan minzu chubanshe, 1999.

Zhang Shengzhen 張聲震, ed. *Zhuangzu tongshi* 壯族通史. 3 vols. Beijing: Minzu chubanshe, 1997.

Zhang Zengqi 張增祺. *Dianguo yu dian wenhua* 滇國與滇文化. Kunming: Yunnan meishu chubanshe, 1997.

Zhang Zhoulai 張周來. "Guangxi rongxian faxian liangqian nian qian datonggu—tixing shuoda wenshi jingzhi" 廣西容縣發現兩千年前大銅鼓—體型碩大紋飾精緻. *Xinhua wang guangxi pindao* 新華網廣西頻道. December 13, 2010. http://www.gx.xinhuanet.com/dtzx/2010-12/13/content_21621008.htm.

Zheng Chaoxiong 鄭超雄. "Guanyu lingnan yetie qiyuan de ruogan wenti" 關於嶺南冶鐵業起源的若干問題. *Guangxi minzu yanjiu* 廣西民族研究 45, no. 3 (1996): 50–56.

Zheng Chaoxiong 鄭超雄 and Tan Fang 覃芳. *Zhuangzu lishi wenhua de kaoguxue yanjiu* 壯族歷史文化的考古學研究. Beijing: Minzu chubanshe, 2006.

Zhongguo gudai tonggu yanjiuhui 中國古代銅鼓研究會. *Zhongguo gudai tonggu* 中國古代銅鼓. Beijing: Wenwu chubanshe, 1988.

Zhongguo lianhe zhunbei yinhang diaocha shi 中國聯合準備銀行調查室. *Tangsong shidai jinyin zhi yanjiu* 唐宋時代金銀之研究. Beijing: Zhongguo lianhe zhunbei yinhang diaocha shi, 1944.

Zhou Ruyu 周如雨. "Wuming xian luobo zhen cunmin wa chu qiannian tonggu" 武鳴縣羅波鎮村民挖出千年銅鼓. *Nanguo zaobao* 南國早報 (June 17, 2014): 11.

Zhou Yiliang 周一良. "Nanchao jingnei zhi gezhong ren ji zhengfu duidai zhi zhengce" 南朝境内之各種人及政府對待之政策. In *Weijin nanbei chao shilunji* 魏晉南北朝史論集, 30–93. Beijing: Zhonghua shuju, 1963.

Zhu Xia 朱夏. *Zhongguo de jin* 中國的金. Shanghai: Shangwu chubanshe, 1953.

Zhu Dawei 朱大渭. "Nanchao shaoshu minzu gailun ji qi yu hanzu de ronghe" 南朝少數民族概況及其與漢族的融合. *Zhongguo shi yanjiu* 中國史研究 no. 1 (1980): 57–76.

Index

administrative titles: change in meaning of, 113; Chinese application to Li and Lao, 17, 22, 31, 103–104, 108–109, 112, 171, 177, 179, 185–186, 192; in Red River plain, 29; significance of use of, 35, 92, 116–117, 171–172, 177, 179, 192–193. *See also* local officials

administrative units (Chinese): absence of, 59, 69, 71, 107; change in sizes of, 15, 110, 113; concentrations of, 10, 55, 105, 128; comparison with *dong*, 112; disparities in size and nature of, 110–111, 113, 117; increase in number of, 65, 67, 72, 108, 109–111, 130, 133, 155, 189, 192; specific to Li and Lao, 104–107, 108; reforms of, 110–111, 113, 183–184; retrospective inclusion of territory into, 69. *See also* left-hand commanderies; proto-commanderies

Allard, Francis, 144

alliances (Li-Lao and Chinese), 18, 36–37, 103–105, 107, 108–109, 111, 131, 137, 141, 143–144, 172, 186, 203–204; advantages for Li and Lao of, 18, 118, 131, 143–144, 161–162, 174–175, 204; Chinese depictions of, 107, 109; conditions

of, 108–109; effects of, 108, 111–112, 117–118, 131, 143–144, 161–162, 172, 178, 203–204; necessity for Chinese of, 137

Anchang Commandery, 131

Anjing Commandery, 191

Annan duhu fu. See Protectorate of the Pacified South

Annan Commandery, 159

Anzhou (province), 133, 183–184

Austroasiatic languages, 12, 33, 85

Baizhou (province), 157, 186, 187. *See also* Changzhou; Nanzhou

bamboo: *Bambusa stenostachya*, 160; hedges of, 160; weaponry, 129; words for, 160–161

Bamboo emissary seals, 194

Bamboo King (Zhu Wang), 88

bandits, 127

Bao Gang, 106

Beiliu (river), 57

Beiliu County, 5, 109, 129, 148

betel chewing, 12

Binzhou (province), 194

Boliang Commandery, 131

bronze drums, 5–12, *passim*; beginning of Li-Lao casting tradition, 8, 31, 34; connection with Li and Lao peoples,

About the Author

Catherine Churchman is a historian specializing in premodern East and Southeast Asia. She received her PhD from the Research School of Pacific and Asian Studies at the Australian National University and lectures on Asian studies at Victoria University of Wellington in New Zealand.

CPSIA information can be obtained at www.ICGtesting.com
Printed in the USA
BVOW04*2346020916

460913BV00002B/3/P